Bernard Shaw

ARMS AND THE MAN

Bernard Shaw

ARMS AND THE MAN

[Edited with Complete Introduction, Biography, Author's Background, Complete Text, Study Questions, Select Criticism and Bibliography]

Mansi Sachdeva
B.A. English (Hons), Delhi University;
M.A., M. Phil. (English), IGNOU

ANMOL PUBLICATIONS PVT. LTD.
NEW DELHI - 110 002 (INDIA)

ANMOL PUBLICATIONS PVT. LTD.

H.O.: 4374/4B, Ansari Road, Darya Ganj,
New Delhi-110 002 (India)
Ph.: 23278000, 23261597

B.O.: No. 1015, Ist Main Road, BSK IIIrd Stage
IIIrd Phase, IIIrd Block
Bangalore - 560 085 (India)
Visit us at: www.anmolpublications.com

Arms and the Man

First Published, 2009

PRINTED IN INDIA

Printed at Balaji Offset Press, Delhi.

Contents

Preface

George Bernard Shaw was born on 26 July 1856, in Dublin, as the son of George Carr Shaw, who was in the wholesale grain trade, and Lucinda Elisabeth Shaw, the daughter of an impoverished landowner. Shaw's childhood was troubled.

Shaw was a Irish dramatist, literary critic, a socialist spokesman, and a leading figure in the 20th century theater. Shaw was a freethinker, defender of women's rights, and advocate of equality of income.

A few of his popular works are immaturity, 1879, the irrational knot, 1880, love among artist, 1881, our corner; cashel byron's profession, 1882, an unsocial socialist, 1883, fabian essays on socialism, 1889, the quintessence of ibsenlsm, 1891 (- see henrik ibsen), widower's houses, 1892, arms and the man, 1894 etc.

Author

Chapter 1

English Literature

Literature written in English since c.1450 by the inhabitants of the British Isles; it was during the 15th cent. that the English language acquired much of its modern form. For the literature of previous linguistic periods, see the articles on Anglo-Saxon literature and Middle English literature For literature written by English speakers elsewhere, see American literature; Australian literature; Canadian literature, English; New Zealand literature; and South African literature.

The Tudors and the Elizabethan Age

The beginning of the Tudor dynasty coincided with the first dissemination of printed matter. William Caxton 's press was established in 1476, only nine years before the beginning of Henry VII's reign. Caxton's achievement encouraged writing of all kinds and also influenced the standardization of the English language. The early Tudor period, particularly the reign of Henry VIII, was marked by a break with the Roman Catholic Church and a weakening of feudal ties, which brought about a vast increase in the power of the monarchy.

Stronger political relationships with the Continent were also developed, increasing England's exposure to Renaissance culture. Humanism became the most important force in English literary and intellectual life, both in its narrow sense—the study and imitation of the Latin classics—and in its broad sense—the affirmation of the secular, in addition to the otherworldly, concerns of people. These forces produced during the reign (1558–1603) of Elizabeth I one of the most fruitful eras in literary history.

The energy of England's writers matched that of its mariners and merchants. Accounts by men such as Richard Hakluyt, Samuel Purchas, and Sir Walter Raleigh were eagerly read. The activities and literature of the Elizabethans reflected a new nationalism, which expressed itself also in the works of chroniclers (John Stow, Raphael Holinshed, and others), historians, and translators and even in political and religious tracts. A myriad of new genres, themes, and ideas were incorporated into English literature. Italian poetic forms, especially the sonnet, became models for English poets.

Sir Thomas Wyatt was the most successful sonneteer among early Tudor poets, and was, with Henry Howard, earl of Surrey, a seminal influence. *Tottel's Miscellany* was the first and most popular of many collections of experimental poetry by different, often anonymous, hands.

A common goal of these poets was to make English as flexible a poetic instrument as Italian. Among the more prominent of this group were Thomas Churchyard, George Gascoigne, and Edward de Vere, earl of Oxford. An ambitious and influential work was *A Mirror for Magistrates,* a historical verse narrative by several poets that updated the medieval view of history and the morals to be drawn from it.

The poet who best synthesized the ideas and tendencies of the English Renaissance was Edmund Spenser. His unfinished epic poem *The Faerie Queen* is a treasure house of romance, allegory, adventure, Neoplatonic ideas, patriotism, and Protestant morality, all presented in a variety of literary styles. The ideal English Renaissance man was Sir Philip Sidney —scholar, poet, critic, courtier, diplomat, and soldier—who died in battle at the age of 32.

His best poetry is contained in the sonnet sequence *Astrophel and Stella* and his *Defence of Poesie* is among the most important works of literary criticism in the tradition. Many others in a historical era when poetic talents were highly valued, were skilled poets. Important late Tudor sonneteers include Spenser and Shakespeare, Michael Drayton, Samuel Daniel, and Fulke Greville. More versatile even than Sidney was Sir Walter Raleigh—poet, historian, courtier, explorer, and soldier—who wrote strong, spare poetry. Early Tudor drama owed much to both medieval morality plays and classical models. *Ralph Roister Doister* (c.1545) by Nicholas Udall and *Gammer Gurton's Needle* (c.1552) are considered the first English comedies, combining elements of classical Roman comedy with native burlesque. During the late 16th and early 17th cent., drama flourished in England as never before or since. It came of age with the work of the University Wits, whose sophisticated plays set the course of Renaissance drama and paved the way for Shakespeare.

The Wits included John Lyly, famed for the highly artificial and much imitated prose work *Euphues;* Robert Greene, the first to write romantic comedy; the versatile Thomas Lodge and Thomas Nashe; Thomas Kyd, who popularized neo-Senecan tragedy; and Christopher Marlowe, the greatest dramatist of the group. Focusing on heroes whose very greatness leads to their downfall, Marlowe wrote in blank verse with a rhetorical brilliance and eloquence superbly equal to the demands of high drama.

William Shakespeare, of course, fulfilled the promise of the Elizabethan age. His history plays, comedies, and tragedies set a standard never again equaled, and he is universally regarded as the greatest dramatist and one of the greatest poets of all time.

The Jacobean Era, Cromwell and the Restoration

Elizabethan literature generally reflects the exuberant self-confidence of a nation expanding its powers, increasing its wealth, and thus keeping at bay its serious social and religious problems. Disillusion and pessimism followed, however, during the unstable reign of James I. The 17th cent. was to be a time of great upheaval—revolution and regicide, restoration of the monarchy, and, finally, the victory of Parliament, landed Protestantism, and the moneyed interests.

Jacobean literature begins with the drama, including some of Shakespeare's greatest, and darkest, plays. The dominant literary figure of James's reign was Ben Jonson, whose varied and dramatic works followed classical models and were enriched by his worldly, peculiarly English wit. His satiric dramas, notably the great *Volpone,* all take a cynical view of human nature. Also cynical were the horrific revenge tragedies of John Ford, Thomas Middleton, Cyril Tourneur, and John Webster (the best poet of this grim genre). Novelty was in great demand, and the possibilities of plot and genre were exploited almost to exhaustion. Still, many excellent plays were written by men such as George Chapman, the masters of comedy Thomas Dekker and Philip Massinger, and the team of Francis Beaumont and John Fletcher. Drama continued to flourish until the closing of the theaters at the onset of the English Revolution in 1642.

The foremost poets of the Jacobean era, Ben Jonson and John Donne, are regarded as the originators of two diverse poetic traditions—the Cavalier and the metaphysica. Jonson and Donne shared not only a common fund of literary resources, but also a dryness of wit and precision of expression. Donne's poetry is distinctive for its passionate intellection, Jonson's for its classicism and urbane guidance of passion.

Although George Herbert and Donne were the principal metaphysical poets, the meditative religious poets Henry Vaughan and Thomas Traherne were also influenced by Donne, as were Abraham Cowley and Richard Crashaw. The greatest of the Cavalier poets was the sensuously lyrical Robert Herrick. Such other Cavaliers as Thomas Carew, Sir John Suckling, and Richard Lovelace were lyricists in the elegant Jonsonian tradition, though their lyricism turned political during the English Revolution. Although ranked with the metaphysical poets, the highly individual Andrew Marvell partook of the traditions of both Donne and Jonson.

Among the leading prose writers of the Jacobean period were the translators who produced the classic King James Version of the Bible and the divines Lancelot Andrewes, Jeremy Taylor, and John Donne.

The work of Francis Bacon helped shape philosophical and scientific method. Robert Burton 's *Anatomy of Melancholy* offers a varied, virtually encyclopedic view of the moral and intellectual preoccupations of the 17th cent. Like Burton, Sir

Thomas Browne sought to reconcile the mysteries of religion with the newer mysteries of science. Izaak Walton, author of *The Compleat Angler*, produced a number of graceful biographies of prominent writers. Thomas Hobbes wrote the most influential political treatise of the age, *Leviathan*.

The Jacobean era's most fiery and eloquent author of political tracts (many in defence of Cromwell's government, of which he was a member) was also one of the greatest of all English poets, John Milton. His *Paradise Lost* is a Christian epic of encompassing scope. In Milton the literary and philosophical heritage of the Renaissance merged with Protestant political and moral conviction.

With the restoration of the English monarchy in the person of Charles II, literary tastes widened. The lifting of Puritan restrictions and the reassembling of the court led to a relaxation of restraints, both moral and stylistic, embodied in such figures as the Earl of Rochester.

Restoration comedy reveals both the influence of French farce (the English court spent its exile in France) and of Jacobean comedy. It generously fed the public's appetite for broad satire, high style, and a licentiousness that justified the worst Puritan imaginings. Such dramatists as Sir George Etherege, William Wycherley, and William Congreve created superbly polished high comedy. Sparkling but not quite so brilliant were the plays of George Farquhar, Thomas Shadwell, and Sir John Vanbrugh.

John Dryden began as a playwright but became the foremost poet and critic of his time. His greatest works are satirical narrative poems, notably *Absalom and Achitophel*, in which prominent contemporary figures are unmistakably and devastatingly portrayed. Another satiric poet of the period was Samuel Butler, whose *Hudibras* satirizes Puritanism together with all the intellectual pretensions of the time. During the Restoration Puritanism or, more generally, the Dissenting tradition, remained vital.

The most important Dissenting literary work was John Bunyan 's *Pilgrim's Progress*, an allegorical prose narrative that is considered a forerunner of the novel. Lively and illuminating glimpses of Restoration manners and mores are provided by the diaries of Samuel Pepys and John Evelyn.

The Eighteenth Century

The Glorious Revolution of 1688 firmly established a Protestant monarchy together with effective rule by Parliament. The new science of the time, Newtonian physics, reinforced the belief that everything, including human conduct, is guided by a rational order. Moderation and common sense became intellectual values as well as standards of behavior. These values achieved their highest literary expression in the poetry of Alexander Pope. Pope—neoclassicist, wit, and master of the heroic couplet—was critical of human foibles but generally confident that order and happiness in human affairs were attainable if excesses were eschewed and rational dictates heeded. The brilliant prose satirist Jonathan Swift was not so sanguine. His "savage indignation" resulted in devastating attacks on his age in A Tale of a Tub, Gulliver's Travels, and A Modest Proposal.

Middle-class tastes were reflected in the growth of periodicals and newspapers, the best of which were the *Tatler* and the *Spectator* produced by Joseph Addison and Sir Richard Steele. The novels of Daniel Defoe, the first modern novels in English, owe much to the techniques of journalism. They also illustrate the virtues of merchant adventure vital to the rising middle class. Indeed, the novel was to become the literary form most responsive to middle-class needs and interests.

The 18th cent. was the age of town life with its coffeehouses and clubs. One of the most famous of the latter was the Scriblerus Club, whose members included Pope, Swift, and John Gay (author of *The Beggar's Opera*). Its purpose was to defend and uphold high literary standards against the rising tide of middle-class values and tastes. Letters were a popular form of polite literature. Pope, Swift, Horace Walpole, and Thomas Gray were masters of the form, and letters make up the chief literary output of Lady Mary Wortley Montagu and Lord Chesterfield. The novels of Samuel Richardson, including the influential *Clarissa,* were written in epistolary form. With the work of Richardson, Fanny Burney, Henry Fielding, Tobias Smollett, and Laurence Sterne the English novel flourished.

Probably the most celebrated literary circle in history was the one dominated by Samuel Johnson. It included Joshua Reynolds, David Garrick, Edmund Burke, Oliver Goldsmith, and James Boswell, whose biography of Johnson is a classic of the genre. Other great master prose writers of the period were the historian Edward Gibbon and the philosopher David Hume. Dr. Johnson, who carried the arts of criticism and conversation to new heights, both typified and helped to form mid-18th-century views of life, literature, and conduct. The drama of the 18th cent. failed to match that of the Restoration. But Oliver Goldsmith and Richard Brinsley Sheridan rose above the prevalent "weeping comedy"—whose sentimentalism infected every literary genre of the period—to achieve polished comedy in the Restoration tradition.

Among the prominent poets of the 18th cent. were James Thomson, who wrote in *The Seasons* of nature as it reflected the Newtonian concept of order and beauty, and Edward Young, whose *Night Thoughts* combined melancholy and Christian apologetics. Anticipations of romanticism can be seen in the odes of William Collins, the poems of Thomas Gray, and the Scots lyrics of Robert Burns. The work of William Blake, the first great romantic poet, began late in the 18th cent. Blake is unique: poet, artist, artisan, revolutionist, and visionary prophet.

In prose fiction, departures from social realism are evident in the Gothic romances of Horace Walpole, Anne Radcliffe, "Monk" Lewis, Charles Maturin, and others. These works catered to a growing interest in medievalism, northern antiquities, ballads, folklore, chivalry, and romance, also exploited in two masterpieces of forgery—the Ossian poems of James Macpherson and the "medieval" Rowley poems of Thomas Chatterton.

The Romantic Period

At the turn of the century, fired by ideas of personal and political liberty and of the energy and sublimity of the natural world, artists and intellectuals sought to break the bonds of 18th-century convention. Although the works of Jean Jacques Rousseau and William Godwin had great influence, the French Revolution and its aftermath had the strongest impact of all. In England initial support for the Revolution was primarily utopian and idealist, and when the French failed to live up to expectations, most English intellectuals renounced the Revolution. However, the romantic vision had taken forms other than political, and these developed apace.

In *Lyrical Ballads* (1798 and 1800), a watershed in literary history, William Wordsworth and Samuel Taylor Coleridge presented and illustrated a liberating aesthetic: poetry should express, in genuine language, experience as filtered through personal emotion and imagination; the truest experience was to be found in nature.

The concept of the *Sublime* strengthened this turn to nature, because in wild countrysides the power of the sublime could be felt most immediately. Wordsworth's romanticism is probably most fully realized in his great autobiographical poem, "The Prelude". In search of sublime moments, romantic poets wrote about the marvelous and supernatural, the exotic, and the medieval. But they also found beauty in the lives of simple rural people and aspects of the everyday world.

The second generation of romantic poets included John Keats, Percy Bysshe Shelley, and George Gordon, Lord Byron. In Keats's great odes, intellectual and emotional sensibility merge in language of great power and beauty. Shelley, who combined soaring lyricism with an apocalyptic political vision, sought more extreme effects and occasionally achieved them, as in his great drama *Prometheus Unbound*. His wife, Mary Wollstonecraft Shelley, wrote the greatest of the Gothic romances, *Frankenstein*.

Lord Byron was the prototypical romantic hero, the envy and scandal of the age. He has been continually identified with his own characters, particularly the rebellious, irreverent, erotically inclined Don Juan. Byron invested the romantic lyric with a rationalist irony. Minor romantic poets include Robert Southey —best-remembered today for his story "Goldilocks and the Three Bears"—Leigh Hunt, Thomas Moore, and Walter Savage Landor.

The romantic era was also rich in literary criticism and other nonfictional prose. Coleridge proposed an influential theory of literature in his *Biographia Literaria*. William Godwin and his wife, Mary Wollstonecraft, wrote ground–breaking books on human, and women's, rights. William Hazlitt, who never forsook political radicalism, wrote brilliant and astute literary criticism.

The master of the personal essay was Charles Lamb, whereas Thomas De Quincey was master of the personal confession. The periodicals *Edinburgh Review* and *Blackwood's Magazine*, in which leading writers were published throughout the century, were major forums of controversy, political as well as literary.

Although the great novelist Jane Austen wrote during the romantic era, her work defies classification. With insight, grace, and irony she delineated human relationships within the context of English country life. Sir Walter Scott, Scottish nationalist and romantic, made the genre of the historical novel widely popular. Other novelists of the period were Maria Edgeworth, Edward Bulwer-Lytton, and Thomas Love Peacock, the latter noted for his eccentric novels satirizing the romantics.

The Victorian Age

The Reform Bill of 1832 gave the middle class the political power it needed to consolidate—and to hold—the economic position it had already achieved. Industry and commerce burgeoned. While the affluence of the middle class increased, the lower classes, thrown off their land and into the cities to form the great urban working class, lived ever more wretchedly. The social changes were so swift and brutal that Godwinian utopianism rapidly gave way to attempts either to justify the new economic and urban conditions, or to change them. The intellectuals and artists of the age had to deal in some way with the upheavals in society, the obvious inequities of abundance for a few and squalor for many, and, emanating from the throne of Queen Victoria (1837–1901), an emphasis on public rectitude and moral propriety.

The Novel: The Victorian era was the great age of the English novel—realistic, thickly plotted, crowded with characters, and long. It was the ideal form to describe contemporary life and to entertain the middle class. The novels of Charles Dickens, full to overflowing with drama, humour, and an endless variety of vivid characters and plot complications, nonetheless spare nothing in their portrayal of what urban life was like for all classes. William Makepeace Thackeray is best known for *Vanity Fair,* which wickedly satirizes hypocrisy and greed.

Emily Brontë's single novel, *Wuthering Heights,* is a unique masterpiece propelled by a vision of elemental passions but controlled by an uncompromising artistic sense. The fine novels of Emily's sister Charlotte Brontë, especially *Jane Eyre* and *Villette,* are more rooted in convention, but daring in their own ways. The novels of George Eliot (Mary Ann Evans) appeared during the 1860s and 70s. A woman of great erudition and moral fervor, Eliot was concerned with ethical conflicts and social problems.

George Meredith produced comic novels noted for their psychological perception. Another novelist of the late 19th cent. was the prolific Anthony Trollope, famous for sequences of related novels that explore social, ecclesiastical, and political life in England.

Thomas Hardy 's profoundly pessimistic novels are all set in the harsh, punishing midland county he called Wessex. Samuel Butler produced novels satirizing the Victorian ethos, and Robert Louis Stevenson, a master of his craft, wrote arresting adventure fiction and children's verse. The mathematician Charles Lutwidge Dodgson, writing under the name Lewis Carroll, produced the complex and sophisticated children's classics *Alice's Adventures in Wonderland* and *Through the Looking Glass*. Lesser novelists of considerable merit include Benjamin Disraeli, George Gissing, Elizabeth Gaskell, and Wilkie Collins. By the end of the period, the novel was considered not only the premier form of entertainment but also a primary means of analyzing and offering solutions to social and political problems.

Nonfiction

Among the Victorian masters of nonfiction were the great Whig historian Thomas Macaulay and Thomas Carlyle, the historian, social critic, and prophet whose rhetoric thundered through the age. Influential thinkers included John Stuart Mill, the great liberal scholar and philosopher; Thomas Henry Huxley, a scientist and popularizer of Darwinian theory; and John Henry, Cardinal Newman, who wrote earnestly of religion, philosophy, and education. The founders of Communism, Karl Marx and Friedrich Engels, researched and wrote their books in the free environment of England. The great art historian and critic John Ruskin also concerned himself with social and economic problems. Matthew Arnold 's theories of literature and culture laid the foundations for modern literary criticism, and his poetry is also notable.

Poetry

The preeminent poet of the Victorian age was Alfred, Lord Tennyson. Although romantic in subject matter, his poetry was tempered by personal melancholy; in its mixture of social certitude and religious doubt it reflected the age. The poetry of Robert Browning and his wife, Elizabeth Barrett Browning, was immensely popular, though Elizabeth's was more venerated during their lifetimes. Browning is best remembered for his superb dramatic monologues. Rudyard Kipling, the poet of the empire triumphant, captured the quality of the life of the soldiers of British expansion. Some fine religious poetry was produced by Francis Thompson, Alice Meynell, Christina Rossetti, and Lionel Johnson.

In the middle of the 19th cent. the so-called Pre-Raphaelites, led by the painter-poet Dante Gabriel Rossetti, sought to revive what they judged to be the simple, natural values and techniques of medieval life and art. Their quest for a rich symbolic art led them away, however, from the mainstream. William Morris —designer, inventor, printer, poet, and social philosopher—was the most versatile of the group, which included the poets Christina Rossetti and Coventry Patmore.

Algernon Charles Swinburne began as a Pre-Raphaelite but soon developed his own classically influenced, sometimes florid style. A. E. Housman and Thomas Hardy, Victorian figures who lived on into the 20th cent., share a pessimistic view in their poetry, but Housman's well-constructed verse is rather more superficial. The great innovator among the late Victorian poets was the Jesuit priest Gerard Manley Hopkins. The concentration and originality of his imagery, as well as his jolting meter ("sprung rhythm"), had a profound effect on 20th-century poetry.

During the 1890s the most conspicuous figures on the English literary scene were the decadents. The principal figures in the group were Arthur Symons, Ernest Dowson, and, first among them in both notoriety and talent, Oscar Wilde. The Decadents' disgust with bourgeois complacency led them to extremes of behavior and expression. However limited their accomplishments, they pointed out the hypocrisies in Victorian values and institutions. The sparkling, witty comedies of Oscar Wilde and the comic operettas of W. S. Gilbert and Sir Arthur Sullivan were perhaps the brightest achievements of 19th-century British drama.

The Early Twentieth Century

Irish drama flowered in the early 20th cent., largely under the aegis of the Abbey Theatre in Dublin . John Millington Synge, William Butler Yeats, and Sean O'Casey all wrote on Irish themes—mythical in Yeats's poetic drama, political in O'Casey's realistic plays. Also Irish, George Bernard Shaw wrote biting dramas that reflect all aspects of British society. In fact, many of the towering figures of 20th-century English literature were not English; Shaw, Yeats, Joyce, O'Casey, and Beckett were Irish, Dylan Thomas was Welsh, T. S. Eliot was born an American, and Conrad was Polish.

Poetry in the early 20th cent. was typified by the conventional romanticism of such poets as John Masefield,

Alfred Noyes, and Walter de la Mare and by the experiments of the imagists, notably Hilda Doolittle (H. D.), Richard Aldington, Herbert Read, and D. H. Lawrence. The finest poet of the period was Yeats, whose poetry fused romantic vision with contemporary political and aesthetic concerns. Though the 19th-century tradition of the novel lived on in the work of Arnold Bennett, William Henry Hudson, and John Galsworthy, new writers like Henry James, H. G. Wells, and Joseph Conrad expressed the skepticism and alienation that were to become features of post-Victorian sensibility.

World War I shook England to the core. As social mores were shaken, so too were artistic conventions. The work of war poets like Siegfried Sassoon and Wilfred Owen, the latter killed in the war (as were Rupert Brooke and Isaac Rosenberg), was particularly influential. Ford Madox Ford 's landmark tetralogy, *Parade's End,* is perhaps the finest depiction of the war and its effects. The new era called for new forms, typified by the work of Gerard Manley Hopkins, first published in 1918, and of T. S. Eliot, whose long poem *The Waste Land* was a watershed in both American and English literary history. Its difficulty, formal invention, and bleak antiromanticism were to influence poets for decades.

Equally important was the novel *Ulysses,* also published in 1922, by the expatriate Irishman James Joyce. Although his books were controversial because of their freedom of language and content, Joyce's revolutions in narrative form, the treatment of time, and nearly all other techniques of the novel made him a master to be studied, but only intermittently copied. Though more conventional in form, the novels of D. H. Lawrence were equally challenging to convention; he was the first to champion both the primitive and the supercivilized urges of men and women.

Sensitivity and psychological subtlety mark the superb novels of Virginia Woolf, who, like Dorothy Richardson, experimented with the interior forms of narration. Woolf was the centre of the brilliant Bloomsbury group, which included the novelist E. M. Forster, the biographer Lytton Strachey, and many important English intellectuals of the early 20th cent.

Aldous Huxley and Evelyn Waugh satirized the group and the period, while Katharine Mansfield and Elizabeth Bowen captured their flavour in fiction.

Moved by the Great Depression, the rise of fascism, and English policies of appeasement, many writers and intellectuals sought solutions in the politics of the left—or the right. Wyndham Lewis satirized what he thought was the total dissolution of culture in *Apes of Gods*. George Orwell fought with the Republicans in the Spanish Civil War. The experience left him profoundly disillusioned with Communism, a feeling he eloquently expressed in such works as *Animal Farm* and *Nineteen Eighty-four*. The poets W. H. Auden, Christopher Isherwood, Stephen Spender, and C. Day Lewis all proclaimed their leftist respective political commitments, but the pressing demands of World War II superseded these long-term ideals.

The Postwar Era to the Present

After the war most English writers chose to focus on aesthetic or social rather than political problems; C. P. Snow was perhaps the notable exception. The novelists Henry Green, Ivy Compton-Burnett, Joyce Cary, and Lawrence Durrell, and the poets Robert Graves, Edwin Muir, Louis MacNeice, and Edith Sitwell tended to cultivate their own distinctive voices. Other novelists and playwrights of the 1950s, often called the angry young men, expressed a deep dissatisfaction with British society, combined with despair that anything could be done about it.

While the postwar era was not a great period of English literature, it produced a variety of excellent critics, including William Empson, Frank Kermode, and F. R. Leavis. The period was also marked by a number of highly individual novelists, including Kingsley Amis, Anthony Burgess, William Golding, Doris Lessing, Iris Murdoch, and Muriel Spark. Anthony Powell and Richard Hughes continued to work in the expansive 19th-century tradition, producing a series of realistic novels chronicling life in England during the 20th cent.

Some of the most exciting work of the period came in the theater, notably the plays of John Osborne, Harold Pinter, Tom

Stoppard, David Storey, and Arnold Wesker. Among the best postwar British authors were the Welsh poet Dylan Thomas and the Irish expatriate novelist and playwright Samuel Beckett. Thomas's lyricism and rich imagery reaffirmed the romantic spirit, and he was eventually appreciated for his technical mastery as well. Beckett, who wrote many of his works in French and translated them into English, is considered the greatest exponent of the theater of the absurd. His uncompromisingly bleak, difficult plays (and novels) depict the lonely, alienated human condition with compassion and humour.

Other outstanding contemporary poets include Hugh MacDiarmid, the leading figure of the Scottish literary renaissance; Ted Hughes, whose harsh, postapocalyptic poetry celebrates simple survival, and Seamus Heaney, an Irish poet who is hailed for his exquisite style. Novelists generally have found as little in the Thatcher and Major eras as in the previous period to inspire them, but the work of Margaret Drabble, John Fowles, David Lodge stands out, and the Scottish writer James Kelman stands out.

Chapter 2

Western Drama

Plays produced in the Western world. This article discusses the development of Western drama in general; for further information see the various national literature articles.

Greek Drama

The Western dramatic tradition has its origins in ancient Greece. The precise evolution of its main divisions— tragedy, comedy, and satire —is not definitely known. According to Aristotle, Greek drama, or, more explicitly, Greek tragedy, originated in the dithyramb. This was a choral hymn to the god Dionysus and involved exchanges between a lead singer and the chorus. It is thought that the dithyramb was sung at the Dionysia, an annual festival honoring Dionysus.

Tradition has it that at the Dionysia of 534 b.c., during the reign of Pisistratus, the lead singer of the dithyramb, a man named Thespis, added to the chorus an actor with whom he carried on a dialogue, thus initiating the possibility of dramatic action. Thespis is credited with the invention of tragedy. Eventually, Aeschylus introduced a second actor to the drama and Sophocles a third, Sophocles' format being continued by Euripides, the last of the great classical Greek dramatists.

Generally, the earlier Greek tragedies place more emphasis on the chorus than the later ones. In the majestic plays of Aeschylus, the chorus serves to underscore the personalities and situations of the characters and to provide ethical comment on the action. Much of Aeschylus' most beautiful poetry is contained in the choruses of his plays. The increase in the number of actors resulted in less concern with communal problems and beliefs and more with dramatic conflict between individuals. Accompanying this emphasis on individuals' interaction, from the time of Aeschylus to that of Euripides, there was a marked tendency toward realism. Euripides' characters are ordinary, not godlike, and the gods themselves are introduced more as devices of plot manipulation (as in the use of the deus ex machina in *Medea*, 431 b.c.) than as strongly felt representations of transcendent power. Utilizing three actors, Sophocles developed dramatic action beyond anything Aeschylus had achieved with only two and also introduced more natural speech. However, he did not lose a sense of the godlike in man and man's affairs, as Euripides often did. Thus, it is Sophocles who best represents the classical balance between the human and divine, the realistic and the symbolic. Greek comedy is divided by scholars into Old Comedy (5th cent. b.c.), Middle Comedy (c.404–c.321 b.c.), and New Comedy (c.320–c.264 b.c.). The sole literary remains of Old Comedy are the plays of Aristophanes, characterized by obscenity, political satire, fantasy, and strong moral overtones. While there are no extant examples of Middle Comedy, it is conjectured that the satire, obscenity, and fantasy of the earlier plays were much mitigated during this transitional period. Most extant examples of New Comedy are from the works of Menander; these comedies are realistic and elegantly written, often revolving around a love-interest.

Roman Drama

The Roman theater never approached the heights of the Greek, and the Romans themselves had little interest in serious dramatic endeavors, being drawn toward sensationalism and spectacle. The earliest Roman dramatic attempts were simply translations from the Greek. Gnaeus Naevius (c.270–c.199 b.c.) and his successors imitated Greek models in tragedies that never transcended the level of violent melodrama. Even the nlne tragedies of the philosopher and statesman Seneca are gloomy and lurid, emphasizing the sensational aspects of Greek myth; they are noted primarily for their inflated rhetoric. Seneca became an important influence on Renaissance tragedy, but it is unlikely that his plays were intended for more than private readings. Although Roman tragedy produced little of worth, a better judgment may be passed on the comedies of Plautus and Terence. Plautus incorporated native Roman elements into the plots and themes of Menander, producing plays characterized by farce, intrigue, romance, and sentiment. Terence was a more polished stylist who wrote for and about the upper classes and dispensed with the element of farce. The Roman preference for spectacle and the Christian suppression of drama led to a virtual cessation of dramatic production during the decline of the Roman Empire. Pantomimes accompanied by a chorus developed out of tragedy, and comic mimes were popular until the 4th cent. a.d. . It is this mime tradition, carried on by traveling performers, that provided the theatrical continuity between the ancient world and the medieval. The Roman mime tradition has been suggested as the origin of the commedia dell'arte of the Italian Renaissance, but this conjecture has never been proved.

Medieval Drama

While the Christian church did much to suppress the performance of plays, paradoxically it is in the church that medieval drama began. The first record of this beginning is the trope in the Easter service known as the Quem quaeritis [whom you seek. Tropes, originally musical elaborations of the church service, gradually evolved into drama; eventually the Latin lines telling of the Resurrection were spoken, rather than sung, by priests who represented the angels and the two Marys at the tomb of Jesus. Thus, simple interpolations developed into grandiose cycles of mystery plays, depicting biblical episodes from the Creation to Judgment Day. The most famous of these plays is the Second Shepherds' Play. Another important type that developed from church liturgy was the miracle play, based on the lives of saints rather than on scripture. The miracle play reached its peak in France and the mystery play in England. Both types gradually became secularized, passing into the hands of trade guilds or professional actors. The *Second Shepherds' Play,* for all its religious seriousness, is most noteworthy for its elements of realism and farce, while the miracle plays in France often emphasized comedy and adventure . The morality play, a third type of religious drama, appeared early in the 15th cent. Morality plays were religious allegories, the most famous being Everyman. Another type of drama popular in medieval times was the interlude, which can be generally defined as a dramatic work with characteristics of the morality play that is primarily intended for entertainment.

Renaissance Drama

By the advent of the Renaissance in the 15th and 16th cent., most European countries had established native traditions of religious drama and farce that contended with the impact of the newly discovered Greek and Roman plays. Little had been known of classical drama during the Middle Ages, and evidently the only classical imitations during that period were the Christian imitations of Terence by the Saxon nun Hrotswitha in the 10th cent.

Italy

The translation and imitation of the classics occurred first in Italy, with Terence, Plautus, and Seneca as the models. The Italians strictly applied their interpretation of Aristotle 's rules for the drama, and this rigidity was primarily responsible for the failure of Italian Renaissance drama. Some liveliness appeared in the comic sphere, particularly in the works of Ariosto and in Machiavelli 's satiric masterpiece, *La Mandragola*. The pastoral drama—set in the country and depicting the romantic affairs of rustic people, usually shepherds and shepherdesses—was more successful than either comedy or tragedy. Notable Italian practitioners of the genre were Giovanni Battista Guarini (1537–1612) and Torquato Tasso. The true direction of the Italian stage was toward the spectacular and the musical. A popular Italian Renaissance form was the intermezzo, which presented music and lively entertainment between the acts of classical imitations. The native taste for music and theatricality led to the emergence of the opera in the 16th cent. and the triumph of this form on the Italian stage in the 17th cent. Similarly, the commedia dell'arte, emphasizing comedy and improvisation and featuring character types familiar to a contemporary audience, was more popular than academic imitations of classical comedy.

France

Renaissance drama appeared somewhat later in France than in Italy. Estienne Jodelle 's Senecan tragedy *Cleopatre captive* marks the beginning of classical imitation in France. The French drama initially suffered from the same rigidity as the Italian, basing itself on Roman models and Italian imitations. However, in the late 16th cent. in France there was a romantic reaction to classical dullness, led by Alexandre Hardy, France's first professional playwright.

This romantic trend was stopped in the 17th cent. by Cardinal Richelieu, who insisted on a return to classic forms. Richelieu's judgment, however, bore fruit in the triumphs of the French neoclassical tragedies of Jean Racine and the comedies of Molière. The great tragedies of Pierre Corneille, although classical in their grandeur and in their concern with noble characters, are decidedly of the Renaissance in their exaltation of man's ability, by force of will, to transcend adverse circumstances.

Spain

Renaissance drama in Spain and England was more successful than in France and Italy because the two former nations were able to transform classical models with infusions of native characteristics. In Spain the two leading Renaissance playwrights were Lope de Vega and Pedro Calderón de la Barca. Earlier, Lope de Rueda had set the tone for future Spanish drama with plays that are romantic, lyrical, and generally in the mixed tragicomic form. Lope de Vega wrote an enormous number of plays of many types, emphasizing plot, character, and romantic action. Best known for his *La vida es sueño* [life is a dream], a play that questions the nature of reality, Calderón was a more controlled and philosophical writer than Lope.

England

The English drama of the 16th cent. showed from the beginning that it would not be bound by classical rules. Elements of farce, morality, and a disregard for the unities of time, place, and action inform the early comedies *Gammer Gurton's Needle* and *Ralph Roister Doister* (both c.1553) and the Senecan tragedy *Gorboduc.* William Shakespeare 's great work was foreshadowed by early essays in the historical chronicle play, by elements of romance found in the works of John Lyly, by revenge plays such as Thomas Kyd 's *Spanish Tragedy* (c.1586)—again inspired by the works of Seneca—and by Christopher Marlowe 's development of blank verse and his deepening of the tragic perception. Shakespeare, of course, stands as the supreme dramatist of the Renaissance period, equally adept at writing tragedies, comedies, or chronicle plays. His great achievements include the perfection of a verse form and language that capture the spirit of ordinary speech and yet stand above it to give a special dignity to his characters and situations; an unrivaled subtlety of characterization; and a marvelous ability to unify plot, character, imagery, and verse movement. With the reign of James I the English drama began to decline until the closing of the theaters by the Puritans in 1642. This period is marked by sensationalism and rhetoric in tragedy, as in the works of John Webster and Thomas Middleton, spectacle in the form of the masque, and a gradual turn to polished wit in comedy, begun by Francis Beaumont and John Fletcher and furthered by James Shirley. The best plays of the Jacobean period are the comedies of Ben Jonson, in which he satirized contemporary life by means of his own invention, the comedy of humours.

Drama from 1750 to 1800

The second half of the 17th cent. was distinguished by the achievements of the French neoclassicists and the Restoration playwrights in England. Jean Racine brought clarity of perception and simplicity of language to his love tragedies, which emphasize women characters and psychological motivation. Molière produced brilliant social comedies that are neoclassical in their ridicule of any sort of excess.

In England, Restoration tragedy degenerated into bombastic heroic dramas by such authors as John Dryden and Thomas Otway. Often written in rhymed heroic couplets, these plays are replete with sensational incidents and epic personages. But Restoration comedy, particularly the brilliant comedies of manners by George Etherege and William Congreve, achieved a perfection of style and cynical upper-class wit that is still appreciated. The works of William Wycherley, while similar in type, are more savage and deeply cynical. George Farquhar was a later and gentler master of Restoration comedy.

Eighteenth-Century Drama

The influence of Restoration comedy can be seen in the 18th cent. in the plays of Oliver Goldsmith and Richard Brinsley Sheridan. This century also ushered in the middle-class or domestic drama, which treated the problems of ordinary people. George Lillo's *London Merchant; or, The History of George Barnwell,* is an important example of this type of play because it brought the bourgeois tragic hero to the English stage. Such playwrights as Sir Richard Steele and Colley Cibber in England and Marivaux in France contributed to the development of the genteel, sentimental comedy. While the political satire in the plays of Henry Fielding and in John Gay 's *Beggar's Opera* seemed to offer a more interesting potential than the sentiment of Cibber, this line of development was cut off by the Licensing Act of 1737, which required government approval before a play could be produced. The Italian Carlo Goldoni, who wrote realistic comedies with fairly sophisticated characterizations, also tended toward middle-class moralizing. His contemporary, Count Carlo Gozzi, was more ironic and remained faithful to the spirit of the commedia dell'arte. Prior to the surge of German romanticism in the late 18th cent., two playwrights stood apart from the trend toward sentimental bourgeois realism. Voltaire tried to revive classical models and introduced exotic Eastern settings, although his tragedies tend to be more philosophical than dramatic. Similarly, the Italian Count Vittorio Alfieri sought to restore the spirit of the ancients to his drama, but the attempt was vitiated by his chauvinism. The Sturm und Drang in Germany represented a romantic reaction against French neoclassicism and was supported by an upsurge of German interest in Shakespeare, who was viewed at the time as the greatest of the romantics. Gotthold Lessing, Friedrich von Schiller, and Goethe were the principal figures of this movement, but the plays produced by the three are frequently marred by sentimentality and too heavy a burden of philosophical ideas.

Nineteenth-Century Drama

The romantic movement did not blossom in French drama until the 1820s, and then primarily in the work of Victor Hugo and Alexandre Dumas père, while in England the great Romantic poets did not produce important drama, although both Lord Byron and Percy Bysshe Shelley were practitioners of the closet drama. Burlesque and mediocre melodrama reigned supreme on the English stage. Although melodrama was aimed solely at producing superficial excitement, its development, coupled with the emergence of realism in the 19th cent., resulted in more serious drama. Initially, the melodrama dealt in such superficially exciting materials as the gothic castle with its mysterious lord for a villain, but gradually the characters and settings moved closer to the realities of contemporary life.

The concern for generating excitement led to a more careful consideration of plot construction, reflected in the smoothly contrived climaxes of the "well-made" plays of Eugène Scribe and Victorien Sardou of France and Arthur Wing Pinero of England. The work of Émile Augier and Alexandre Dumas fils combined the drama of ideas with the "well-made" play. Realism had perhaps its most profound expression in the works of the great 19th-century Russian dramatists: Nikolai Gogol, A. N. Ostrovsky, Ivan Turgenev,

Leo Tolstoy, Anton Chekhov, and Maxim Gorky. Many of the Russian dramatists emphasized character and satire rather than plot in their works.

Related to realism is naturalism, which can be defined as a selective realism emphasizing the more sordid and pessimistic aspects of life. An early forerunner of this style in the drama is Georg Büchner 's powerful tragedy *Danton's Death,* and an even earlier suggestion may be seen in the pessimistic romantic tragedies of Heinrich von Kleist. Friedrich Hebbel wrote grimly naturalistic drama in the middle of the 19th cent., but the naturalistic movement is most commonly identified with the "slice-of-life" theory of Émile Zola, which had a profound effect on 20th-century playwrights.

Henrik Ibsen of Norway brought to a climax the realistic movement of the 19th cent. and also served as a bridge to 20th-century symbolism. His realistic dramas of ideas surpass other such works because they blend a complex plot, a detailed setting, and middle-class yet extraordinary characters in an organic whole. Ibsen's later plays, such as *The Master Builder,* are symbolic, marking a trend away from realism that was continued by August Strindberg 's dream plays, with their emphasis on the spiritual, and by the plays of the Belgian Maurice Maeterlinck, who incorporated into drama the theories of the symbolist poets .

While these antirealistic developments took place on the Continent, two playwrights were making unique contributions to English theater. Oscar Wilde produced comedies of manners that compare favorably with the works of Congreve, and George Bernard Shaw brought the play of ideas to fruition with penetrating intelligence and singular wit.

Twentieth-Century Drama

During the 20th cent., especially after World War I, Western drama became more internationally unified and less the product of separate national literary traditions. Throughout the century realism, naturalism, and symbolism (and various combinations of these) continued to inform important plays. Among the many 20th-century playwrights who have written what can be broadly termed naturalist dramas are Gerhart Hauptmann (German), John Galsworthy (English), John Millington Synge and Sean O'Casey (Irish), and Eugene O'Neill, Clifford Odets, and Lillian Hellman (American).

An important movement in early 20th-century drama was expressionism. Expressionist playwrights tried to convey the dehumanizing aspects of 20th-century technological society through such devices as minimal scenery, telegraphic dialogue, talking machines, and characters portrayed as types rather than individuals. Notable playwrights who wrote expressionist dramas include Ernst Toller and Georg Kaiser (German), Karel Èapek (Czech), and Elmer Rice and Eugene O'Neill (American). The 20th cent. also saw the attempted revival of drama in verse, but although such writers as William Butler Yeats, W. H. Auden, T. S. Eliot, Christopher Fry, and Maxwell Anderson produced effective results, verse drama was no longer an important form in English. In Spanish, however, the poetic dramas of Federico García Lorca are placed among the great works of Spanish literature.

Three vital figures of 20th-century drama are the American Eugene O'Neill, the German Bertolt Brecht, and the Italian Luigi Pirandello. O'Neill's body of plays in many forms—naturalistic, expressionist, symbolic, psychological—won him the Nobel Prize in Literature in 1936 and indicated the coming-of-age of American drama. Brecht wrote dramas of ideas, usually promulgating socialist or Marxist theory. In order to make his audience more intellectually receptive to his theses, he endcavored—by using expressionist techniques—to make them continually aware that they were watching a play, not vicariously experiencing reality. For Pirandello, too, it was paramount to fix an awareness of his plays as theater; indeed, the major philosophical concern of his dramas is the difficulty of differentiating between illusion and reality.

World War II and its attendant horrors produced a widespread sense of the utter meaninglessness of human existence. This sense is brilliantly expressed in the body of plays that have come to be known collectively as the theater of the absurd. By abandoning traditional devices of the drama, including logical plot development, meaningful dialogue, and intelligible characters, absurdist playwrights sought to convey modern humanity's feelings of bewilderment, alienation, and despair—the sense that reality is itself unreal. In their plays human beings often portrayed as dupes, clowns who, although not without dignity, are at the mercy of forces that are inscrutable.

Probably the most famous plays of the theater of the absurd are Eugene Ionesco 's *Bald Soprano* and Samuel Beckett 's *Waiting for Godot*. The sources of the theater of the absurd are diverse; they can be found in the tenets of surrealism, Dadaism , and existentialism; in the traditions of the music hall, vaudeville, and burlesque; and in the films of Charlie Chaplin and Buster Keaton. Playwrights whose works can be roughly classed as belonging to the theater of the absurd are Jean Genet (French), Max Frisch and Friedrich Dürrenmatt (Swiss), Fernando Arrabal (Spanish), and the early plays of Edward Albee (American). The pessimism and despair of the 20th cent. also found expression in the existentialist dramas of Jean-Paul Sartre, in the realistic and symbolic dramas of Arthur Miller, Tennessee Williams, and Jean Anouilh, and in the surrealist plays of Jean Cocteau.

Somewhat similar to the theater of the absurd is the so-called theater of cruelty, derived from the ideas of Antonin Artaud, who, writing in the 1930s, foresaw a drama that would assault its audience with movement and sound, producing a visceral rather than an intellectual reaction. After the violence of World War II and the subsequent threat of the atomic bomb, his approach seemed particularly appropriate to many playwrights. Elements of the theater of cruelty can be found in the brilliantly abusive language of John Osborne 's *Look Back in Anger* and Edward Albee's *Who's Afraid of Virginia Woolf?*, in the ritualistic aspects of some of Genet's plays, in the masked utterances and enigmatic silences of Harold Pinter 's "comedies of menace," and in the orgiastic abandon of Julian Beck 's *Paradise Now!*; it was fully expressed in Peter Brooks's production of Peter Weiss 's *Marat/Sade*.

During the last third of the 20th cent. a few continental

European dramatists, such as Dario Fo in Italy and Heiner Müller in Germany, stand out in the theater world. However, for the most part, the countries of the continent saw an emphasis on creative trends in directing rather than a flowering of new plays. In the United States and England, however, many dramatists old and new continued to flourish, with numerous plays of the later decades of the 20th cent. (and the early 21st cent.) echoing the trends of the ,ears preceding them.

Realism in a number of guises—psychological, social, and political—continued to be a force in such British works as David Storey 's *Home*, Sir Alan Ayckbourn 's *Norman Conquests* trilogy, and David Hare 's *Amy's View*; in such Irish dramas as Brian Friel's *Dancing at Lughnasa* and Martin McDonagh's 1990s Leenane trilogy; and in such American plays as Jason Miller's *That Championship Season*, Lanford Wilson 's *Talley's Folly*, and John Guare 's *Six Degrees of Separation*. In keeping with the tenor of the times, many of these and other works of the period were marked by elements of wit, irony, and satire.

A witty surrealism also characterized some of the late 20th cent.'s theater, particularly the brilliant wordplay and startling juxtapositions of the many plays of England's Tom Stoppard. In addition, two of late-20th-century America's most important dramatists, Sam Shepard and David Mamet (as well as their followers and imitators), explored American culture with a kind of hyper-realism mingled with echoes of the theater of cruelty in the former's *Buried Child*, the latter's *Glengarry Glen Ross*, and other works. While each exhibited his own very distinctive voice and vision, both playwrights achieved many of their effects through stark settings, austere language in spare dialog, meaningful silences, the projection of a powerful streak of menace, and outbursts of real or implied violence.

The late decades of the 20th century were also a time of considerable experiment and iconoclasm. Experimental dramas of the 1960s and 70s by such groups as Beck's Living Theater and Jerzy Grotowski 's Polish Laboratory Theatre were followed by a mixing and merging of various kinds of media with aspects of postmodernism, improvisational techniques, performance art, and other kinds of avant-garde theater. Some of the era's more innovative efforts included productions by theater groups such as New York's La MaMa and Mabou Mines and Chicago's Steppenwolf Theatre Co.; the Canadian writer-director Robert Lepage's intricate, sometimes multilingual works, e.g. *Tectonic Plates*; the inventive one-man shows of such monologuists as Eric Bogosian, Spalding Gray, and John Leguizamo; the transgressive drag dramas of Charles Ludlam's Ridiculous Theater, e.g., *The Mystery of Irma Vep*; and the operatic multimedia extravaganzas of Robert Wilson, e.g. *White Raven*.

Thematically, the social upheavals of the 1960s, 70s, and 80s—particularly the civil rights and women's movements, gay liberation, and the AIDS crisis—provided impetus for new plays that explored the lives of minorities and women. Beginning with Lorraine Hansberry 's *A Raisin in the Sun*, drama by and about African Americans emerged as a significant theatrical trend. In the 1960s plays such as James Baldwin 's *Blues for Mr. Charley*, Amiri Baraka 's searing *Dutchman*, and Charles Gordone's *No Place to Be Somebody* explored black American life; writers including Ed Bullins (e.g., *The Taking of Miss Janie*, 1975), Ntozake Shange (e.g., *For Colored Girls Who Have Considered Suicide When the Rainbow is Enuf*, 1976) and Charles Fuller (e.g., *A Soldier's Play*, 1981) carried these themes into later decades. One of the most distinctive and prolific of the century's African-American playwrights, August Wilson, debuted on Broadway in 1984 with *Ma Rainey's Black Bottom* and continued to define the black American experience in his ongoing dramatic cycle into the next century.

Feminist and other women-centered themes dramatized by contemporary female playwrights were plentiful in the 1970s and extended in the following decades. Significant figures included England's Caryl Churchill (e.g., the witty *Top Girls*, 1982), the Cuban-American experimentalist Maria Irene Forñes (e.g., *Fefu and Her Friends*, 1977) and American realists including Beth Henley (e.g., *Crimes of the Heart*, 1978), Marsha Norman (e.g., *'Night Mother*, 1982), and Wendy Wasserstein (e.g., *The Heidi Chronicles*, 1988). Skilled monologuists also provided provocative female-themed one-women shows such as Eve Ensler's *The Vagina Monologues* and various solo theatrical performances by Lily Tomlin, Karen Finley, Anna Deveare Smith, Sarah Jones, and others.

Gay themes (often in works by gay playwrights) also marked the later decades of the 20th cent. Homosexual characters had been treated sympathetically but in the context of pathology in such earlier 20th-century works as Lillian Hellman's *The Children's Hour* and Robert Anderson's *Tea and Sympathy*. Gay subjects were presented more explicitly during the 1960s, notably in the English farces of Joe Orton and Matt Crowley's witty but grim portrait of pre-Stonewall American gay life, *The Boys in the Band*. In later years gay experience was explored more frequently and with greater variety and openness, notably in Britain in Martin Sherman's *Bent* and Peter Gill's *Mean Tears* and in the United States in Jane Chambers' *Last Summer at Bluefish Cove*, Harvey Fierstein's *Torch Song Trilogy*, Larry Kramer's *The Normal Heart*, David Henry Hwang's *M. Butterfly*, which also dealt with Asian identity, and Paul Rudnick's *Jeffrey*. Tony Kushner 's acclaimed two-part *Angels in America* is generally considered the century's most brilliant and innovative theatrical treatment of the contemporary gay world

Chapter 3

Introduction

George Bernard Shaw (1856-1950)

Irish dramatist, literary critic, a socialist spokesman, and a leading figure in the 20th century theater. Shaw was a freethinker, defender of women's rights, and advocate of equality of income. In 1925 he was awarded the Nobel Prize for Literature. Shaw accepted the honour but refused the money.

"Just as the historian can teach no real history until he has cured his readers of the romantic delusion that the greatness of a queen consists in her being a pretty woman and having her head cut off, so the playwright of the first order can do nothing with his audience until he has cured them of looking at the stage through the keyhole, and sniffing round the theatre as prurient people sniff round the divorce court."

George Bernard Shaw was born in Dublin, where he grew up in something close to genteel poverty. "I am a typical Irishman; my family came from Yorkshire," Shaw once said. His father, George Carr Shaw, was in the wholesale grain trade. Lucinda Elisabeth (Gurly) Shaw, his mother, was the daughter of an impoverished landowner. She was 16-years younger than her husband.

George Carr was a drunkard - his example prompted his son to become a teetotaller. When he died in 1885, his children and wife did not attend his funeral. Young Shaw and his two sisters were brought up mostly by servants. Shaw's mother eventually left the family home to teach music, singing, in London. When she died in 1913, Shaw confessed to Mrs.

Patrick Campbell: "I must write to you about it, because there is no one else who didn't hate her mother, and even who doesn't hate her children."

In 1866 the family moved to a better neighborhood. Shaw went to the Wesleyan Connexional School, then moved to a private school near Dalkey, and from there to Dublin's Central Model School. Shaw finished his formal education at the Dublin English Scientific and Commercial Day School. At the age of 15, he started to work as a junior clerk. In 1876 he went to London, joining his sister and mother. Shaw did not return to Ireland for nearly thirty years.

Most of the next two years Shaw educated himself at the British Museum. He began his literary career by writing music and drama criticism, and novels, including the semi-autobiographical IMMATURITY, without much success. A vegetarian, who eschewed alcohol and tobacco, Shaw joined in 1884 the Fabian Society, served on its executive committee from 1885 to 1911. The middle-class socialist group attracted also H.G. Wells - the both writers send each other copies of their new books as they appeared. "You are, now that Wilde is dead, the one living playwright in my esteem," wrote Wells after receiving Shaw's THREE PLAYS FOR PURITANS.

A man of many causes, Shaw supported abolition of private property, radical change in the voting system, campaigned for the simplification of spelling, and the reform of the English alphabet. As a public speaker, Shaw gained the status of one of the most sought-after orators in England. In 1895 Shaw became a drama critic for the *Saturday Review*. Articles written for the paper were later collected in OUR THEATRES IN THE NINETIES. Music, art, and drama criticism Shaw wrote for *Dramatic Review, Our Corner, The Pall Mall Gazette, The World,* and *The Star* as 'Corno bi Basetto'. His music criticism were collected in SHAW'S MUSIC. After lacing a shoe too tightly, an operation was performed on his foot for necrosis; Shaw was unable to put his foot on the ground for eighteen months. During this period he wrote CAESAR AND CLEOPATRA and THE PERFECT WAGNERITE. "...I have no reason to believe that they would have been a bit better if they had been written on two legs instead of one," he said in a letter to the playwright St John Ervine. His friend had his leg amputated during WWI after being hit by a shell splinters.

In 1898 Shaw married the wealthy Charlotte Payne-Townshend. They settled in 1906 in the Hertfordshire village of Ayot St. Lawrence. Shaw remained with Charlotte until her death, although he was occasionally linked with other women. He carried on a passionate correspondence over the years with Mrs. Patrick Campbell, a widow and actress, who got the starring role in PYGMALION. All the other actresses refused to say the taboo word 'bloody' that the playwright had put in the mouth of Eliza. When she wanted to publish his love letters to her, Shaw answered: "I will not, dear Stella, at my time of life, play the horse to your Lady Godiva."

The Norwegian playwright Henrik Ibsen had a great influence on Shaw's thinking. For a summer meeting of the Fabian Society in 1890, he wrote THE QUINTESSENCE OF IBSENISM, in which he considered Ibsen a pioneer, "who declares that it is right to do something hitherto regarded as infamous."

Shaw's early plays, WIDOWER'S HOUSES, which criticized slum landlords, as well as several subsequent ones, were not well received. His 'unpleasant plays', ideological attacks on the evils of capitalism and explorations of moral and social problems, were followed with more entertaining but as principled productions. "To a professional critic theatre-going is the curse of Adam.

The play is the evil he is paid to endure in the sweat of his brow; and the sooner it is over, the better." CANDIDA was a comedy about the wife of a clergyman, and what happens when a weak, young poet wants to rescue her from her dull family life.

But it was not until JOHN BULL'S OTHER ISLAND that Shaw gained in England a wider popularity with his own plays. In the Unites States and Germany Shaw's name was already well-known. Between 1904 and 1907 The Royal Court Theatre staged several of his plays, including *Candida*.

MORELL: Man can climb to the highest summits; but he cannot dwell there. MARCHBACKS (springing up): It's false: there can he dwell for ever, and there only. It's in the other moment that he can find no rest, no sense of the silent glory of life. Where would you have spend my moments, if not on the summits?

MORELL: In the scullery, slicing onions and filling lamps.

MAJOR BARBARA depicted an officer of the Salvation Army, who learns from her father, a manufacturer of armaments, that money and power can be better weapons against evil than love. Ironically the producer of the film version of the play, Gabriel Pascal, was eager to do business with Sir Basil Zaharoff, an arms dealer.

PICKERING: Have you no morals, man?

DOOLITTLE: Can't afford them, Governor.

Pygmalion was originally written for the actress Mrs. Patrick Campbell. Later the play became the basis for two films and a musical. (Shaw's correspondence with the actresses Ellen Terry and Stella Campbell are available in book form.) Shaw's popularity declined after his essay 'Common Sense About the War', which was considered unpatriotic.

With SAINT JOAN, his masterpiece, Shaw was again accepted by the post-war public. Now he was regarded as 'a second Shakespeare', who had revolutionized the British theatre. Shaw did not portrait Joan of Arc, his protagonist, as a heroine or martyr, but as a stubborn young woman. And as in classic tragedies, her flaw is fatal and brings about her downfall. Uncommonly Shaw showed some sympathy to her judges. The play was written four years after Joan was declared a saint.

In 1893 Shaw collaborated with Keir Hardie in writing the party programme for the new Independent Labour party. Many of his playes also were philosophical addresses on the subject of individual responsibility or freedom of spirit against the conformist demands of society. Shaw was cofounder with the Webbs of the London School of Economics, and launched the petition against the imprisonment of Oscar Wilde. In 1897 he entered local government.

In his plays Shaw combined contemporary moral problems with ironic tone and paradoxes, "Shavian" wit, which have produced such phrases as "He who can, does. He who cannot, teaches", "England and America are two countries divided by a common language", "Christianity might be a good thing if anyone ever tried it", and "I never resist temptation because I have found that things are bad for me do not tempt me." Discussion and intellectual acrobatics are the basis of his drama, and before the emergence of the sound film, his plays were nearly impossible to adapt into screen. During his long career, Shaw wrote over 50 plays. He continued to write them even in his 90s. George Bernard Shaw died at Ayot St. Lawrence, Hertfordshire, on November 2, 1950. He was cremated and it was his wish that his ashes be mixed with those of his wife, Charlotte - she had died seven years before, "an old woman bowed and crippled, furrowed and wrinkled," as Shaw depicted her in a letter to H.G. Wells.

Since the days of the silent films, Shaw had been a fan of motion-picture. He also played in the film *Rosy Rapture - The Pride of the Beauty*. Shaw did not like much of the German film version of *Pygmalion,* and the penniless producer and director Gabriel Pascal persuaded the author to give him the rights to make films from his plays. "Mr Pascal, you're the first honest film producer I have ever met," Shaw told him at their first meeting and gave him a pound note. *Pygmalion,* produced by Pascal and directed by Anthony Asquith and David Lean (uncredited), was a great success. In one article, Pascal was picked with the Pope and Hitler as one of the ten most famous men of 1938, but his career ended in the financial fiasco of the spectacle *Caesar and Cleopatra.* Among several other films inspired by Shaw's plays are *Saint Joan, How He Lied to Her Husband, Arms and the Man, Major Barbara,* and *My Fair Lady.* Pascal's co-director in *Major Barbara* was David Lean, but for thousand pounds Lean agreed to give the full credit to Pascal.

Selected Works:

- Immaturity, 1879
- The irrational knot, 1880

- Love among artist, 1881
- Our corner; cashel byron's profession, 1882
- An unsocial socialist, 1883
- Fabian essays on socialism, 1889
- The quintessence of ibsenism, 1891 (- see henrik ibsen)
- Widower's houses, 1892
- Arms and the man, 1894 - sankareita - film 1932, dir. By cecil lewis, starring barry jones, anne grey, angela baddeley
- Cashel byron's profession, 1885 - herra byronin ammatti
- Candida, 1987 - suomentajina mm. Helmi setälä, helvi erjakka
- The man of destiny, 1897 - kohtalon mies
- The devil's disciple, 1897 - pirun oppipoika - film 1959, dir. By guy hamilton, starring burt lancaster, kirk douglas, laurence olivier, eva le gallienne
- The perfect wagnerite, 1898
- Plays pleasant and unpleasant, 1898
- The philander, 1898
- You never can tell, 1899
- Fabianism and the empire, 1900
- Captain brassbound's conversion, 1900 - kapteeni brassboundin kääntymys
- Caesar and cleopatra, 1901 - caesar ja cleopatra - film 1945, dir. By gabriel pascal, starring claude rains, vivien leigh, cecil parker, stewart granger
- Three plays for puritans, 1901
- Mrs. Warren's profession, 1902 - rouva warrenin ammatti
- John bull's other island, 1904 (stage play 1907)
- The common sense of municipal trading, 1904
- Man and superman, 1905
- On going to church, 1905
- Major barbara, 1905 - majuri barbara - film 1941, dir. By gabriel pascal, starring wendy hiller, rex harrison, robert morley, robert newton, marie lohr, deborah kerr

- Doctor's dilemma, 1906 - lääkäri pulassa - film 1958, dir. By anthony asquith, starring leslie caron, dirk bogarde, john robinson
- Dramatic opinions and essays, 1906
- Getting married, 1908
- Misalliance, 1910
- Socialism and superior brains, 1910
- Fanny's first play, 1911 - fannyn ensi-ilta
- Overruled, 1912
- Androcles and the lion, 1912 - androkles ja leijona
- Great catherine, 1913 - suuri katariina
- Pygmalion, 1913 - suom. - Film 1935, dir. By erich engel; film 1938, dir. By anthony asquith, starring leslie howard, wendy hiller, wilfrid lawson, scott sunderland; my fair la dy in 1964, dir. By ceorge cukor, starring rex harrison, audrey hepburn, stanley holloway, wilfrid hyde white
- Peace conference hints, 1919
- Heartbreak house, 1920 - särkyneiden sydänten talo
- Back to metuselah, 1922
- Saint joan, 1923 - pyhä johanna (trans. By matti norri) - film 1957, dir. By otto preminger, starring jean seberg, anton walbrook, richard widmark - movie version utilized a screen version by graham greene - "i always wanted to make a picture of it. Perhaps that was the great mistake: I loved the play so much that i didn't analyse it. I realized only later that the play is actually a very intellectual, analytical rendition of the story of saint joan. It's not a emotional story, and it just wasn't moving enough to get the masses to follow. Even the play, as i found out later, was never a big popular success." (Otto preminger in *who the devil made it* by peter bogdanovich, 1997)
- Imprisonment, 1925
- The socialism of shaw, 1926
- The intelligent woman's guide to socialism and capitalism, 1928

- The apple cart, 1929 - amerikan keisari
- Bernard shaw and karl marx, 1930
- What i really wrote about the war, 1931
- Screenplay (with frank launder): How he lied to her husband, 1931 - *film dir. By cecil lewis*
- Doctor's delusions, crude criminology, and sham education, 1932
- Essays in fabian socialism, 1932
- The works of bernard shaw, 1930-32 (30 vols., revised as ayot st. Lawrence edition, 1931-32; standard edition, 36 vols., 1947-52)
- Major critical essays, 1932
- Too true to be good, 1932
- Our theatres in the nineties, 1932
- Music in london, 1890-94, 1932
- American boobs, 1933
- Prefaces, 1934
- Village wooing, 1934
- The simpleton of the unexpected isles, 1935
- William morris as i knew him, 1936
- The millionairess, 1936 - miljoonaperijätär - film 1961, dir. By anthony asquith, starring sophia loren, peter sellers, alistari sim, vittorio de sica
- London music in 1888-1889, 1937
- "In good king charles's golden days", 1939
- Everybody's political what's what, 1944
- Sixteen self-sketches, 1948
- Buoyant billions, 1948 (perf. And pub. Zurich)
- Farfetched fables, 1950
- Plays and players, 1952
- Selected prose, 1953
- Shaw on music, 1955
- The illusions of socialism, 1956
- Shaw on the theatre, 1958
- An unfinished novel, 1958
- Shaw's dramatic criticism: 1895-1898, 1959
- How to become a musical critic, 1960
- Platform and pulpit, 1961

- Shaw on shakespeare, 1961 (ed. By e. Wilson)
- The matter with ireland, 1962
- G.b.s. On music, 1962
- Religious speeches, 1963
- Heartbreak house, 1964
- The complete prefaces of bernard shaw, 1965
- Shaw on religion, 1967
- Shaw: An autobiography, 1969-70 (2 vols.)
- The road to equality, 1971
- Collected music criticism, 1973
- Bernard shaw's practical politics, 1976
- The portable bernard shaw, 1977
- The great composers, 1978
- The collected screenplays of bernard shaw, 1980
- Early texts, 1981 (12 vols.)
- Shaw's music, 1981 (3 vols.)
- Shaw on dickens, 1984
- Agitations, 1985
- The diaries, 1885-1897, 1985
- Selected shorter plays, 1987
- Collected letters, 1965-88 (4 vols.)
- Bernard shaw's book reviews, 1991
- The complete prefaces, 1993
- The drama observed, 1993
- Unpublished shaw, 1996

Chapter 4

Bernard Shaw, 1856-1950

A Descriptive Chronology of His Plays,
Theatrical Career, and Dramatic Theories

1856 July: George Bernard Shaw is born on July 26 in Dublin.

1876 April: Shaw moves to London (and disdainfully casts off his first name).

1884 August: Shaw begins writing a play based on romantic plot materials supplied by William Archer, with working titles of *The Way to a Woman's Heart*, then *Rheingold* and *Rhinegold*, but eventually *Widowers' Houses*.

1885 March: After seeing a performance of *As You Like It*, Shaw writes to Archer: "The decadence of the stage is awful. We have our work cut out for us, I can tell you. My opinion of Shakspere has gone up prodigiously: my opinion of stage culture is below zero."

1887 October: Having finished the first two acts of *Rheingold*, Shaw forewarns Archer that he "has brought the romantic notion which possessed you, into vivid contact with real life," and that "the title *Rheingold* ought to be saved for a romantic play. This is realism." When he reads the completed portion to Archer two days later, he records in his diary that a "long argument ensued, Archer having received it with contempt."

1889 August: Shaw writes the journalist/novelist Tighe Hopkins, "Some time ago I tried novelizing again, and wrote a chapter & a half; but I could not stand the form: it is too clumsy and unreal. Sometimes in spare moments I write dialogues; and these are all working up to a certain end (a sermon, of course) my imagination playing the usual tricks meanwhile of creating visionary persons &c. When I have a few hundred of these dialogues worked up and interlocked, then a drama will be the result—a moral, instructive, suggestive comedy of modern society, guaranteed correct in philosophic & economic detail, and unactably independent of theatrical considerations. Meanwhile, *I live.* Point out to me any 'brilliant' person who can say as much. I repudiate brilliant promise, fiction & political economy as ends. My business is to incarnate the Zeitgeist, whereby I experience its impulse and universality, and it experiences the personal raptures of music and copulation" (the last two words, not printed in the *Collected Letters*, have a single line drawn through them in the ms. of the letter at Cornell).

1890 July: Shaw lectures on Ibsen to the Fabian Society, opening fire "from the depths of my innermost soul against [the] confounded ideals of Truth, Duty, Self-Sacrifice, Virtue, Reason and so on."

1891 July: In a music review, Shaw says that W. S. Gilbert, "at his best, was a much cleverer man than most of the playwrights of his day: he could always see beneath the surface of things; and if he could only have seen through tnem, he might have made his mark as a serious dramatist instead of having, as a satirist, to depend for the piquancy of his ridicule on the general assumption of the validity of the very things he ridiculed.... Nevertheless, there was a substratum of earnest in Mr Gilbert's joking."

November: Shaw expands his Fabian lecture on Henrik Ibsen into *The Quintessence of Ibsenism,* defining the realistic social dramas as "ideal-destroying plays," the mode of his own plays of the 1890s. With some justification, critics have quipped that the book is virtually "The Quintessence of Shaw." He interprets Ibsen's implicit beliefs in the light of his own developing philosophy that the human will should be the determinant of actions rather than external pressures that parade as "ideals": conventions of duty and the dictates of religious, rationalist, and materialist doctrines ("Ideals are only swaddling clothes which man has outgrown, and which insufferably impede his movements"). His call for women to "repudiate duty altogether" marks him as an early feminist. His revision 22 years later will bring his discussion up to date and extend it to "the Ibsen school"—which includes himself.

1892 August: Shaw completes the evolution of *Rhinegold* into an antiromantic exposé of slum landlordism and retitles it *Widowers' Houses: An Original Didactic Realistic Play.* That Autumn J. T. Grein complains to Shaw of the dearth of new British plays, and Shaw submits his play to him for the Independent Theatre.

December: Shaw's *Widowers' Houses* is given two performances by the Independent Theatre Society at the Royalty Theatre in London. It arouses intense and prolonged discussion, much of it directed at its negative portrayal of capitalist society, with some drama critics complaining that it is not a "play" at all. Shaw observes that "the men who find my sociology wrong are also the men who find my dramatic workmanship bad; and *vice versa*". The first of his three "propagandist dramas" subtly undermining capitalism, the play portrays the transformation of an altruistic medical student into a conscious exploiter of the poor in collaboration with experienced profiteers, not only because he learns that his security is tied up in slum properties but also because others convince him that poverty is an inevitable social condition. The play is published with a preface by Shaw in May 1893 (the 1898 version in *Plays Pleasant and Unpleasant* will be significantly revised). After reading it Oscar Wilde writes to Shaw, "I admire the horrible flesh and blood of your creatures" and "I like your superb confidence in the dramatic value of the mere facts of life" (May 1893). The shorthand and holograph manuscripts of the play are published in the 12-volume set of Shaw's *Early Texts: Play Manuscripts in Facsimile.*

In stark contrast to Shaw's theatrical achievement is the success met by Brandon Thomas's facetious farce *Charley's Aunt* beginning nine days later, a run of 1,469 performances.

1893 May: Widowers' Houses is published with Shaw's defence of the play (his third), "The Author to the Dramatic Critics." To the widespread contention that he is emulating

Ibsen, he replies that the first two acts of the play were written when he "knew nothing of Ibsen," and it has "no trace" of Ibsen's retrospective technique; furthermore, the subjects which supposedly reflect the Norwegian's influence—heredity, the emancipation of women, marriage laws and customs, and a "mixture of wickedness and goodness in the same character"—can be more easily traced to "half a dozen English writers than to Ibsen," which he proceeds to specify. To the equally recurring complaint that virtually all of the characters in the play are unpleasant and immoral, Shaw uses the example of the slum landlord Sartorius to point out that, as in real life, his plea that he does not repair his tenements because the tenants would burn his improvements "is perfectly well founded"; his "rascality—for from the social point of view he certainly is a callous rascal—.... lies altogether in his indifference to defects in our social system which produce a class of persons so poor that they are driven by constant physical privation to turn everything they can lay hands on into more fuel and more food." Shaw praises Wilde in a letter to Lady Colin Campbell for "teaching the theatrical public that 'a play' may be a playing with ideas instead of a feast of sham emotions compounded from dog's eared prescriptions." Later he twits, "there are only two literary schools in England today: the Norwegian school and the Irish school."

June: Shaw finishes *The Philanderer: A Topical Comedy* for J. T. Grein's Independent Theatre, incorporating satires of the Ibsen and New Woman fads, and featuring a critique of marriage laws that people evade by instituting "grotesque sexual compacts." Shaw calls it "an extremely advanced farcical comedy" and says it "exudes brimstone at every pore." Grein tacitly rejects it, and the play is not performed until 1907. Its reputation will be heightened by a revival in November 1991 which restores Shaw's highly discursive original last act, unknown until the holograph manuscript is published in *Early Texts: Play Manuscripts in Facsimile*. Shaw next composes *Mrs Warren's Profession*, partly in reaction to Arthur Wing Pinero's *The Second Mrs Tanqueray*. The drama, which deals with a brothel manager and her strong-minded daughter, is too daring to be suitable for performance, and in 1898 is refused a licence by the Lord Chamberlain's Office. The Stage Society produces it in 1902, but it is not licensed until August 1924 (and then "reluctantly") or performed publicly in England until September 1925. In November Shaw turns to a romantic theme and starts writing *Arms and the Man*, his first "pleasant play."

1894 April: Shaw's *Arms and the Man* is presented at the Avenue Theatre, the first of 50 performances. (Shaw does not learn for ten years that the "angel" who leased the theatre was A. E. F. "Annie" Horniman, making the first of her many notable ventures into financing the "higher drama.") The comedy, an attempt to discredit romantic ideals of war and love, features a thoroughly prosaic military antihero who packs grub instead of bullets and whose blunt common sense finally wins everyone's admiration. His abrupt intrusion into a glamorous lady's bedroom starts a series of events that explodes her idealization of a handsome major she refers to as "my hero!" and converts her to the businesslike captain. The deposed "hero," just as aware as the captain that his success in battle was the result of dumb luck, realizes that his ideal of womanhood is less desirable to him than a delectable servant. At the finale he expresses his admiration for his oddly constituted replacement by declaring, "What a man! Is he a man?" (In early editions, simply "What a man! What a man!") Watching his first Shaw play prompted Yeats to record that it caused a nightmare in which he was "haunted by a sewing machine" that "clicked and shone" while it "smiled, smiled perpetually." The holograph manuscript of the play is published in *Early Texts: Play Manuscripts in Facsimile.*

In response to Archer's criticism that *Arms and the Man* is "a fantastic, psychological extravaganza, in which drama, farce, and Gilbertian irony keep flashing past the bewildered eye," Shaw retorts in a long letter, "Gilbert is simply a paradoxically humorous cynic. He accepts the conventional ideals implicitly, but observes that people do not really live up to them. This he regards as a failure on their part at which he mocks bitterly.... I do not accept the conventional ideals.

To them I oppose in the play the practical life & morals of the efficient, realistic man.... My whole secret is that I have got clean through the old categories of good & evil, and no longer use them even for dramatic effect. Sergius is ridiculous through the breakdown of his ideals, not odious from his falling short of them. As Gilbert sees, they dont work; but what Gilbert does not see is that there is something else that does work, and that in that something else there is a completely satisfactory asylum for the affections. It is this positive element in my philosophy that makes *Arms & the Man* a perfectly genuine play about real people, with a happy ending and hope & life in it, instead of a thing like [Gilbert's] *Engaged* which is nothing but a sneer at people for not being what Sergius & Raina play at being before they find one another out."

July: Responding to negative reviews of *Arms and the Man*, Shaw in his long essay "A Dramatic Realist to His Critics" (*New Review*) declares that his play amounts to a "comedy of the collision of the realities represented by the realist playwright with the preconceptions of stageland." Whereas stage life "is artificially simple and well understood by the masses" and is thus not only "totally unsuggestive of thought" but "constantly in conflict with the real knowledge which the separate members of the audience derive from their own daily occupations," real life is so poorly understood "that no sort of consistency is discoverable in it"; on the contrary, "it is credible, stimulating, suggestive, various, free from creeds and systems-in short, it is real."

September: Arms and the Man becomes the first Shaw play to be presented in America. Introduced into the actor-manager Richard Mansfield's repertory, it attracts good notices but few spectators.

December: Shaw finishes writing *Candida*, designing it partly as "a counterblast to Ibsen's *Doll's House*, showing that in the real typical doll's house it is the man who is the doll." In structure the play is a traditional romantic comedy involving a *ménage à trois*, with a guest/intruder becoming infatuated with a handsome married woman. Marital conventions voiced by the husband, an urbane but conventional preacher, are attacked both by the guest, a fiercely perceptive young poet, and by the down-to-earth wife he is entranced with. After an auction scene in which the two males express their contending claims, the woman sits her two "babies" down and explains that her spoiled and confident husband needs her much more than the youth does, and incidentally shatters the poet's notion of ideal domesticity. What Shaw detects in Ibsen's realistic plays, "a conflict of unsettled ideals," occurs prominently in *Candida*: the two contestants for Candida's love misconstrue her true nature because of contrasting, but no less delusory, ideals of marriage and womanhood. Shaw conceived of her as the ultimate mother-woman, "the Virgin Mother and nobody else": a "calm dispassionate queen who hands out her favours to those who need her most." The play will not be given a full production in London for ten years (the Stage Society performs it once in July 1900), but it becomes one of Shaw's most popular. The holograph manuscript is published in *Early Texts: Play Manuscripts in Facsimile* along with that of his 1904 short play *How He Lied to Her Husband*.

1895 January: Shaw's first drama criticisms for the *Saturday Review* appear, beginning his full-fledged "siege laid to the theatre of the XIXth Century by an author who had to cut his own way into it at the point of a pen, and throw some of its defenders into the moat" ("The Author's Apology," preface to *Dramatic Opinions and Essays*, 1906). His weekly reviews will continue until May 1898.

March: On the occasion of the death of E. F. Smyth Pigott, Examiner of Stage Plays since 1874, Shaw writes in the *Saturday Review* that it has been "frightful" to see "the greatest thinkers, poets, and authors of modern Europe—men like Ibsen, Wagner, Tolstoi, and the leaders of our own literature—delivered helpless into the vulgar hands of such a noodle as this amiable old gentleman," and predicts that his successor will be the same kind of incompetent. George Redford, a bank manager and friend of Pigott, is appointed and lasts until 1911.

March-April: Richard Mansfield tentatively accepts Shaw's *Candida*, but rejects it when rehearsals convince him that it is "not a play" but "three long acts of talk—talk—talk." His letter, highly symptomatic of the theatrical milieu in America at the time, continues: "It isn't right to try and build a play out of a mere incident.... All the world is crying out for deeds—for action! When I step upon the stage I want to act—I'm willing to talk a little to oblige a man like you—but I must act—and hugging my ankles for three mortal hours won't satisfy me in this regard.... Shaw—if you will write for me a strong, hearty—earnest—noble—genuine play—I'll play it.... You'll have to write a play that a *man* can play and about a woman that heroes fought for and a bit of ribbon that a knight tied to his lance. The stage is for romance and love and truth and honor. To make men better and nobler. To cheer them on the way— Life is real. Life is earnest. And the grave is not its goal.... Be not like dumb, driven cattle. Be a hero in the fight!"

May: Contributing to a symposium on the question, "Should social problems be freely dealt with in the Drama?" ("The Problem Play," *Humanitarian*), Shaw acknowledges that "a drama with a social question for the motive cannot outlive the solution of that question." However, since "the huge size of modern populations and the development of the press make every social question more momentous than it was formerly," we are "witnessing a steady intensification in the hold of social questions on the larger poetic imagination." The great example is Ibsen, turning deliberately from "dramatic poems on the grandest scale" to "the most obviously transitory social questions, finding in their immense magnitude under modern conditions the stimulus which, a hundred years ago,... he would only have received from the eternal strife of man with his own spirit. *A Doll's House* will be as flat as ditchwater when *A Midsummer Night's Dream* will still be as fresh as paint; but it will have done more work in the world; and that is enough for the highest genius, which is always intensely utilitarian."

June: Reviewing two plays by Victorien Sardou, Shaw pins the term "Sardoodledom" on well-made plays which are no more than "claptraps" contrived for suspense and easy gratification.

July: In response to Max Nordau's attack on artists in

Degeneration (1893; English translation, 1895), Shaw replies at length in "A Degenerate's View of Nordau," revised as *The Sanity of Art* in 1898. He eloquently proclaims his basic humanistic and evolutionary aesthetic: "The claim of art to our respect must stand or fall with the validity of its pretension to cultivate and refine our senses and faculties until seeing, hearing, feeling, smelling, and tasting become highly conscious and critical acts with us.... Further, art should refine our sense of character and conduct, of justice and sympathy, greatly heightening our self-knowledge, self-control, precision of action, and considerateness, and making us intolerant of baseness, cruelty, injustice, and intellectual superficiality or vulgarity.... The great artist is he who goes a step beyond [serving the demands of the physical and moral senses] and, by supplying works of a higher beauty and a higher interest than have yet been perceived, succeeds after a brief struggle with its strangeness, in adding this fresh extension of sense to the heritage of the race. This is why we value art: this is why we feel that the iconoclast and the Philistine are attacking something made holier, by solid usefulness, than their own theories of purity and practicality."

October: Arthur Wing Pinero's comedy *The Benefit of the Doubt* is performed badly, but it evokes Shaw's well-qualified praise (along with an object lesson for other conventional playwrights) in the *Saturday Review*: "This time Mr Pinero has succeeded. *The Benefit of the Doubt* is worth *The Profligate, Mrs Tanqueray*, and *Mrs Ebbsmith* rolled into one and multiplied by ten.... Mr Pinero, concentrating himself on a phase of life and sentiment which he thoroughly understands, has extracted abundant drama from it, and maintained it at an astonishingly high and even pressure for two hours, without for a moment being driven back on the woman with a past, the cynical libertine peer, the angel of purity, the Cayley Drummle confidant, or any other of the conventional figures which inevitably appear in his plays whenever he conceives himself to be dealing as a sociologist with public questions of which he has no solid knowledge, but only a purely conventional and theatrical conceit.

In *The Benefit of the Doubt* he keeps within the territory he has actually explored; and the result is at once apparent in the higher dramatic pressure, the closer-knit action,... and the comparative originality, naturalness, and free development of the characters.... Consciously or unconsciously, he has this time seen his world as it really is: that is, a world which never dreams of bothering its little head with large questions or general ideas."

November: Shaw finishes his short play *The Man of Destiny: A Trifle*. He wrote his "beautiful little one act play for Napoleon and a strange lady" for the American actor-manager Richard Mansfield and as a lure for Ellen Terry, but Mansfield turns it down and Terry cannot quite induce Henry Irving to perform it. It will not be given a full performance until June 1907.

In answer to a query about *Mrs Warren's Profession* from the critic Golding Bright when the Independent Theatre was considering it for production, Shaw first describes it in terms of his intentions: "The play is a cold bloodedly appalling one; but not in the least a prurient one. Mrs Warren is much worse than a prostitute. She is an organism of prostitution—a woman who owns & manages brothels in every big city in Europe & is proud of it. With her gains she has had her daughter highly educated and respectably brought up in complete ignorance of the source of her mother's income.

The drama, of course, lies in the discovery and its consequences. These consequences, though cruel enough, are all quite sensible & sobre, no suicide nor sensational tragedy of any sort. Nobody's conscience is smitten except, I hope, the conscience of the audience. My intention is that they shall go home thoroughly uncomfortable.... The play has horrified everyone who has heard it, but only as an honest treatment of such a subject ought to horrify them. I want to make an end, if I can, of the furtively lascivious Pharisaism of stage immorality, by a salutary dramatisation of the reality." Shaw goes on to proclaim his invention of a distinctive New Woman, Mrs Warren's daughter:

"I have sought to put on the stage for the first time (as far as I know) the highly educated, capable, independent young woman of the governing class as we know her today, working, smoking, preferring the society of men to that of women simply because men talk about the questions that interest her and not about servants & babies, making no pretense of caring much about art or romance, respectable through sheer usefulness & strength, and playing the part of the charming woman only as the amusement of her life, not as its serious occupation."

1896 May: Shaw finishes writing *You Never Can Tell*, having begun it in mid-1895 and interrupted it by starting *The Devil's Disciple* in April. A "humanized" farcical comedy aimed at the West End, it is not performed there until May 1900, and then only six times. (The newly formed Stage Society gives it a Sunday night performance in November 1899.) Shaw will become ashamed of its "tricks and laughs and popularities" and declare it a "potboiler," but it will be frequently revived. Its "duel of the sexes," with the female overcoming the resistant male, looks forward to *Man and Superman*; the tensely comic situation of an imperious lady introducing her children to their father for the first time has its counterpart in *Major Barbara*; the highly sensible advice emerging from an unexpected source begins with the play's mellifluous waiter and evolves into the soothing greengrocer in *Getting Married;* and the scene in which his son, an eminent Q.C., serves as a deus ex machina for the young couple by provoking the lady to grant her impecunious lover a marriage settlement is approximated in *Misalliance* when a woman determined to marry an aviator who 'just dropped in' asks her father to "buy the brute" for her. The holograph manuscript of *You Never Can Tell* is published in *Early Texts: Play Manuscripts in Facsimile.*

In the *Saturday Review*, Shaw clarifies his objections to farcical comedy (notably Oscar Wilde's *The Importance of Being Earnest*): "Beware how you laugh when you do not enjoy. To laugh without sympathy is a ruinous abuse of a noble function; and the degradation of any race may be measured by the degree of their addiction to it. In its subtler forms it is dying very hard: for instance, we find people who would not join in the laughter of a crowd of peasants at the village idiot, or tolerate the public flogging or pillorying of a criminal, booking seats to shout with laughter at a farcical comedy, which is, at bottom, the same thing—namely, the deliberate indulgence of that horrible, derisive joy in humiliation and suffering which is the beastliest element in human nature."

June: Informing Golding Bright that *Mrs Warren's Profession* no longer has a prospect of being produced by the Independent Theatre, Shaw states: "The facts are rather funny, in a way. My first three plays, *Widowers' Houses, The Philanderer,* and *Mrs Warren's Profession* were what people call realistic. They were dramatic pictures of middle class society from the point of view of a Socialist who regards the basis of that society as thoroughly rotten economically and morally. In *Widowers' Houses* you had the rich suburban villa standing on the rents of the foul rookery. In *The Philanderer* you had the fashionable cult of Ibsenism and 'New Womanism' on a real basis of clandestine sensuality. In *Mrs Warren's Profession* you had the procuress, the organizer of prostitution, convicting society of her occupation. All three plays were criticisms of a special phase, the capitalist phase, of modern social organization, and their purpose was to make people thoroughly uncomfortable whilst entertaining them artistically. But my four subsequent plays, *Arms & the Man, Candida, The Man of Destiny* (the one-act Napoleon piece) and the unnamed four act comedy just finished [*You Never Can Tell*], are not 'realistic' plays. They deal with life at large, with human nature as it presents itself through all economic and social phases.... These later plays are of course infinitely more pleasing, more charming, more popular than the earlier three. And of course the I.T. now wants one of those pleasant plays to make a popular success with, instead of sticking to its special business & venturing on the realistic ones.... You must understand, however, that we are all on the friendliest terms, and that I am rather flattered than otherwise at the preference of my friends for those plays of mine which have no purpose except the purpose of all poets & dramatists as against those which are exposures of the bad side of our social system."

November: Shaw describes his rhetorical *modus operandi* in a memorable way that applies to his writings as well as his speeches: "When I first began to promulgate my opinions, I found that they appeared extravagant and even insane. In order to get a hearing, it was necessary for me to attain the footing of a privileged lunatic, with the license of a jester. Fortunately the matter was very easy. I found that I had only to say with perfect simplicity what I seriously meant just as it struck me, to make everybody laugh. My method is to take the utmost trouble to find the right thing to say, and then say it with the utmost levity. And all the time the real joke is that I am in earnest" (*Chap-Book*).

December: Shaw declares in the *Saturday Review*: "No great play can ever be written by a man who will allow the public to dictate to him." The business of the playwright is "to strive incessantly with the public; to insist on earnest relations with it, and not merely voluptuous ones; to lead it, nerve it, withstand its constant tendency to relapse into carelessness and vulgar familiarity; in short, to attain to public esteem, authority, and needfulness to the national welfare (things undreamt of in the relations between the theatrical profession and the public today), instead of to the camp-follower's refuge of mere popularity."

1897 January: Shaw writes to Ellen Terry: "The theatre is my battering ram as much as the platform or the press: that is why I want to drag it to the front. My capers are part of a bigger design than you think: Shakespear, for instance, is to me one of the towers of the Bastille, and down he must come."

February: Shaw puts the finishing touches on *The Devil's Disciple,* written for the home of popular melodrama, the Adelphi Theatre. As Shaw says in 1930, "The play was stuffed with everything from the ragbag of melodrama: reading of a will, heroic sacrifice, court martial, gallows, eleventh-hour reprieve, and all complete with... just that little bit of my own that made all the difference" (letter in George W. Bishop, *My Betters,* 1957). The Shavian "bit" is the play's reversal of Sidney-Carton motives for the hero's willingness to be hanged for another man; he is not doing it for the man's doting wife or as a heroic self-sacrifice, but because his own nature dictates it.

Originally a "devil's disciple," he evolves into a preacher because he proves superior not only to religion, morality, and love but also to gentility (embodied in General Burgoyne)—to Shaw, "the whole ideal of modern society." The play is accepted by Richard Mansfield in America and staged in October (with the Shavian motives muddled, leading to a run of 64), but is not presented in London until two years later, and then not at the Adelphi but in suburban Kennington. The first West End production will not occur until October 1907, with a run of 74. The holograph manuscript of the play is published in *Early Texts: Play Manuscripts in Facsimile.*

April-May: Rehearsals of Shaw's *You Never Can Tell*, accepted for production at the Haymarket Theatre, disrupt the acting company and Shaw considerately withdraws the play.

June: On the occasion of a revival of T. W. Robertson's "epoch-making play," *Caste*, Shaw reflects in the *Saturday Review*: "A very little epoch and a very little play, certainly.... I see now clearly enough that the eagerness with which it was swallowed long ago was the eagerness with which an ocean castaway... would pounce on a spoonful of flat salutaris and think it nectar. After years of sham heroics and superhuman balderdash, *Caste* delighted everyone by its freshness, its nature, its humanity." The touches of nature, "in the windows, in the doors, in the walls," were then "inexpressibly welcome because they were the most unexpected of novelties." These marks of cup-and-saucer drama "are now spurned because they are commonplaces."

July: Shaw comments in the *Saturday Review* on the evolution of audience reactions: "The most advanced audiences to-day, taught by Wagner and Ibsen..., cannot stand the drop back into decoration after the moment of earnest life. They want realistic drama of complete brainy, passional texture all through.... The decorative play, with its versified rhetoric, its timid little moments of feeling and blusterous big moments of raving nonsense, must now step down to the second-class audience, which is certainly more numerous and lucrative than the first-class, but is being slowly dragged after it.... And so even the second-class public, though it still likes plenty of pictorial beauty and distinction... in the setting, and plenty of comfortable optimistic endearment and cheap fun in the substance, nevertheless needs far more continuous drama to bind the whole together and compel sustained attention and interest than it did twenty years ago."

1898 April: Shaw publishes *Plays Pleasant and Unpleasant*, with stage directions designed to enhance the readability of the plays and with explanatory didactic prefaces. His rationale is that "in the present condition of the theatre it is evident that a dramatist like Ibsen, who absolutely disregards the conditions which managers are subject to, and throws himself on the reading public, is taking the only course in which any serious advance is possible." Shaw labels the first three plays "unpleasant," he says in the preface, because "their dramatic power is used to force the spectator to face unpleasant facts." And though his next plays are "pleasant" romantic comedies, they embody his "conception of romance as the great heresy to be rooted out from art and life-as the root of modern pessimism and the bane of modern self-respect." *Three Plays for Puritans* will print the rest of his plays of the 1890s.

December: Shaw finishes his chronicle play *Caesar and Cleopatra*, having begun it on Shakespeare's birthday in April. The script far exceeds the prevailing norm for length, but he has planned Act III to be completely removable. Conceived partly as a counter to *Julius Caesar* and *Antony and Cleopatra*, the drama reflects the German historian Friedrich Mommsen's portrait of a Caesar who came to spurn vengeance rather than Plutarch's more bloodthirsty conqueror, and offers a teenager sadly in need of a father-figure in place of a mature vamp. In his attempt to revive the genre of heroic drama, Shaw designed the play to highlight the qualities of the person he considered "the greatest man that ever lived," an antitype of the prevailing "gentlemanly hero," including provocations for several long speeches. (He does the same much later with the more naive Joan of Arc.) His Caesar is "heroic in the true human fashion: that is, touching the summits only at rare moments, and finding the proper level of all occasions, condescending with humour and good sense to the prosaic ones, as well as rising to the noble ones." Caesar's attitude toward vengeance is expressed in one of his noblest moments: "And so, to the end of history, murder shall breed murder, always in the name of right and honor and peace, until the gods are tired of blood and create a race that can understand." The play will not be performed in London until 1907; for a 1912 production Shaw replaces the present Prologue with an oration by the god Ra. The holograph manuscript of the play is published in *Early Texts: Play Manuscripts in Facsimile* along with that of his short play about Napoleon, *The Man of Destiny*.

1899 July: Shaw completes *Captain Brassbound's Conversion*, whose protagonist Lady Cicely is expressly designed for Ellen Terry; in fact, he wrote it "to please her and not as a matter of business." She is not to play the role until 1906, the first major London performances after two by the Stage Society in December 1900. In this melodramatic comedy, the charmingly self-possessed but manipulative heroine is the female counterpart of Shaw's Caesar: "not merely the maternal, managing woman who likes everybody and loves nobody," but also "the adventurous, fearless woman, seeking new countries and new people to play with." In three highly comic scenes highlighting her qualities, she talks a brigand out of his romantic commitment to vengeance, then talks his captors out of convicting him, and finally talks herself out of accepting his proposal of marriage. In August Shaw tells Terry, "And now no more plays—at least no more practicable ones. None at all, indeed, for some time to come: it is time to do something more in Shaw-philosophy, in politics & sociology. Your author, dear Ellen, must be more than a common dramatist." The holograph manuscript of *Captain Brassbound's Conversion* is published in *Early Texts: Play Manuscripts in Facsimile*.

November: The Stage Society, following the pattern of J. T. Grein's Independent Theatre, begins its forty-year existence by presenting Shaw's *You Never Can Tell*. The Society will subsequently provide first hearings in London for several other Shaw plays, including *Mrs Warren's Profession* (already censored).

1900 May: Shaw begins planning a play provisionally

entitled *The Superman,* "an immense play, but not for the stage of this generation," and starts writing the Don Juan in Hell dream scene.

1901 January: In a letter to an actor, Shaw sums up his theatrical fortunes so far: "In short, for the last eight or nine years, I have written a play whenever anyone asked me to—ten in all. Not one of these plays has been produced by the people for whom they were written: in fact, except for a few scratch matinees, a provincial tour which had to take a play of mine because it could get nothing else, a flutter at a suburban theatre, and the shows of forlorn hopes like the Independent Theatre &c &c, they have not been produced at all.... So I published the plays, and gave up the theatre as a bad job."

1902 January: Shaw's most impressive anticapitalist propaganda play, *Mrs Warren's Profession,* is produced by the Stage Society for two performances nine years after its completion. The Independent Theatre had refused to produce the play, and its producer J. T. Grein now finds it "unnecessary and painful" in performance. The drama forcefully depicts a smug, energetic "New Woman" working, smoking, and dallying with infatuation until she is shaken by learning the source of her income: her rarely present mother is a wealthy brothel manager. She scorns the dowdy woman but is further shaken when her mother explains that she escaped an exploitative job necessitated by poverty, and avoided marriage within her class, by becoming a prostitute and finally rising to the position of chief madame. This poisons love for the daughter (who also hears that her boyfriend may be her half-brother), and at the finale she isolates herself from both people who care for her. Shaw states in a programme note to the first West End production in 1926: "when a woman of bold character and commercial ability applies to herself the commercial principles that are ruthlessly applied to her in the labour market, the result is Kitty Warren.... You will hear her justify herself completely on those principles." The holograph manuscript of the play is published in *Early Texts: Play Manuscripts in Facsimile.*

Shaw publishes *The Author's Apology from Mrs Warren's*

Profession. Besides describing the play's rationale at length, he generalizes eloquently: "I am convinced that fine art is the subtlest, the most seductive, the most effective means of moral propagandism in the world, excepting only the example of personal conduct; and I waive even this exception in favour of the art of the stage, because it works by exhibiting examples of personal conduct made intelligible and moving to crowds of unobservant, unreflecting people to whom real life means nothing.... So effective do I find the dramatic method that I have no doubt I shall at last persuade even London to take its conscience and its brains with it when it goes to the theater, instead of leaving them at home with its prayer book as it does at present."

June: Shaw finishes writing *Man and Superman: A Comedy and a Philosophy*, complete with preface and "Revolutionists' Handbook and Pocket Companion." It is published in August 1903, but the "Comedy" will wait for performance until 1905, the "Philosophy" until 1907, and the whole drama until 1925. The four-act play, considered by some the greatest English-language comic drama of the century, is not only richly iconoclastic and rhetorically riveting, but highly innovative in form. Its hour-and-a-half dream sequence commonly referred to as "the Don Juan in Hell scene" is an actionless argument between the Devil and Juan, a spokesman for Shaw's religion of Creative Evolution, set in a Hell which is a kind of rest home for romantic idealists. The scene is completely detachable so that the "Comedy," itself over three hours long, can be performed without it (Shaw specified minor changes that make it self-contained). The modern drawing-room comedy of manners is Shaw's first in a series of highly discursive plays. It is so mainly because of its reformist hero's propensity to sermonize eloquently against reigning conventions, including marriage, and to explain at length his radical views on unmarried pregnancy, the "struggle between the artist man and the mother woman," and the effect of the "Life Force" on unwary males. But he is a true comic protagonist: his volubility only makes him more susceptible to the conventional but crafty lady determined to marry him, especially when he blindly urges her to defy her (helplessly passive) mother and come with him on a long excursion. Even when his chauffeur makes him realize that she is the pursuer and he the pursued, which sends him fleeing for Granada, he cannot evade her relentless tracking. The lady finally casts off her hypocritical poses and stands boldly before him as what he perceives as the Life Force personified, and he yields, wincing only when she urges him to "go on talking," which is (somehow) followed by "universal laughter." Shaw explains her nature in a December 1904 letter to a woman who had deplored the play's blatant treatment of the "bestial" sexual instinct: "Ann is the Mother Woman. She is a breeder of men, specialized by Nature to that end and endowed with enormous fascination for it; and all the twaddling little minor moralities that stand between her and her purpose—as, for instance, that she must not be a naughty girl and tell fibs,... —all become the merest impertinences. As she says in her transfiguration 'I believe in the life to come'; and when you feel the mightiness of that belief and the vital Force of all Forces that is behind it, you will blush at having had no more to say to it than 'How unladylike!'" The full text of the volume *Man and Superman*, which Shaw tells Henry Salt is "one of the most colossal efforts of the human mind," and Archer "a blinding brain display as has not occurred in the British drama since Shakespear's advent" (August 1903 letters), is widely recognized as a landmark of modern dramatic literature.

London Times critic A. B. Walkley sums up the progress of English drama from Robertson to Shaw in "Modern English and French Drama" (reprinted in *Drama and Life* in 1907). He credits Robertson with "the first intelligent employment in England of the picture-stage" to attain "a plausible representation of actual life and manners and speech, with all rhetoric and rhetorical conventions abolished," but deplores his drama for its major defect: "it was 'unidea'd'"; while he "observed his time and responded to its pressure, he had no critical ideas about it." The radical shock of Ibsen "for a brief moment frighted the isle from its propriety" until it petered out, but it prompted the "serious plays" of Pinero, Jones,

[Sydney] Grundy, and Shaw. In the nineties Pinero's plays became "the high-water mark of our modern English drama" as "our closest approximation to the theatre of ideas, to a criticism of life through the medium of drama." But he "lacked the courage to defy his audience," so that he gives us only "half-ideas, or adumbrations of ideas." Thus it is refreshing to come to "a man with real ideas and a definite purpose," Bernard Shaw. His plays "are so many attacks upon what he considers our false ideals, and so many attempts to illustrate what he calls a scientific natural history." The problem is that "'with such a being as man, in such a world as the present,' Mr Shaw's plays do not count as plays at all. They offer such a criticism of life as the average man cannot even begin to understand." He "addresses himself to the pure reason; his characters do not love or hate, laugh or cry, they merely argue it out.... The essential law of the theatre is thought *through emotion*. No character exhibits real emotion (though occasionally there is a show of 'temper') in those fascinating exercises in dialectic which Mr Shaw miscalls plays."

1903 January: Shaw declares in a letter to William Archer that the "extraordinarily happy command of classes & grades of civilization" in his plays deserves greater appreciation. "The one overwhelming characteristic of my plays is the friction between people on different planes of thought, of character, of civilization & of class prejudice," whereas that of "the ordinary Pinero-Jones-Grundy play [is] that all the characters are on exactly the same planes in these respects."

September: A trial matinee of Shaw's *Candida* in New York, mounted at their own expense by Arnold Daly and a young actor, gains such a positive reception that additional performances are arranged so that the play is finally given over a hundred times. *The Man of Destiny* sometimes supplements the evening.

Shaw responds to fellow Fabian John Burns's praise for *Man and Superman* (copying it to Sidney Webb): "I'm glad you like the Superman: it has relieved me of a great deal that has been on my chest for a long time. However, it is not really pessimistic: quite the contrary. All that it says is that we shall not get any further until we get rid of property and of promiscuous breeding in that hopeless little rabbit-hutch the British home.... I am going to see whether I cannot sink those two rotten old ships Property and Promiscuity with pedigree dynamite. That may succeed or it may not succeed; but the attempt is not pessimism: there is more life left in the old dog than that gentlemanly fatuity."

1904 April: Shaw's *Candida* receives its first public performance for six matinees at the Royal Court Theatre as a trial balloon for a major venture designed to bring English theatre into the modern era. It is revived in late November when the venture is under way.

October: The most important theatrical development in early modern British drama, the Vedrenne-Barker management at the Court Theatre, begins with the performance of Gilbert Murray's version of Euripides' *Hippolytus* for six matinees. Early in 1904 Harley Granville Barker, William Archer, and Murray had issued *Scheme and Estimates for a National Theatre* (privately printed), the ideas of which underlie this effort. Strongly backed by Shaw, the theatre manager John E. Vedrenne and Granville Barker leased the Court to present plays whose "advanced" content and dramaturgy made them unlikely to be produced in the West End, including foreign plays by Ibsen, Hauptmann, Schnitzler, and Maeterlinck. Repertory scheduling and ensemble acting by minimally paid actors preclude the usual emphasis on long runs and star appeal. The response from cultured playgoers is highly favorable—the term "congregation" will be applied to Court audiences—and the enterprise will last until June 1907: 988 performances, 701 of which are devoted to eleven Shaw plays. In *The Old Drama and the New,* Archer will look back on those years as a period of "almost miraculous renascence."

November: Shaw's new disquisitory drama about the relations between the Irish and English, *John Bull's Other Island,* is presented at the Court. (Although written partly for the opening of the Abbey Theatre in Dublin, the play exceeded the resources of that venture, and W. B. Yeats deemed it "uncongenial to the whole spirit of the neo-Gaelic movement." When he sees it in London, moreover, he calls it "fundamentally ugly and shapeless.") It attracts great publicity for the Court, partly because King Edward VII—who (as the Prince of Wales) had snarled that Shaw "must be mad" at the 1894 premiere of *Arms and the Man*—requested a Command Performance and laughed so boisterously that he broke his chair. A materialistic, always upbeat Englishman accompanies a dour, iconoclastic Irish expatriate to Ireland presumably to visit the Irishman's home town but actually to bestow the fruits of free enterprise upon the land. In spite of his narrowminded capitalist views and comic antics, the Englishman gains acceptance of his plan to replace tenant farms with a hotel and golf course, his proposal to an attractive young lady (whose love for his companion continues unrequited), and a nomination for Parliament. He is sharply contrasted to an unfrocked Irish priest who philosophizes to a grasshopper and is considered deranged, but whose "dream of a madman" for his country is "a godhead in which all life is human and all humanity divine."

Shaw responds to the critic A. B. Walkley, who charged him with "wilful, perverse disregard of anything like construction" in *John Bull's Other Island*: "I never achieved such a feat of construction in my life. Just consider my subject—the destiny of nations! Consider my characters—personages who stalk on the stage impersonating millions of real, living, suffering men and women.

Good heavens! I have had to get all England and Ireland into three hours and a quarter. I have shown the Englishman to the Irishman and the Irishman to the Englishman, the Protestant to the Catholic and the Catholic to the Protestant. I have taken that panacea for all the misery and unrest of Ireland—your Land Purchase Bill—as to the perfect blessedness of which all your political parties and newspapers were for once unanimous; and I have shown at one stroke its idiocy, its shallowness, its cowardice, its utter and foredoomed futility" (*Tatler*).

1905 January: Arnold Daly, following his success with

Shaw plays in September 1903 and a year later, gives *You Never Can Tell* its American premiere and scores another success. With revivals of his previous Shaw offerings starting in September and the premieres of *John Bull's Other Island* and *Mrs Warren's Profession* in October, Daly helps makes the year a notable one for the growing acceptance of Shaw in America, which newspapers attribute to a "Shaw cult."

May: Shaw's *Man and Superman* is performed as a three-act comedy (without the dream scene) at the Court 14 times. Granville Barker is made up to resemble Shaw for his role as Tanner. With *John Bull's Other Island* and *You Never Can Tell,* the Comedy of *Man and Superman* becomes one of the plays most frequently presented during Shaw's reign at the Court.

September: Shaw's *Man and Superman* (the Comedy) is performed in New York, with Robert Loraine as Tanner, and runs for six months.

October: Shaw's *Mrs Warren's Profession* is performed in New York and is closed by police. The theatre company is arrested but released on bail, then acquitted at the trial (and gives thirteen more performances). Anthony Comstock, long-time secretary for the Society for the Suppression of Vice, who had influenced the New York Public Library to remove a copy of *Man and Superman* from its shelves, takes the occasion to call Shaw the "Irish smut dealer"; Shaw counters in a letter to the *New York Times* that "Comstockery is the world's outstanding joke at the expense of the United States."

November: One of Shaw's most powerful and challenging plays, *Major Barbara,* written expressly for the Court, enters its repertory. Subtitled "a discussion" and culminating in a brain-racking argument between the principal characters, with the demonic munitions-maker triumphant, the play stirs fierce controversy among critics. Shaw struggled through its composition from March to October, and will never be fully satisfied with the last act. The first two acts, a comedic reunion of an imperious upper-class woman and her long-estranged titan-of-industry husband, with her children and their beaus looking on, then a melodramatic portrayal of unfortunates at a Salvation Army shelter, with the affluent characters arguing over the means of saving their souls, grip the audience and critics. But the conversions that follow, showing the evangelist daughter and her scholar-humanist fiancé overcoming "an abyss of moral horror" and allying themselves with "Undershaft" (the "Prince of Darkness") because he represents reality and raw power, prove well-nigh unendurable—to some extent even to Shaw. Curiously, Shaw tells Beatrice Webb that his central theme is "the need for preliminary good physical environment before anything could be done to raise the intelligence and morality of the average sensual man." But the doctrine that "poverty is the worst of crimes" is preached by a character who ruthlessly liberated himself from poverty to become an arch-capitalist, and the play revolves around the effects of his insidious charisma and persuasiveness, which are sufficient to compel the much more humane characters to abandon their benevolent missions and join his "factory of death" (the gentle scholar must even take his surname). Shaw told the actor who played the role that it will be "TREMENJOUS"; "Undershaft is diabolically subtle, gentle, self-possessed, powerful, stupendous, as well as amusing and interesting. There are the makings of ten Hamlets and six Othellos in his mere leavings" (July 1905 letter). In January 1906 he responds to Archer's review ("the worst you ever wrote") by proclaiming "It is a MAGNIFICENT play, a summit in dramatic literature." The holograph manuscript is published in *Early Texts: Play Manuscripts in Facsimile.*

A month before the premiere of *Major Barbara*, Shaw had written to the model for the new Undershaft, the classical scholar Gilbert Murray, "I want to get Cusins beyond the point of wanting power.... The fascination that draws him is the fascination of reality, or rather—for it is hardly a fascination—the impossibility of refusing to put his hand to Undershaft's plough, which is at all events doing something, when the alternative is to hold aloof in a superior attitude and beat the air with words.... I have taken rather special care to make Cusins the reverse in every respect of the theatrical strong man. I want him to go on his quality wholly, and not to make the smallest show of physical robustness or brute determination.

His selection by Undershaft should be a puzzle to people who believe in the strong-silent-still-waters-run-deep hero of melodrama." Shaw also explains the "daimonic" finale: "As to the triumph of Undershaft, that is inevitable because I am in the mind that Undershaft is in the right, and that Barbara and Adolphus [Cusins]... are very young, very romantic, very academic, very ignorant of the world. I think it would be unnatural if they were able to cope with him. Cusins averts discomfiture & scores off him by wit & humorous dexterity; but the facts are too much for him; and his strength lies in the fact that he, like Barbara, refuses the Impossibilist position... even when the alternative is the most sensationally anti-moral department of commerce." During rehearsals Shaw threw more light on the finale when he instructed the actress playing Barbara when to show that she is her mother's daughter: "It comes very natural to her to order people about. There is a curious touch of aristocratic pride at the very end, where she says she does not want to die in God's debt, and will forgive him 'as becomes a woman of her rank' for all the starvation & mischief he is responsible for. Barbara has great courage, great pride & high temper at the back of her religious genius; and you need not hesitate to let them flash through at moments."

December: The first book about Shaw is published: H. L. Mencken's *George Bernard Shaw: His Plays*. It touches off a international flurry of full-length studies written before the war, chief among them Holbrook Jackson's *Bernard Shaw,* G. K. Chesterton's *George Bernard Shaw*, Julius Bab's *Bernard Shaw* (1910; in German), Renée M. Deacon, *Bernard Shaw as Artist-Philosopher: An Exposition of Shavianism,* Archibald Henderson's *George Bernard Shaw: His Life and Works: A Critical Biography* (1911; authorized by Shaw), Charles Cestre's *Bernard Shaw et son oeuvre,* Augustin Hamon's *Le Molière du XXe siècle: Bernard Shaw* (1913; translated in 1915 as *The Twentieth Century Molière: Bernard Shaw*), and Joseph McCabe's *George Bernard Shaw: A Critical Study.*

1906 February: Asked to comment on the question "What Is the Finest Dramatic Situation?" (for *Strand Magazine*), Shaw points to the contemporary examples of Granville Barker's *The*

Voysey Inheritance, St John Hankin's *Return of the Prodigal,* and his own *Candida* and asserts that "the best plays consist of a single situation, lasting several hours.... This expansion of the old momentary claptraps, introduced by tedious explanations between servants, and followed by a final act which was seldom more than a more or less adroitly covered up collapse into episodes of sufficient significance, richness, and variety to form whole plays, is the most hopeful sign about our modern drama."

March: Shaw's *Captain Brassbound's Conversion* has its first London performances at the Court. The actress Shaw visualized as Lady Cicely, Ellen Terry, plays the role at last.

April: In a three-week triple bill, J. M. Barrie includes a one-act called *Punch: A Toy Tragedy*. The main character is Superpunch—made up to resemble Shaw.

October: Shaw's *Caesar and Cleopatra* has its English-language world premiere in New York (in March a German translation had appeared), with the "classic actor of our day" for whom Shaw wrote the part of Caesar, Johnston Forbes-Robertson, playing the role. The production will not reach London until November 1907.

A two-volume selection of Shaw's articles from the *Saturday Review* is published with his prefatory note, "The Author's Apology." His concerted aim, he says, was to compel the theatre to take itself seriously as "a factory of thought, a prompter of conscience, an elucidator of social conduct, an armoury against despair and dullness, and a temple of the Ascent of Man."

November: Shaw's highly discursive exposé of the medical profession, *The Doctor's Dilemma,* which he dubbed "a tragedy" despite the farcical cast of its death scene, is staged at the Court 50 times. Shaw composed the play "at hurricane speed" (between August 11 and September 3) to keep the theatre flourishing. While depicting a cross section of physicians from the comedic underside, the play focuses seriously upon the inventor of an antitoxin for tuberculosis which can kill if it is not properly administered.

Since he must choose between patients competing for the

time-consuming treatment, he is faced with a severe ethical crisis when an attractive woman begs him to save her husband, a Bohemian artistic genius (and "disciple of Bernard Shaw"). The doctor decides to play God and get his way by putting the artist in the hands of a bumbling colleague, who in effect kills him; but he has his comeuppance later when he learns that the woman has already remarried. Shaw explains in his preface that the play demonstrates the crying need for public control of the medical profession; its present state is one reason he subtitled the play a "tragedy." The other reason pertains to the irresponsible artist: "'a man of genius who is not also a man of honor' is the most tragic of all themes" (March 1918 letter to Archibald Henderson). The holograph manuscript of the play is published in *Early Texts: Play Manuscripts in Facsimile.*

Shaw forewarns the critic A. B. Walkley that the "scientific side" of *The Doctor's Dilemma* is "correct and up to date." The hero is based directly upon Dr Almroth Wright, recently knighted for his opsonic discovery, the description of which in Act I " is accurate in every detail." Moreover, "the situation of the doctor having more cases than he could treat, and consequently having to choose whom to cure & whom to let go, actually existed last year." The blunders of the physician who causes the artist's death are founded on confusion between vaccines and anti-toxins; he "imagines that vaccines stimulate the phagocytes instead of buttering the baccili. His cardinal error is sufficiently explained in the play."

1907 February: The Court gives Shaw's second play, *The Philanderer,* its first public performances.

June: Reviewing Shaw's collected drama criticism in *The Fortnightly Review,* St John Hankin takes issue with current critics who seem to have learned nothing since the mid-nineties, as evidenced especially in their naive reviews of Ibsen revivals and of Shaw's recent plays. They seem "quite unconscious" of the fact that Ibsen is acknowledged as "the most famous dramatist whom the nineteenth century produced," and that Shaw is "indisputably the most distinguished living English dramatist. His plays... are read and discussed and defended and attacked wherever men of letters are gathered together who take any serious interest in the theatre."

The dream scene of Shaw's *Man and Superman*, entitled *Don Juan in Hell* for separate production, is staged for eight matinees at the Court. Set in an afterlife of "utter void," the long one-act is a fantasy that develops into a pure discussion drama. Shaw will later refer to it as his "beginning of a bible for Creative Evolution."

The four principals—Juan, Doña Ana, her father (bedecked as a statue), and the Devil—engage in a concerted argument about the main issues in that philosophy, with Juan passionately upholding the creed of aligning oneself with the *élan vital* or Life Force and the Devil advocating a hedonistic life contemplating ideals of beauty and love that are no longer contradicted by brute realities. (The two sides mark "the difference between the angelic and the diabolic temperament.") Juan provokes Ana to shed her earthly illusions and help the Life Force in its struggle upward as only a mother-woman can: by heading for heaven to locate "a father! a father for the Superman!"; the Devil, clearly bettered in the debate although his rebuttal speeches are stunning until the last phase, wins the pleasure-seeking Statue as a consolation prize.

A highlight of the discussion is Juan's pointed recollection of an attempt to cut short an affair with a seductive woman: "whilst I was in the act of framing my excuse to the lady, Life seized me and threw me into her arms as a sailor throws a scrap of fish into the mouth of a seabird."

The same, in effect, happens to his 20th-century counterpart in the Comedy. Shaw had specified that the stage designer for the production must create "a really artistic fantastic picture, with top lighting in the manner of [Gordon] Craig, and cunning costumes—a violet velvet Don Juan..., a crimson scarlet Mephistopheles, a masterpiece of white marble sculpture, and a radiant female"—else "the thing will be unendurable" (December 1905 letter). He later commends Charles Ricketts for fulfilling this task brilliantly.

Shaw's one-act Napoleon play, *The Man of Destiny: A Trifle,* is finally given a full production in London to fill out the bill with *Don Juan in Hell* at the Court. After his first notable success in battle, General Napoleon is faced with a dilemma which could ruin his career in its infancy. A letter proving that his wife has been unfaithful with a prominent official has been intercepted, and when he catches the culprit—an attractive "strange lady"—she warns him that reading it would force him into a duel, risking his life and reputation. By clever and unscrupulous machinations, he manages both to read the letter and leave no evidence that he has.

The play is a logical successor to *Arms and the Man,* with its opposed idealistic and realistic "heroes." In this case, the focus on a single "man of destiny" allows for discussions of what motivates a hero and verbal assaults on the currently accredited view (upheld most conspicuously by the English). The play is in effect a dramatized essay on willful versus theatrical motivation.

The Vedrenne-Barker management at the Court ends, but moves into West End theatres (the Savoy and Haymarket) for performances of a few plays, among them Shaw's *Getting Married* in 1908.

October: A letter to the *London Times* protesting the censorship of plays, prompted by the refusal to license Granville Barker's drama *Waste,* is signed by 71 writers, among them W. S. Gilbert, Arthur Wing Pinero, J. M. Barrie, Shaw, W. B. Yeats, John Millington Synge, John Galsworthy, and Somerset Maugham.

This, and the deputation to the Prime Minister's office that followed, is the first step in a concerted campaign, tirelessly stage-managed by Shaw, to end or significantly revise the governmental examination of plays.

Yeats reports to Florence Farr that he saw Shaw's *Caesar and Cleopatra* twice in one week and was "delighted and what I never thought [to] be with a work of his, moved. There is vulgarity, plenty of it, but such gay heroic delight in the serviceable man. Ah if he had but style, distinction, and was not such a barbarian of the barricades."

November: Shaw's *Caesar and Cleopatra* is finally produced in London and has a run of 28.

December: Shaw's *Arms and the Man* is performed in London for the first time since 1894 and has a run of 77.

1908 May: In an interview before the opening of *Getting Married,* Shaw declares that he is going to be revenged upon critics for "their arrant Philistinism, their shameless intellectual laziness, their low tastes, their hatred of good work, their puerile romanticism, their disloyalty to dramatic literature.... There will be nothing but talk, talk, talk, talk, talk—Shaw talk. The characters will seem to the wretched critics to be simply a row of Shaws, all arguing with one another on totally uninteresting subjects. The whole thing will be hideous, indescribable—an eternity of brain-racking dullness. And yet they will have to sit it out" (*Daily Telegraph*).

Shaw's *Getting Married,* a "disquisitory play" with a vengeance, is staged at the Haymarket and manages a run of 54 in spite of (or by now, perhaps because of) its discursiveness. Shaw wrote it between August 1907 and March 1908, finally rejecting its provisional title, "Any Just Cause or Impediment?" A seriocomic analysis of the institution of marriage in England, the three-hour drama obeys the classical unities of time (a wedding day) and place (an oversized kitchen), but its structure is argumentative rather than "well made" to an extent unequaled at the time except in the dream scene of *Man and Superman.* Critics greet it with what Shaw calls a "torrent of denunciation" largely because of its torrent of talk. The many fascinating characters, from a bishop and a beadle to a general and a clairvoyant, exist primarily as conflicting viewpoints on and exemplars of the institution of marriage and divorce. (The greengrocer/alderman's contention that "Marriage is tolerable enough in its way if youre easygoing and don't expect too much from it. But it doesnt bear thinking about" fails to stem the debate.) The group has assembled before a wedding when the young couple informs them that they have learned about the deficiencies of present marriage laws, especially the provisions for divorce, and are changing their plans. Led by the broad-minded bishop, the kitchenful of people try to agree on a marriage contract which will accommodate a wide range of views—except for celibacy, advocated by the bishop's assistant—and allow for divorce on reasonable grounds. Their prolonged attempt finally has no effect whatever on the couple; they abandon the debate, work out a contract that satisfies them, and get married offstage. A highlight of the play is the impassioned aria of the clairvoyant to men in general, concluding: "I gave you your own soul: you ask me for my body as a plaything. Was it not enough? Was it not enough?"

November: Admonishing an actress playing Ann in a touring production of *Man and Superman*, Shaw instructs her in the "particular kind of English ladylikeness" she must strive for: "No matter how improperly she may behave, an English lady never admits she is behaving improperly. Just as there are lots of women who are good-hearted and honest and innocent in an outrageously rowdy way, so there are ladies who do the most shocking things with a dignity and gentility which a bishop might envy.... Ann's dignity, her self-control, her beautifully measured speed, her impressive grief for her father, which absolutely forbids her to smile until she is out of mourning, a sort of rich, chaste, noble self-respect about her... must be splendidly and very firmly handled on the stage in order to give effect to her audacity" (letter to Frances Dillon).

1909 May: In a plea for a national theatre, Shaw contends: "The theatre is literally making the minds of our urban populations to-day. It is a huge factory of sentiment, of character, of points of honour, of conceptions of conduct, of everything that finally determines the destiny of a nation. And yet it is openly said that the theatre is only a place of amusement. It is nothing of the kind; a theatre is a place of culture, a place where people learn to think, act, and feel; more important than all the schools in Christendom" (London *Times*).

July: A governmental revaluation of the function of the Lord Chamberlain's Office as examiner of plays begins with meetings of the Joint Select Committee of House of Lords and House of Commons on Stage Plays. Similar committees had met in 1892 and 1906 with negligible results, but this time dozens of well-known writers are clamoring for reform. Shaw is to be interviewed on July 30; in preparation he draws up an 11,000-word statement to supplement and clarify his answers to the questions they have posed, almost surely the most thoughtful analysis of the existing censorship and possible alternatives ever written. The statement is not admitted into evidence (which would have mandated its appearance in the Select Committee's transcript of proceedings); after protesting repeatedly and being refused, Shaw prints it in his Preface to *The Shewing-up of Blanco Posnet* (published in 1911). It states, "I am a specialist in immoral and heretical plays. My reputation has been gained by my persistent struggle to force the public to reconsider its morals," and insists on "those rights of liberty of speech and conscience which are matters of course in other professions." After fifteen meetings the Committee publishes its half-a-million-word final report. Shaw calls it an example of "the art of contriving methods of reform which will leave matters exactly as they are," but it does lessen the powers of the Examiner of Plays and incorporates other suggestions from Shaw and his allies.

August: Shaw's one-act *The Shewing-up of Blanco Posnet* is performed at the Abbey after the Lord Chamberlain's Office refused to license it in England. Written in three weeks early in 1909 on commission to benefit a children's charity, the "religious tract in dramatic form" (of a creative evolutionist) was censored for blasphemy. Shaw used the decision as another means of prompting an inquiry into the policy of censorship. Partly to point up its absurdity, he has the play performed in Dublin, where touchy audiences jam the theatre and find little to scandalize or titillate them. A variation on the plot of *The Devil's Disciple*, the courtroom melodrama features an American drifter in pioneer days who inadvertently steals the sheriff's horse, then cannot resist giving it to a woman who is trying to reach a doctor because her child is dying. When these secrets are disclosed and he is acquitted, Blanco preaches a Shavian sermon that he "played the rotten game, but the great game was played on [him]"—

by the same cosmic force that made the child's disease. The Stage Society gives the play two private performances in London in December, but it will not have a West End performance until July 1921.

After putting Shaw's *The Shewing-up of Blanco Posnet* into rehearsal, Lady Gregory is informed by Dublin Castle officials that producing it will violate the restrictions placed upon the Abbey Theatre by the Patent, and will thus nullify their license. Gregory, W. B. Yeats, and Shaw determine to take the risk and go ahead with the performance. When the audience finds the play innocuous, the Castle capitulates silently.

November: Shaw begins writing *Misalliance,* evidently inspired by hearing Granville Barker read his newly completed play *The Madras House.* At about this time he also finishes writing a long preface to a volume not published until 1911, *Three Plays by Brieux,* in which he proclaims the basic aesthetic principle underlying his drama: "Life as it occurs is senseless: a policeman may watch it and work in it for thirty years in the streets and courts of Paris without learning as much of it or from it as a child or a nun may learn from a single play by Brieux. For it is the business of Brieux to pick out the significant incidents from the chaos of daily happenings, and arrange them so that their relation to one another becomes significant, thus changing us from bewildered spectators of a monstrous confusion to men intelligently conscious of the world and its destinies. This is the highest function that man can perform—the greatest work he can set his hand to; and this is why the great dramatists of the world, from Euripides and Aristophanes to Shakespear and Molière, and from them to Ibsen and Brieux, take that majestic and pontifical rank which seems so strangely above all the reasonable pretensions of mere strolling actors and theatrical authors."

1910 February: Shaw's *Misalliance: A Debate in One Sitting,* a seriocomic exploration of relations between parents and children, enters the repertory at the Duke of York's with eleven performances. It is severely criticized for the apparent formlessness of its "debate."

In Shaw's opinion, the main reason is that the producer

Charles Frohman "cut out what he considered the highbrow parts and made the rest unintelligible," and revivals faithful to the play in 1930 and 1953 will be better received. As in *Getting Married*, the unities of time and space are observed and the structure is that of an argument. But in this play striking things happen to introduce new points of view, notably a plane crash into the greenhouse that brings an attractive, aggressively independent Polish acrobat, and a stickup by a young intruder with melodramatic notions who intends to avenge his mother by killing the master of the house. Moreover, looking forward to *Heartbreak House*, infatuations and flirtations galore (including several directed at the acrobat) alternate with brief discussions on an array of topics ("Let's argue about something intellectual," a character says; one of the many topics is the superman, which evokes the comment, "Read Whatshisname").

The title relates to a topsy-turvy sentiment of the play's elder statesman, who objected to a young man marrying his daughter "on the ground that a marriage between a member of the great and good middle class with one of the vicious and corrupt aristocracy would be a misalliance."

Count Leo Tolstoy responds to Shaw's gift of an inscribed volume of *Man and Superman* with praise for Don Juan's speeches and the "attitude towards civilisation and progress" shown in "The Revolutionist's Handbook," but urges him not to "speak jestingly of such a subject as the purpose of human life, the causes of its perversion, and the evil that fills the life of humanity today." Shaw retorts that making people laugh in the "most earnest moments" of the play is a valid strategy: "Why should humour and laughter be excommunicated? Suppose the world were only one of God's jokes, would you work any the less to make it a good joke instead of a bad one?" Tolstoy replies that he "received a very painful impression" from these words.

November: Shaw's one-act featuring a confrontation between Shakespeare and Queen Elizabeth, *The Dark Lady of the Sonnets*, is performed at the Haymarket for two matinees. He wrote it as an appeal for the establishment of a national theatre, which is the appeal that Shakespeare makes (in vain) to the Queen.

1911 April: Shaw's *Fanny's First Play* is produced, its author unidentified, at the Little Theatre, then is transferred to the Kingsway for a total run of 623. The play, its author *also* unidentified, presents Fanny's Ibsenite drama of youthful rebellion from conventions and ensuing self-discovery, partly designed to bring her father up-to-date. (It is performed in his elegant country house.)

A framework of "Induction" and Epilogue—sometimes omitted in performance—presents the wrongheaded anticipations and reactions of her father and the invited audience of four prominent drama critics. Her father, an aesthete completely unfamiliar with current drama, is roundly shocked; the critics, three of them caricatures of living men and one representing "the man in the street," voice conflicting extreme opinions. They inevitably discuss Shaw as the possible author: "A giant brain... but no heart"; all his characters are "mere puppets stuck up to spout Shaw"; "All he wants to do is to insult everybody all round and set us talking about him." Shaw calls the play a "potboiler," and it turns out to be his first commercial success.

December: Shaw states that Synge's satirical dramas have a "joyousness and a wild wealth of poetic imagery" (*Gaelic American*).

1912 July: Shaw writes to the actress Pat Campbell, "My plays must be acted, and acted hard. They need a sort of bustle and crepitation of life which requires extraordinary energy and vitality, and gives only glimpses and movements of the poetry beneath. The lascivious monotony of beauty which satisfies those who are slaves of art instead of masters of it is hideous in my plays."

December: Writing to his French translator, Augustin Hamon, about his script of *Man and Superman*, Shaw suggests using Bergson's term, *l'élan vital*, for Life Force. He adds: "It is quite probable that if I had heard the expression... when I was writing *Man and Superman*, I would have called the Life Force, the Life Impulse." He also comments that he was the first to use the word "superman": "Everybody uses it now. But for a year or two a few men of letters here persisted in ignoring it and using such alternatives as Overman and even Beyondman. Exactly the same thing would happen to us if we attempted to ignore Bergson's term; we should be forced eventually to adopt it."

1913 August: Shaw's expanded edition of *The Quintessence of Ibsenism* is published. Much commentary from the perspective of two decades later is appended, including analyses of the late plays and the seminal essay "The Technical Novelty in Ibsen's Plays." The "novelty" that Shaw identifies is the discussion, which "conquered Europe" in Ibsen's A *Doll's House*. "Formerly you had in what was called a well made play an exposition in the first act, a situation in the second, and unravelling in the third.

Now you have exposition, situation, and discussion; and the discussion is the test of the playwright." This technique has evolved so that in some contemporary plays, including his own, "the discussion interpenetrates the action from beginning to end."

September: Shaw's *Androcles and the Lion: A Fable Play*, written during January 1912, is staged and has a run of 63. Shaw will comment much later that he wrote it "as a sample of what children like in contrast to Barrie's Peter Pan,... [rather than] a sample of what adults think children like." It also contrasts strongly with Wilson Barrett's solemn Christian martyr play *The Sign of the Cross*; its comic and irreverent treatment of religious themes elicit accusations of blasphemy. In the farcical frame-tale, Androcles removes a thorn from a lion's paw and then confronts the same lion in the arena; both times the two waltz offstage. The play's serious dimensions expose the religious hypocrisy of the Roman persecutors, who urge the captured Christians to save themselves simply by pretending homage to their pagan gods, and portray two strong-minded Christians, a beautiful noblewoman and an indomitable warrior, coming to realize under stress that their true natures befit them for service to Rome rather than to "the God who is not yet."

Anticipating *Saint Joan* (December 1923) on a trip to Orleans, Shaw writes to Pat Campbell: "I shall do a Joan play some day, beginning with the sweeping up of the cinders and orange peel *after* her martyrdom, and going on with Joan's arrival in heaven. I should have God about to damn the English for their share in her betrayal and Joan producing an end of burnt stick in arrest of Judgment. 'What's this? Is it one of the faggots?' says God. 'No,' says Joan 'it's what is left of the two sticks a common English soldier tied together and gave me as I went to the stake; for they wouldnt even give me a crucifix; and you cannot damn the common people of England, represented by that soldier[,] because a poor cowardly riff raff of barons and bishops were too futile to resist the devil.' That soldier is the only redeeming figure in the whole business."

1914 April: Shaw's *Pygmalion: A Romance,* written in June 1912, starts a run of 118 at His Majesty's Theatre, his first success in the West End. (The play had first been presented in Vienna in November 1913.) The reception derives in part from the sensation caused by the use (and re-use) of the word "bloody," but also from Shaw's comically antiromantic inversion of the myth of Pygmalion and Galatea. The play goes beyond a sound-sculpting Pygmalion fashioning the raw material of a female into an admirable mate for him; it shows her transcending the ladylike stage and becoming a genuinely independent woman—partly because of her resistance to her overbearing teacher. And he likes her the better for it: "By George, Eliza, I said I'd make a woman of you; and I have." A highly comic subplot involves Eliza's dustman-father, a contented member of the "undeserving poor" class who pleads his distinctive ethics when he confronts the phonetician about his daughter (not to get her back, but for money). A few months later he learns to his chagrin that her mentor has caused him to win a large bequest by recommending him as the most original moralist in England, thus delivering him over to middle-class morality. Among other deplorable consequences, he will have to marry the woman he has been living with. To keep people from deducing that Eliza and the bullying phonetician are headed for marriage, Shaw will add a postscript to the book (published in 1916) saying that Eliza later married the young man who adores her, then in 1939 he will change the curtain scene to have her mentor roar with jeering laughter at that prospect.

1916 March: Shaw begins writing *Heartbreak House,* tentatively entitled "The Studio in the Clouds," with the war pervading his consciousness to the extent that he speaks of "creeping through a new [play] (to prevent myself crying) at odd moments, two or three speeches at a time." He will not complete it until mid-1917, and then he will wait until after the war to have it produced. (Shaw apparently misleads people, among them his chosen biographer Archibald Henderson, into believing he had written the play before the war, which accounts for the statement in several sources that he began it in 1913.) A 1910 comment by Henry James about Shaw is reported in the New York *Sun*: "I do not think highly of him. Wilde wrote a better play, I think, *Lady Windermere's Fan*. It is a distinctly good play, better than anything Shaw has written. Shaw has the sort of success that consists in being talked about, but I do not think him great."

November: When Frank Harris comments that Shaw's plays are not passionate or sexual the dramatist replies in a letter: "I know of no writer who has dealt as critically with sex as I have. Archer's early complaint that my plays reeked with sex was far more sensible than the virgin-eunuch theory which the halfpenny journalists delight in.... You had better avoid the subject, as you will certainly botch it frightfully."

1917 July: After a performance of *The Outcry* by Henry James, Shaw responds to an actress who deplored its failure: "Nothing can make H.J. intelligible on the stage. The difficulty is not in the least that his dialogue is artificial and affected and involved: it is not more so than Congreve's now appears.... It is simply that he uses sounds that are not intelligible to the ear, though they are quite lucid on paper.... I did not, with all my literary expertness and knowledge of James's style, catch more than two thirds of the dialogue as it was spoken, though I could have read it without difficulty."

October: After completing *Heartbreak House,* Shaw replies to his puzzled Swedish translator, Hugo Vallentin: "You say you do not understand it; but there is nothing to understand beneath the surface: it is a picture of a certain sort of life that our civilization tends to produce among people of extraordinary vitality and sensibility.... The only part of society which is not a quicksand is the life of the equestrian country house class and the frankly autocratic Crown-Colony-Governing-Class extolled by the daughter of the house who happens to be born conventional. The old Captain is your prophet Jeremiah bawling the judgment of God on all this insanity. And you have the undercurrent of sex continually reproducing quicksand as fast as the welter tries to consolidate itself.... I think what makes it puzzling is that the people seem to be so interesting and attractive and novel at first sight that one is led to expect great things from them; and when they are all reduced to absurdity, and even the solution of blowing them to bits misses fire, the spectator feels baffled and disappointed, as if something very promising had been wantonly spoilt."

1918 March: In New York Shaw's *Mrs Warren's Profession* is revived by the Washington Square Players, this time free of police raids.

Shaw begins writing his dramatic magnum opus, the five-play cycle *Back to Methuselah*; he will finish it (and its 30,000-word preface) two years later.

1919 August: Among Shaw's many deploring retorts to statements of his aspiring (but eventually stillborn) biographer, Thomas Demetrius O'Bolger, is the following: "My plays are no more economic treatises than Shakespear's plays.... It is clear that *Widowers' Houses* and *Major Barbara*, being dramas of the cash nexus (in plot), could not have been written by a non-economist. It is also clear that *Mrs Warren's Profession* is the work of an economist. There is an economic link between Cashel Byron [in the novel *Cashel Byron's Profession*], Sartorius, Mrs Warren & Undershaft, all of them engaged very capably in infamous activities prosperously and proudly. But would anyone but a buffle headed idiot of a university professor, half crazy with correcting examination papers (another infamous activity pursued under economic pressure) immediately shriek that all my plays were written as economic essays, and that I did not know that they were plays of life, character, and human destiny as much as Shakespear's or Euripides's?"

1920 February: Just before a revival of *Pygmalion* in the West End, Shaw insists in a letter to Pat Campbell that in playing Eliza she "must not relapse" after she emancipates herself ("when Galatea comes to life"). She must retain her pride to the end. When Higgins compares her to a consort battleship and takes her arm, she "must instantly throw him off with implacable pride; and this is the note until the final 'Buy them yourself.'" In this production Higgins was to "come back triumphantly into the room" and exclaim "Galatea!" For a Spanish production at the same time, Higgins was to exclaim, "Finished, and come to life! Bravo, Pygmalion!" (letter to Julio Brouta). Shaw will not settle on the final version, which has no mythic allusion, until August 1939.

April: St John Ervine generalizes about Shaw in the *North American Review*: "when all the discount is made that can be made for possible charlatanry in Shaw's character, there remains this indisputable fact that he has left a mark on the thought and life not only of the English-speaking world, but of the whole of Western civilization, which cannot be eradicated. We may go to the theatre to laugh at Bernard Shaw, but we remain to think with him."

November: Shaw's *Heartbreak House: A Fantasia in the Russian Manner on English Themes*, written in 1916-17, is produced at last after having been published in September 1919. The recently incorporated Theatre Guild of America presents the play (uncut, at Shaw's insistence) in New York for a run of 125. It will not be performed in London (with a few excisions allowed) until October 1921, when the Court stages it 63 times. The subtitle points primarily to Shaw's attempt to emulate the fluid dramaturgy of Anton Chekhov's *The Cherry Orchard*, which he had admired in 1911, and to attain musical effects; he tells Edward Elgar in 1929 that it is "by far the most musical work of the lot." Archer tells Granville Barker in 1923 that it is an "unconstructed play" which "lives from moment to moment by the mere shillelagh-whirling of its dialogue."

This comic tragedy—which he will also dare to call his own *King Lear* in his 1949 puppet play *Shakes versus Shav*—is uncharacteristically enigmatic as well as sad. The portrayal of "cultured, leisured Europe before the war" which has not learned how to "navigate" the ship of state (symbolized by the design of the former sea-captain's house) is made even more poignant by the several romantic infatuations and heartbreaks that occur. The chief sufferer is a susceptible middle-class young lady who is rudely initiated into this strange, decadent society. First she must undergo the loss of her dream-lover, who turns out to be her hostess's ultra-romantic husband, addicted to heroic posturing under aliases in front of pretty women. Then, with help from the worldly and tolerant hostess, she must overcome the initial effect of her heartbreak: a cynical determination to "make a domestic convenience" of a bloated capitalist to whom her father thinks he is indebted by holding him to his proposal of marriage. Finally, she chooses to become the spiritual wife of the 88-year-old sea captain who, while subsisting on rum, aspires to attain "the seventh degree of concentration" and invent an ultimate weapon, but whose erratic wisdom soothes her. His transforming message to her is: "At your age I looked for hardship, danger, horror, and death, that I might feel the life in me more intensely." The play's finale, with the most promising characters lighting the house to welcome German bombs because proximity to death renews one's sense of being alive, is as paradoxical and ungratifying as that of *Major Barbara. Heartbreak House* will become the favourite of Shavians who prefer tragic to comic drama, and Shaw will often declare it his best play. The revised typescript is published in *Early Texts: Play Manuscripts in Facsimile.*

When St John Ervine in a review of *Heartbreak House* contends that Shaw's choice of actress for the heroine was "seriously miscast" (*Observer*, October 1921), Shaw responds that the part "fits her like a glove." Ellie Dunn is *not* the ingenue, a "sweet little sexual attraction," but "the heavy lead";

her part is written "with obvious operatic solos in it," and the objection to her "recitations" and "pontificating" are oddly misplaced when "Hector declaims all through" and the Captain "prophesies like a Druid," and no one objects. Moreover, the complaint that Ellie does not seem to be "in her element" in the play is misguided: "I took the greatest care that she should not be—that she should be in the sharpest contrast to all the heart-breakers, and that when she is lured into it she should walk over Hector and Hesione straight to the Captain, the positive efficient man on whose shoulders the whole structure is carried." The actress presents Ellie "precisely as I planned her: as the strong respectable woman of the play, virginal by contrast with the demon daughters, and yet audaciously passionate and imaginative."

1921 June: Shaw's most imposing and imaginative work, *Back to Methuselah: A Metabiological Pentateuch,* is published. The book sells very well, but the huge drama will not be performed until February 1922. Composed of five full-length plays, the whole spans 35,000 years, from the Garden of Eden ("In the Beginning") to postwar London ("The Gospel of the Brothers Barnabas") to 2170 A.D. ("The Thing Happens") to 3000 A.D. ("The Tragedy of an Elderly Gentleman") and finally to 31,920 A.D. ("As Far as Thought Can Reach"). Shaw advertised it as his "scientific, religious, and political testament as well as his supreme exploit in dramatic literature," and linked it to the "beginning" of his bible of Creative Evolution, the Don Juan in Hell scene of *Man and Superman.* The central line of action is touched off when two contemporary believers in that creed discuss their "gospel": in order to attain genuine knowledge and power, men and women must *will* themselves a life span of at least 300 years. Two politicians, a young rector, and a parlormaid listen, wondering at the advocates' sanity. However, 250 years later, "The Thing" has happened: a few people have unconsciously willed themselves into longlivers. The President of the land learns to his dismay that the Archbishop and four other famous people who had been reported drowned in past ages are all one and the same man: the rector, 283 years old but looking 50. Moreover, their

Domestic Minister turns out to be the former parlormaid, who has also lived several lives. In the next 35 millennia life evolves so that seventeen-year-old children emerge from eggs and reach maturity in four years. As they grow into "Ancients," they are destined to live forever, barring an accident, and to spend their time in a state of contemplation that becomes more profound and ecstatic as they progress toward the goal they visualize: a bodiless "vortex of pure thought." The mythical figure of Lilith is attributed in part one with creation: by a mighty effort of imagination and will she divided herself into Adam and Eve. At the end of the drama she is pleased with the present results of her deed, and urges man onward toward "the whirlpool in pure intelligence" and whatever lies beyond that. "It is enough that there is a beyond." In a postscript to a 1945 revised edition Shaw declares that the play "is a world classic or it is nothing."

1921 October: The Macdona Players, led by the actor-manager Charles Macdona, secure the touring rights for Shaw's plays, form the Shaw Touring Repertory Company, and produce thirteen of his plays in the provinces and Paris. After Esmé Percy becomes their director in 1924, they begin London seasons which bring their repertory to the West End. Notable first productions there include *Mrs Warren's Profession* in September 1925 and the whole of *Man and Superman* in October. Shaw speaks of Percy as having "led the forlorn hope of advanced drama in England" after the war.

1922 February-March: To Shaw's great surprise, the New York Theatre Guild mounts a production of the full play-cycle *Back to Methuselah* at a special Shaw Festival in the Garrick Theatre. The five parts of the twelve hour performance are presented over a two-week period; in nine weeks the whole is performed 25 times. The "fanatic" who proposed the event, Lawrence Langner, is followed by Barry Jackson, founder of the Birmingham Repertory Theatre; his group presents the cycle beginning in October 1923 for four performances in Birmingham, then for four more in London at the Court in February 1924. Reactions to the book and drama are of course mixed; T. S. Eliot deplores its doctrinaire strain, Arnold Bennett falls asleep at a performance, and Shaw himself admits that he had been "too damned discursive."

1923 June: Responding to Archer's preference for "constructed" plays in his recent book, *The Old Drama and the New*, Shaw declares: "The plain fact is that there are two sorts of plays: natural growths and constructions, just as there are two sorts of flowers, natural ones and artificial ones.... When you are writing a play it is of the first importance that you should not for a moment allow your attention and interest to be diverted from the interest proper to drama: that is, an interest common to yourself and your audience. Now the interest of carrying out a scenario is like the interest of piecing together a jigsaw puzzle: it has nothing whatever to do with dramatic interest, and though it is absorbing to the operator, it is unbearably dull to the looker-on. You must always go where the dramatic interest takes you; and if you do this you will find that the dramatic interest, a live thing, will organize itself so marvellously (like the natural flower) that the final result will be held up by critics as a triumph of construction."

December: Shaw's compelling historical drama, *Saint Joan*, is staged in New York by the Theatre Guild, has a run of 214, then in March 1924 starts a run of 244 in London. The play transforms many critics' opinions of Shaw as a playwright incapable of writing serious drama, and largely accounts for his being awarded the Nobel Prize in Literature for 1925 after several previous nominations. Written in four months after a long period of gestation, the play is firmly based on Jules Quicherat's transcription of Joan's trial and rehabilitation—that is, on recorded history rather than legend. (Because of this Shaw will say that he is "not inordinately proud of it" because "it was very easy to write" [February 1924 letter].) Still, the play is suffused with Shavian ideas: as a "genius," Joan "has a different set of ethical valuations" than other people and manifests "an appetite for evolution"; her trial was conducted not by villains but by men with just as good intentions as hers; she was burnt not only for her heretical Protestantism and Nationalism, but also "for what we call unwomanly and insufferable presumption"—her form of classic pride or hubris, conveyed by direct allusions to Aristotelian theory. He also subtly undercuts the validity of Joan's voices and the miracle of the changing wind. The three-and-a-half-hour drama traces her full career in three contrasting movements: as Shaw describes them, "the romance of her rise, the tragedy of her execution, and the comedy of the attempts of posterity to make amends for that execution." In effect he burns Joan again to force people to ask themselves, "Must then a Christ perish in torment in every age to save those that have no imagination?" Several reviewers object to the partly farcical Epilogue, and T. S. Eliot remonstrates that Shaw had committed "the greatest sacrilege" against Joan by turning her into "a great middle-class reformer." But Pirandello calls the play "a work of poetry from beginning to end."

1924 January: On the occasion of the production of *Saint Joan*, Luigi Pirandello offers his perspective on Shaw's career: "I have a strong impression that for some time past George Bernard Shaw has been growing more and more serious. He has always believed in himself, and with good reason. But in a number of plays, after his first successes, he did not seem to believe very much in what he was doing. This, at least, may properly be suspected, since it cannot be denied that in his eagerness to defend his own intellectual position against the so-called 'bourgeois morality,' he not infrequently abandoned all pretensions to seriousness as an artist. Now, however, he seems to be believing less in himself, and more in what he is doing." The strongest evidence is his portrait of Joan, which reflects a "new tolerance and pity" that "rise from the most secret depths of poetry that exist in Shaw." In sum, "There is a truly great poet in Shaw; but this combative Anglo-Irishman is often willling to forget that he is a poet, so interested is he in being a citizen of his country, or a man of the twentieth century society, with a number of respectable ideas to defend, a number of sermons to preach, a number of antagonists to rout from the intellectual battlefield" (*New York Times Sunday Magazine*).

March: Shaw tells his biographer Archibald Henderson, "My plays are *sui generis*; and to say that they are comedies or tragedies or tragi-comedies or dramas is like saying that I am a Caucasian: it says nothing about them that does not apply to thousands of plays not a bit like them" (*Table-Talk of G.B.S.*).

December: A New York revival of Shaw's *Candida*, starring Katharine Cornell, starts as a matinee and ends as a regular offering with a run of 143.

1925 July: Shaw's *Mrs Warren's Profession* is performed in Birmingham, the Lord Chamberlain having finally granted a Licence for Representation. In September it enters the repertory of Regent Theatre in London and is staged 21 times; in March 1926 it moves to the Strand and has a run of 68. Writing to Edith Evans about the Examiner's unexpected act in August 1924, Shaw urged her to accept the role of Mrs Warren (she declined), and noted that the play "is as old fashioned as Ibsen, and much cruder; but Mrs W. has two very powerful scenes.... Fancy my feelings at having this horror shoved on me when I am in the very odor of sanctity after *St Joan*."

October: The whole of Shaw's *Man and Superman* is performed for the first time when the Macdona Players present it at the Regent Theatre in a repertory season.

1926 April: Shaw outlines the structure of some of his disquisitory dramas in the *Fortnightly Review*, echoing his chapter "The Technical Novelty in Ibsen's Plays" in his 1913 revision of *The Quintessence of Ibsenism*. Like Ibsen's *A Doll's House, Candida* has its discussion of ideas at the end of the last act, but that element "soon spreads itself over the whole play." In those plays "you have action producing discussion; in *The Doctor's Dilemma* you have discussion producing action, and that action being finally discussed. In other plays you have discussion all over the shop. Sometimes the discussion interpenetrates the action from beginning to end. Sometimes, as in *Getting Married* and *Misalliance*, the whole play, though full of incident, is a discussion and nothing else.... The public now demands a case and an argument, vehemently conducted."

November: Shaw is awarded the Nobel Prize in Literature for 1925. He first refuses the money (about £7000), but upon learning that it would simply revert to the Nobel fund he uses it to help establish an Anglo-Swedish Literary Foundation, largely to finance English translations of Swedish literary works.

1929 August: Barry Jackson opens the first annual Malvern Festival, set in a resort town in western England with a new theatre and dedicated to presenting the plays of Shaw and others in idyllic conditions. Shaw's futuristic "political extravaganza" *The Apple Cart*, which he wrote (in two months) expressly for the occasion although the premiere was held in Warsaw, is performed in repertory four times. It is transferred to London the next month, where its relevance to current issues and near-caricatures of political figures insure its popularity so that it attains a run of 258. But it will be the last of Shaw's plays to be frequently revived. An attempt to expose the subjection of both democracy and royalty to plutocratic enterprises, this highly discursive drama culminates in the king (whom Shaw modeled partly on himself) countering demands to make himself subordinate to Parliament by threatening to abdicate and run for Prime Minister as a private citizen. In 1949 Thomas Mann will describe the play as a "stunningly clairvoyant political satire." Between two long political discussions is an "Interlude" in which the king's aspiring mistress misbehaves much as the actress Pat Campbell had with Shaw in 1913. Within a fortnight, *Back to Methuselah, Caesar and Cleopatra,* and *Heartbreak House* are also performed at the Festival; English premieres of *Too True to be Good, The Simpleton of the Unexpected Isles, Geneva, 'In Good King Charles's Golden Days'*, and *Buoyant Billions* are held there in subsequent years.

1932 February: Shaw's *Too True to be Good,* another "political extravaganza" but more of a fantasy than a realistic debate over issues, is performed in New York by the Theatre Guild, at the Malvern Festival in August, then in London in September, where it has a run of 47. Beginning with a bedridden young lady dreaming that she hears a Microbe complain that she has given a disease to him, yet he gets the blame; proceeding to her flight from deadening respectability on a hedonistic sojourn with a burglar-lover, which soon becomes as boring as life was at home; and concluding with the lover, a former clergyman, bewailing that mankind is "falling endlessly and hopelessly through a void in which they can find no footing," the play is received as an often-enjoyable curio marked by apparent pessimism and formlessness. The Microbe anticipates this reception in Act I when he says, "The play is now virtually over, but the characters will discuss it at great length for two acts more."

Writing to the drama historian Allardyce Nicoll some time later, Shaw comments on "the great length to which *Too True* carries my practice of making my characters say not what in real life they could never bring themselves to say, even if they understood themselves clearly enough, but the naked soul truth, quite objectively and scientifically presented, thus combining the extreme of unnaturalness with the greatest attainable naturalness.... The highest drama is nothing but a striving towards this feat of interpretation."

September: Shaw is unanimously elected President of the newly formed Irish Academy of Letters, with Yeats as Vice President. He remains in this figurehead position until 1935.

1933 November: Shaw's *On the Rocks: A Political Comedy* is presented in London and manages a run of 73. A hypothetical fantasy set inside10 Downing Street with mobs of the unemployed outside, the play poses a conflict between two contrasting ways of trying to save the country: a series of socialist reforms or rule by a right-thinking dictator like Moses, Lenin, or Mussolini. The amiable Prime Minister finds himself unable to gain acceptance for his reforms or to accept dictatorial powers and, to the sound of riots, retires from politics.

1935 February: Shaw's "vision of judgment," *The Simpleton of the Unexpected Isles*, is performed in New York by the Theatre Guild, then at the Malvern Festival in July. A futuristic and allegorical fantasy, the play portrays attempts to improve the race by merging West and East, then to avoid the consequences of Judgment Day (announced by angels) by proving one's social usefulness. Many people disappear, among them children named Love, Pride, Heroism and Empire and many doctors and politicians, and the remainder are incited to dedicate themselves to work and thought for the improvement of life.

March: Shaw suggests the permeation strategy of his last three plays in responding to Joseph Wood Krutch's assertion that spectators will spoil their enjoyment if they search for their serious meaning, since none exists:

"People come to a play as they come to all forms of art, to have their minds agreeably occupied in their hours of leisure." As for speculating on the meaning of his plays, "I can only say that I object to it strenuously.... If I have ulterior designs, if in occupying the playgoer's mind agreeably I take advantage of his pre-occupation to extirpate his worn-out convictions and substitute fresh ones: in short, if I not only occupy his mind but change it, then the last thing I desire is that he should be conscious of the operation.... I like my patients to leave the hospital without a suspicion that they have been operated on and are leaving it with a new set of glands" (*Malvern Festival Book*).

1936 November: After remote productions in Vienna and Australia, Shaw's *The Millionairess: A Jonsonian Comedy* (written in 1935), is performed in Sussex. It will not reach London until 1944 and the West End until 1952, when it will manage a run of 98. The problematic portrait of a domineering arch-capitalist—a female counterpart of Undershaft in *Major Barbara*—the play depicts the relentless lady setting out to prove her capacities to the reluctant man of her choice, a compassionate Egyptian doctor. Starting from scratch as a scullery maid, in six months she has applied her ruthlessly efficient methods to become prosperous, which convinces "the guardian of life" to unite with "the exploiter of misery" because she also manifests the "pulse of Allah." For the standard edition of the play Shaw adds a brief alternative ending showing how the story would end in Communist countries.

1938 August: Shaw's *Geneva: A Fancied Page of History* (another "political extravaganza") is performed at the Malvern Festival. Transferred to London, it attains a run of 237, largely due to its relevance to the current world crisis on the threshold of World War II. The drama includes problematic portrayals of Franco, Mussolini, and Hitler, who appear before a world tribunal in satirical guises but are granted strong presentations of their points of view. (Shaw comments, "Instead of making the worst of all the dictators, which only drives them out of the League [of Nations], I have made the best of them, and may even challenge them to live up to their portraits if they can.") Shaw will revise the play several times to preserve its topicality, adding a more substantial climax at the declaration of war in 1939 and a new act in 1945 that prophesies a world catastrophe made likely by the "quantrum theory."

November: Shaw views a West End performance of *Geneva* and writes to the director, "What a horrible, horrible play! Why had I to write it? To hear those poor devils spouting the most exalted sentiments they were capable of, and not one of them fit to manage a coffee stall, sent me home ready to die."

1939 February: Shaw explains the origin of the term "Shavian" in a letter to the biographer Hesketh Pearson: "The word Shavian began when William Morris found in a medieval MS by one Shaw the marginal comment 'Sic Shavius, sed inepte.' It provided a much needed adjective; for Shawian is obviously impossible and unbearable."

August: Shaw's *'In Good King Charles's Golden Days': A True History that Never Happened* is performed at the Malvern Festival. In two London venues in April and May 1940, it manages only brief runs, but revivals will confirm that it is probably the most durable of what Shaw will call the "dramas of my dotage." The play, set in 1680, depicts a lively intellectual debate between an amiable King Charles II (in disguise), his disagreeable brother (a "man of principle"), the scientist Isaac Newton, the artist Godfrey Kneller, and the Quaker founder George Fox. Interruptions from Charles's three mistresses and a confrontation between the King and his wife (who knows about them but calls him "the very best husband who ever lived") provide spice and variety.

1945 December: A virtual Shaw boom begins in New York with a revival of *Pygmalion*. In the next eleven years (through his centennial) further revivals will appear: *Man and Superman* (without the dream scene, which is performed as *Don Juan in Hell* in October 1951), *John Bull's Other Island, You Never Can Tell, Caesar and Cleopatra, The Devil's Disciple, Captain Brassbound's Conversion, Getting Married, Saint Joan, Candida, The Millionairess, Misalliance, The Apple Cart,* and even *'In Good King Charles' s Golden Days'.*

1946 July: Maxwell Anderson reads his essay on Shaw, printed as "St. Bernard" in *Off Broadway,* at a celebration of the playwright's ninetieth birthday in New York. He admits that before he became a dramatist, he considered Shaw "a brilliant writer but no playwright." But now he sets him "at the head of all modern playwrights. He is a more considerable figure than Molière or Schiller or Chekhov or Strindberg or Ibsen, or any Irishman or American so far.... I base my revised opinion on the fact that Shaw has illuminated a larger area of the modern intellectual landscape than anybody else. Reading or seeing his plays... is like viewing our civilization by flashes of lightning." Primarily a dialectical dramatist, Shaw "pushed dialectic over into the realms of the spirit and considered every aspect of man and superman with a logic and a wit so flashing as often to seem superhuman."

September: Writing in the *London Observer* in his ninetieth year, Shaw looks back on his first years of playwriting in reaction to Allardyce Nicoll's assumption that in the evolution of English drama he developed in the school of Pinero, Jones, and Wilde and "learned my art from them." He retorts that he was "furiously opposed to their method and principles," those of the well-made play, and "went back to Shakespear, to the Bible, to Bunyan, Walter Scott, Dickens, and Dumas *père,* Mozart, and Verdi, in whom I had been soaked from my childhood. Instead of planning my plays I let them grow as they came, and hardly ever wrote a page foreknowing what the next page would be." In sum, "I did the old stuff in the old way, because, as it happened, I could do it superlatively well."

1949 August: Shaw's *Buoyant Billions: A Comedy of No Manners* (written in 1947) is performed at the only postwar

Malvern Festival after having its premiere in Switzerland in October 1948. Starting in September it will be staged in London 40 times. The play features a young "world betterer" who wants to use atomic energy to solve many of the earth's problems, and his (successful) pursuit of a rich recluse who believes that love is illusory.

1950 April: Sean O'Casey apotheosizes Ibsen and Shaw as the two dramatists who "brought a dead drama back to a serious and singing life again. The zeal for the theatre that had eaten them up gave them the courage and strength to drive, helterskelter, the foolish, fustian plays that had cluttered the stage for so long.... The previous playwrights had made a simpering whore of the drama, and it took Shaw and Ibsen—though they didn't make her a lady, thank God—to change her into a vigorous, dignified, and intelligent woman, able and ready to give an answer for the hope that was in her" (*New Statesman and Nation*).

May: Shortly before his death, Shaw responds to Terence Rattigan's contention that his plays are "plays of ideas" and thus not plays (*New Statesman and Nation*) by reminding him of the great tradition of theatre to which he belongs, including opera. "Opera taught me to shape my plays into recitatives, arias, duets, trios, ensemble finales, and bravura pieces to display the technical accomplishments of the executants, with the quaint result that all the critics, friendly and hostile, took my plays to be so new, so extraordinary, so revolutionary, that the *Times* critic [A. B. Walkley] declared they were not plays at all as plays had been defined for all time by Aristotle." But "I was, and still am, the most old-fashioned playwright outside China and Japan."

September: Shaw's *Farfetched Fables* is performed 30 times by the Shaw Society in London. The six brief fables, directly prompted by the atomic arms race, project a non-atomic world holocaust and a remote future of creative evolution edging close to the ultimate "vortex of pure thought" hypothesized in *Back to Methuselah.*

November: Shaw dies on November 2 at age 94 from complications incurred after breaking his leg. Shortly afterwards his amusing short play *Why She Would Not* is discovered. The 20-minute "comedietta" is first kept from being published or performed because executors of his estate assume it is incomplete. However, scholars subsequently determine that both internal and external evidence point not only to its completeness but also to Shaw's desire to make it public.

1951 April: In T. S. Eliot's influential essay "Poetry and Drama," the author introduces the complexities that may beset any poet attempting to write verse dramas by tracing the problems he encountered in composing his first three full-length plays. Among other observations, he declares that "if we are to have a poetic drama, it is more likely to come from poets learning how to write plays, than from skilful prose dramatists learning to write poetry." He pronounces Shaw the greatest prose stylist among modern dramatists and admits that when he wrote the prose speeches of the knights in *Murder in the Cathedral* he "may, for aught I know, have been slightly under the influence of *St. Joan* [sic]."

October: The dream scene of Shaw's *Man and Superman,* entitled *Don Juan in Hell* for separate performance, is given a single staged reading in Carnegie Hall, New York, with Charles Boyer as Don Juan and Charles Laughton as The Devil. It excites such enthusiasm that it is presented in commercial theatres 105 times and subsequently recorded.

1954 August: Ronald Duncan's verse comedy *The Death of Satan* is performed at the Devon Festival of the Arts. This little-known play is noteworthy for its variations on the Don Juan in Hell scene of Shaw's *Man and Superman*. Set in Hell as a dingy men's club reading room, the first scene reveals Byron, Wilde, and Shaw playing poker, as they will for all eternity, using the Ten Commandments as chips. Don Juan broods about his lost love, Dona Ana, and the Devil broods about his inability to torment his modern guests. He sends Juan to earth to find out why, and learns that people have rationalized sin out of existence. The news causes Satan to die of remorse.

1956: The English dramatist and critic John Whiting comments on Shaw: "the plays are the work of a great artist.

We are made aware of an argument, but it is the argument of a man, not of a sect; of a single human voice, not the crowd. He was a virtuoso, with Picasso and Yeats, the great example in his time of the supremely unselfconscious artist." However, Whiting grants Shaw only a "single masterpiece," *Heartbreak House*, and even that, "with its extraordinary overtones of the present time, its uneasiness and chill, does not quite convince."

March: Sean O'Casey's collection of reprinted and new essays, *The Green Crow,* is published in America. Notable inclusions are "National Theatre Bunkum [I and II]", "Murdher in the Theatre", "The Green Goddess of Realism", three 1936 essays on Noël Coward, treatments of Pinero, Shaw, and several drama critics, and defenses of several of his plays. The English edition published in February 1957 adds a 1956 essay on Shaw and another on himself, "Playwright in Exile." A noteworthy comment on Shaw as an Irishman appears in "A Whisper About Bernard Shaw," written in 1946: "We Irish, when we think, and we often do this, are just as serious and sobre as the Englishman; but we never hesitate to give a serious thought the benefit and halo of a laugh. That is why we are so often thought to be irresponsible, whereas, in point of fact, we are critical realists, while Englishmen often mistake sentimental mutterings for everlasting truths. This silvery thread of laughter runs through all of Shaw's plays."

June: Samuel Beckett comments briefly on Shaw, Yeats, Synge, and O'Casey in a letter to Cyril Cusack, who had asked him for a tribute to G.B.S. for a centenary programme: "I wouldn't suggest that G.B.S. is not a great play-wright, whatever that is when it's at home. What I would do is give the whole unupsettable apple-cart for a sup of the Hawk's Well, or the Saints', or a whiff of Juno, to go no further. Sorry."

August: Shaw's last play, *Why She Would Not,* is published in the *London Magazine,* making it available to a wide audience.

1957 November:In *Thoughts in the Wilderness,* J. B. Priestley says that one reason why Shaw was such a fine dramatist is that he never seemed to be "emotionally committed" to his ideas. "Because he could hold his beliefs in his own peculiar fashion, keeping them free of negative emotions, he was able to create his own kind of comedy, good enough to put him among the world's great dramatists. This comedy of his has light without heat. The superbly theatrical wit crackles and dazzles and strikes without wounding. Behind the cut-and-thrust of the talk... is a vast golden good humour. The master quite early of a magnificent debating style, he heightened it and orchestrated it to provide us with this comedy of argument, the Mozartian opera of witty debate."

Chapter 5

More On Shaw

To the irreverent—and which of us will claim entire exemption from that comfortable classification?—there is something very amusing in the attitude of the orthodox criticism toward Bernard Shaw. He so obviously disregards all the canons and unities and other things which every well-bred dramatist is bound to respect that his work is really unworthy of serious criticism (orthodox). Indeed he knows no more about the dramatic art than, according to his own story in "The Man of Destiny," Napoleon at Tavazzano knew of the Art of War. But both men were successes each in his way—the latter won victories and the former gained audiences, in the very teeth of the accepted theories of war and the theatre. Shaw does not know that it is unpardonable sin to have his characters make long speeches at one another, apparently thinking that this embargo applies only to long speeches which consist mainly of bombast and rhetoric. There never was an author who showed less predilection for a specific medium by which to accomplish his results. He recognized, early in his days, many things awry in the world and he assumed the task of mundane reformation with a confident spirit. It seems such a small job at twenty to set the times aright. He began as an Essayist, but who reads essays now-a-days?—he then turned novelist with no better success, for no one would read such preposterous stuff as he chose to emit. He only succeeded in proving that absolutely rational men and women—although he has created few of the latter—can be most extremely disagreeable to our conventional way of thinking.

As a last resort, he turned to the stage, not that he cared

for the dramatic art, for no man seems to care less about "Art for Art's sake," being in this a perfect foil to his brilliant compatriot and contemporary, Wilde. He cast his theories in dramatic forms merely because no other course except silence or physical revolt was open to him. For a long time it seemed as if this resource too was doomed to fail him. But finally he has attained a hearing and now attempts at suppression merely serve to advertise their victim.

It will repay those who seek analogies in literature to compare Shaw with Cervantes. After a life of heroic endeavor, disappointment, slavery, and poverty, the author of "Don Quixote" gave the world a serious work which caused to be laughed off the world's stage forever the final vestiges of decadent chivalry.

The institution had long been outgrown, but its vernacular continued to be the speech and to express the thought "of the world and among the vulgar," as the quaint, old novelist puts it, just as to-day the novel intended for the consumption of the unenlightened must deal with peers and millionaires and be dressed in stilted language. Marvellously he succeeded, but in a way he least intended. We have not yet, after so many years, determined whether it is a work to laugh or cry over. "It is our joyfullest modern book," says Carlyle, while Landor thinks that "readers who see nothing more than a burlesque in 'Don Quixote' have but shallow appreciation of the work."

Shaw in like manner comes upon the scene when many of our social usages are outworn. He sees the fact, announces it, and we burst into guffaws. The continuous laughter which greets Shaw's plays arises from a real contrast in the point of view of the dramatist and his audiences. When Pinero or Jones describes a whimsical situation we never doubt for a moment that the author's point of view is our own and that the abnormal predicament of his characters appeals to him in the same light as to his audience. With Shaw this sense of community of feeling is wholly lacking. He describes things as he sees them, and the house is in a roar. Who is right? If we were really using our own senses and not gazing through the glasses of convention and romance and make-believe, should we see things as Shaw does? Must it not cause Shaw to doubt his own or the public's sanity to hear audiences laughing boisterously over tragic situations? And yet, if they did not come to laugh, they would not come at all. Mockery is the price he must pay for a hearing. Or has he calculated to a nicety the power of reaction? Does he seek to drive us to aspiration by the portrayal of sordidness, to disinterestedness by the picture of selfishness, to illusion by disillusionment? It is impossible to believe that he is unconscious of the humour of his dramatic situations, yet he stoically gives no sign. He even dares the charge, terrible in proportion to its truth, which the most serious of us shrinks from—the lack of a sense of humour. Men would rather have their integrity impugned.

In "Arms and the Man" the subject which occupies the dramatist's attention is that survival of barbarity—militarism—which raises its horrid head from time to time to cast a doubt on the reality of our civilization. No more hoary superstition survives than that the donning of a uniform changes the nature of the wearer. This notion pervades society to such an extent that when we find some soldiers placed upon the stage acting rationally, our conventionalized senses are shocked. The only men who have no illusions about war are those who have recently been there, and, of course, Mr. Shaw, who has no illusions about anything.

It is hard to speak too highly of "Candida." No equally subtle and incisive study of domestic relations exists in the English drama. One has to turn to George Meredith's "The Egoist" to find such character dissection. The central note of the play is, that with the true woman, weakness which appeals to the maternal instinct is more powerful than strength which offers protection. Candida is quite unpoetic, as, indeed, with rare exceptions, women are prone to be. They have small delight in poetry, but are the stuff of which poems and dreams are made. The husband glorying in his strength but convicted of his weakness, the poet pitiful in his physical impotence but strong in his perception of truth, the hopelessly de-moralized manufacturer, the conventional and hence emotional typist make up a group which the drama of any language may be challenged to rival. In "The Man of Destiny" the object of the dramatist is not so much the destruction as the explanation of the Napoleonic tradition, which has so powerfully influenced generation after generation for a century. However the man may be regarded, he was a miracle. Shaw shows that he achieved his extraordinary career by suspending, for himself, the pressure of the moral and conventional atmosphere, while leaving it operative for others. Those who study this play—extravaganza, that it is—will attain a clearer comprehension of Napoleon than they can get from all the biographies.

"You Never Can Tell" offers an amusing study of the play of social conventions. The "twins" illustrate the disconcerting effects of that perfect frankness which would make life intolerable. Gloria demonstrates the powerlessness of reason to overcome natural instincts. The idea that parental duties and functions can be fulfilled by the light of such knowledge as man and woman attain by intuition is brilliantly lampooned. Crampton, the father, typifies the common superstition that among the privileges of parenthood are inflexibility, tyranny, and respect, the last entirely regardless of whether it has been deserved. The waiter, William, is the best illustration of the man "who knows his place" that the stage has seen. He is the most pathetic figure of the play. One touch of verisimilitude is lacking; none of the guests gives him a tip, yet he maintains his urbanity. As Mr. Shaw has not yet visited America he may be unaware of the improbability of this situation.

To those who regard literary men merely as purveyors of amusement for people who have not wit enough to entertain themselves, Ibsen and Shaw, Maeterlinck and Gorky must remain enigmas. It is so much pleasanter to ignore than to face unpleasant realities—to take Riverside Drive and not Mulberry Street as the exponent of our life and the expression of our civilization. These men are the sappers and miners of the advancing army of justice. The audience which demands the truth and despises the contemptible conventions that dominate alike our stage and our life is daily growing. Shaw and men like him—if indeed he is not absolutely unique—will not for the future lack a hearing

1894: Shaw was already a celebrity arts critic and socialist lecturer when he wrote *Arms and the Man* in 1894. One of Shaw's earliest attempts at writing for the theatre, it was also his first commercial success as a playwright. Although it played for only one season at an avant-garde theatre, thanks to the financial backing of a friend, it was later produced in America in 1895. Accustomed to the melodramas of the age, however, even sophisticated audiences often did not discern the serious purpose of Shaw's play. Thus, Shaw considered it a failure.

True success did not come until 1898, when *Arms and the Man* was published as one of the "pleasant" plays in Shaw's collection called *Plays: Pleasant and Unpleasant*, and it subsequently gained popularity as a written work. Included in this collection of plays are lengthy explanatory prefaces, which note significant issues in the plays and which have been invaluable to critics. In place of brief stage directions, Shaw's plays also included lengthy instructions and descriptions. Another unique aspect of *Arms and the Man* was its use of a woman as the central character.

Set during the four-month-long Serbo-Bulgarian War that occurred between November 1885 and March 1886, this play is a satire on the foolishness of glorifying something so terrible as war, as well as a satire on the foolishness of basing your affections on idealistic notions of love. These themes brought reality and a timeless lesson to the comic stage. Consequently, once Shaw's genius was recognized, *Arms and the Man* became one of Shaw's most popular plays and has remained a classic ever since

Chapter 6

Characters

Captain Bluntschli

A professional soldier from Switzerland. He is roughly 35 years old. He is working as an officer for the Servian military fighting for hire against the Bulgarian army. When his line was broken and his forces scattered by a Bulgarian cavalry charge, he took refuge in Raina's room. He is worldly, cool-headed, and pragmatic, with a sense of humour about his situation and the world.

Raina Petkoff

The only daughter of one of the wealthiest families in Bulgaria.Her father is a major in the Bulgarian army. She is young and beautiful and intensely conscious of that fact. She has many romantic ideals about love, nobility, courage and beauty, but she is not above using them to get what she wants.

Catherine Petkoff

Raina's mother. She has a powerful and commanding presence that even her husband respects. She is a smart and capable woman over forty, who is determined to be a Viennese lady. To that end, she wears a fashionable tea gown on all occasions.

Major Petkoff

Raina's Father. He is a cheerful, excitable, insignificant, unpolished man of about 50, naturally unambitious except when it comes to his income and his importance in local society. Just now he is greatly pleased with the military rank which the war has thrust on him as it makes him a man of consequence in his town.

Major Sergius Saranoff

Engaged to Raina. He is dashing and romantically handsome. He is observant, but what he observes constantly disappoints his romantic ideals for the world.

Not even he can live up to his ideals. This has created an ironic and slightly cynical air of general brooding that suits him well.

Louka

Louka is a maidservant in the Petkoff household. She is handsome, but proud. She is so defiant that her servility to Raina is almost insolent. She is afraid of Catherine, but even with her goes as far as she dares. Very ambitious, she has the greatest contempt for those who serve willingly.

Nicola

Head Servant in the Petkoff household. He is a middle-aged man of cool temperament and low but clear and keen intelligence. He is complacent about his station as a servant and values himself on his rank in servility. He has the imperturbability of the accurate calculator who has no illusions. A very intelligent and capable man, he plans to open his own shop eventually.

Chapter 7

Plot Summary

ACT I

The play begins in Raina's bedroom. It is an odd mix of the expensively grand and tastelessly cheap. Raina stands out on her balcony enjoying the idea that she makes the lovely evening even more so. She wears a fur dressing gown worth three times the room's furniture. Catherine, her mother, enters and tells Raina that there has been a great battle. The war between Bulgaria and Servia may have been decided by this great victory. Leading the daring charge was Raina's fiancée: Major Sergius Saranoff.

The routed forces of the enemy are being hunted through the streets of the city. Their maid servant, Louka, enters and informs the rejoicing mother and daughter of orders that the windows must be kept shuttered and barred, lest escaping soldiers or errant bullets get in. Raina's window does not bolt, but she closes the shutter and hides from the gunfire under her covers. It is then that a bedraggled-looking Servian officer climbs in her window. Raina is not about to be intimidated and the two talk for quite a while. An officer of the Bulgarian army requests to search the room, as some people reported seeing a man climb in. Raina hides the Servian officer and convinces the other soldiers that there is nobody there.

The soldier reveals that his gun has no cartridges and that, in fact, he generally carries chocolates where they should be. He is a professional soldier and knows that chocolates and food are more important in the long run than bullets. Raina contemptuously gives him the last of her chocolate cremes and he gratefully eats them. Rather than allowing him to take the chance of capture and execution, Raina convinces the Officer (he isn't hard to convince) to rely upon her and her mother's good will. She leaves to enlist the help of her mother and when Raina and Catherine return to the room, the Officer has fallen asleep from stress and exhaustion. They wake him, dress him in an old coat of the Major's, and sneak him out safely.

ACT II

In the courtyard of the Petkoff house, Nicola is lecturing Louka about her insolence towards her employers. She scorns Nicola for his servility, but he knows the way things are and talks to her of practicalities and the real world. She will hear none of it. Major Petkoff comes into the garden. He has just returned from the newly finished war. Treaties have been signed, and the two sides have begun diplomatic relations again. Petkoff is very glad to be home. Catherine runs out to greet him and they talk about the state of the two nations and of their own social status.

Sergius Saranoff arrives. Before he is brought around to the courtyard, Catherine presses Petkoff to arrange a promotion for their daughter's fiancée, but Petkoff assures her that it will not be very likely. Though his charge was brave, and worked, it was only through luck. It was actually a foolish move that only succeeded because of a technical problem in the enemy's machine guns.

Nobody will give Saranoff a higher rank which would mean even more men to risk. Saranoff realizes that his charge was "the cradle and the grave" of his military career and he announces his intention to retire. Raina arrives right on cue (Catherine remarks that her daughter waits for such moments). Talking to Petkoff, Saranoff mentions an odd Swiss soldier they met during a prisoner exchange. He was an interesting fellow and definitely got the better of them in the trade. He told them a very interesting story about a spectacular escape from the Bulgarian forces. It involved crawling in the window of a young lady's bedroom and, with the assistance of the young lady and her mother, his escape in an old house-coat.

This shocks Raina and Catherine, but both hide it well. The major heads to the library to finish some plans for the military movements as they head back home. Saranoff and Raina are left alone. They trade romantic endearments and mutually worship each other's qualities. Raina convinces Saranoff to go for a walk with her and runs into the house to change dresses for the walk.

Saranoff takes the opportunity to drop his façade of courtly love and flirts with Louka. He is conflicted about the propriety of his own actions and varies between loving Louka and chastising himself, flirting and then apologizing. She is attracted to him, but also insulted by his actions. She hints that Raina isn't as innocent as Saranoff thinks, and he becomes angry, bruising her arms in his grip.

Raina enters to take Saranoff for a walk, but Catherine interrupts them, telling Saranoff that the Major needs his help with figuring out the troop movements. Saranoff promises to return in five minutes and runs into the Library. Raina admits to her mother that she isn't really as taken with Saranoff as she pretends to be. Raina leaves as Louka re-enters to inform Catherine that a Servian Officer named Bluntschli has come to visit. It quickly becomes clear that this is the "Chocolate Crème Soldier"- the man they helped to escape. He has come to return the old house coat.

Catherine sees him secretly in the courtyard and asks him to leave as quickly as possible. He says he understands and begins to leave as Major Petkoff and Saranoff enter. Recognizing the soldier, they greet him warmly and insist that he stay at the Petkoff home. He tries to back out, but they are insistent. Raina runs in and, recognizing Bluntschli, calls him her "Chocolate Crème Soldier" in shock. She and Catherine have to cover quickly for her slip. Finally, with Raina insisting that he stay as well, Bluntschli agrees to prolong his visit for a few days.

ACT III

The library, later that afternoon. It really isn't much of a 'library' but the Petkoffs are enormously proud of it as a symbol of their wealth. Major Petkoff sits reading a paper. Bluntschli is studiously focused on writing the orders for troop movements that Petkoff and Saranoff couldn't figure out. He hands each completed order to Saranoff to sign.

Saranoff is at once awed and jealous of Bluntschli's military knowledge. Catherine sits working on sewing, while Raina poses gazing out the window. The major complains that he misses his old house-coat. He can't find it anywhere. Little does he know that his wife gave it to Bluntschli in his escape. Now returned, Catherine tells Petkoff to look in an upstairs closet, but the major insists that he's checked the closet a dozen times. He sends a servant to check once more, and Nicola enters with the house-coat. Amazed and a bit confused, the major happily dons his favourite garment.

Finishing the orders, Bluntschli sends the Major and Sergius out to dispatch them to the troops. Left alone, Raina teases Bluntschli about the coat and his escape. The conversation becomes serious as she blames Bluntschli for forcing her to tell the only two lies she has ever told- one to the officer searching her room in Act I, and the other to her father to cover for calling him her "chocolate crème soldier". Bluntschli laughs at the idea that she could be so innocent. Indeed, she is not. Once she is through raging at him, she admits that he's right. She is impressed- he is the only person to actually take her so seriously.

She asks him if he liked the portrait she sneaked into the pocket of the house-coat, but Bluntschli has never seen it. He did not go through the pockets of the coat when he escaped. Raina realizes that the portrait, which she inscribed "to my chocolate crème soldier" is likely still in the pocket of the coat. Louka enters with mail for Bluntschli. He receives a telegram informing him of his father's death and his inheritance. He exits to pack, as he must be leaving very soon to take care of the arrangements.

Louka compares him unfavorably to Saranoff and Raina leaves, offended. Nicola again tries to curb Louka's ambition and insolence. They are engaged, and he would like her to be content with the life ahead of her. If she can not be, she will quickly be discharged. She keeps getting more and more insolent with Raina. Louka, however, just despises Nicola's servility all the more. Sergius enters and Nicola leaves to let them be alone. Sergius apologizes for hurting her, but says that he is "never sorry" for anything. Again, he varies between his desires and his ideals.

Louka calls him a coward. She says that he refuses to marry her simply because of station, and that is cowardly. Were she Empress of Russia, she claims, she would marry whom she pleased and show her own bravery. Getting carried away, Louka tells Saranoff that Raina is really in love with Bluntschli and that it was Raina who helped him escape. Saranoff at first refuses to believe it, then rages. Louka continues to taunt him about his own infidelities. Incensed, Saranoff swears to Louka that if he ever holds her again, it will be as his fiancée.

Bluntschli enters and Sergius challenges him to a duel. He is shocked and hasn't any idea why, but if Sergius is determined, he will fight. Raina enters and Sergius makes his grievance clear. He accuses Raina of secretly trysting with Bluntschli. They both deny this and it is true, neither has done anything inappropriate.

Bluntschli tries to help Sergius repair things with Raina, but it is too late. Saranoff's philandering with Louka comes out, and Louka is found eavesdropping on the conversation. Now both Louka and Raina proceed to berate Sergius who, while deserving, is totally incapable of defending himself. Petkoff enters and everything comes out. The portrait addressed to "the chocolate crème soldier" is found, Sergius breaks off his engagement with Raina.

Then, he takes Louka's hand and, once she reminds him of his oath, he swears to marry her. Nicola quietly gives up his claim on her. Bluntschli, recognizing Nicola's intelligence and dedication suggests that he has an excellent position running hotels for him.

Bluntschli intends to leave, but Saranoff deduces the Officer's real reason for his visit. He must be in love with Raina. Since he can not deny this, Bluntschli then tells Petkoff that he intends to court Raina for his wife. Catherine objects to her daughter marrying a poor officer in the Swiss Army. Now Bluntschli admits to his inheritance and makes it clear that he is a VERY wealthy man. Raina initially objects, saying that it was the poor officer that she was interested in, but Bluntschli makes it clear that he is quite the same man, regardless of wealth. He is her "chocolate crème soldier."

Chapter 8

Complete Text

ACT I

The window is hinged doorwise and stands wide open. Outside, a pair of wooden shutters, opening outwards, also stand open. On the balcony a young lady, intensely conscious of the romantic beauty of the night, and of the fact that her own youth and beauty are part of it, is gazing at the snowy Balkans. She is in her nightgown, well covered by a long mantle of furs, worth, on a moderate estimate, about three times the furniture of her room. Her reverie is interrupted by her mother, Catherine Petkoff, a woman over forty, imperiously energetic, with magnificent black hair and eyes, who might be a very splendid specimen of the wife of a mountain farmer, but is determined to be a Viennese lady, and to that end wears a fashionable tea gown on all occasions.

CATHERINE [entering hastily, full of good news] Raina! [She pronounces it Rah-eena, with the stress on the ee]. Raina! [She goes to the bed, expecting to find Raina there]. Why, where—? [Raina looks into the room]. Heavens, child! are you out in the night air instead of in your bed? Youll catch your death. Louka told me you were asleep.

RAINA [dreamily] I sent her away. I wanted to be alone. The stars are so beautiful! What is the matter?

CATHERINE. Such news! There has been a battle.

RAINA [her eyes dilating] Ah! [She comes eagerly to Catherine].

CATHERINE. A great battle at Slivnitza! A victory! And it was won by Sergius.

RAINA [with a cry of delight] Ah! [They embrace rapturously] Oh, mother! [Then, with sudden anxiety] Is father safe?

CATHERINE. Of course: he sends me the news. Sergius is the hero of the hour, the idol of the regiment.

RAINA. Tell me, tell me. How was it? [Ecstatically] Oh, mother! mother! mother! [She pulls her mother down on the ottoman; and they kiss one another frantically].

CATHERINE [with surging enthusiasm] You cant guess how splendid it is. A cavalry charge! think of that! He defied our Russian commanders—acted without orders—led a charge on his own responsibility—headed it himself—was the first man to sweep through their guns. Cant you see it, Raina: our gallant splendid Bulgarians, with their swords and eyes flashing, thundering down like an avalanche and scattering the wretched Serbs and their dandified Austrian officers like chaff. And you! you kept Sergius waiting a year before you would be betrothed to him. Oh, if you have a drop of Bulgarian blood in your veins, you will worship him when he comes back.

RAINA. What will he care for my poor little worship after the acclamations of a whole army of heroes? But no matter: I am so happy! so proud! [She rises and walks about excitedly]. It proves that all our ideas were real after all.

CATHERINE [indignantly] Our ideas real! What do you mean?

RAINA. Our ideas of what Sergius would do. Our patriotism. Our heroic ideals. I sometimes used to doubt whether they were anything but dreams. Oh, what faithless little creatures girls are! When I buckled on Sergius's sword he looked so noble: it was treason to think of disillusion or humiliation or failure. And yet—and yet—[She sits down again suddenly] Promise me youll never tell him.

CATHERINE. Dont ask me for promises until I know what I'm promising.

RAINA. Well, it came into my head just as he was holding me in his arms and looking into my eyes that perhaps we only had our heroic ideas because we are so fond of reading Byron and Pushkin, and because we were so delighted with the opera that season at Bucharest. Real life is so seldom like that! indeed never, as far as I knew it then. [Remorsefully] Only think, mother: I doubted him: I wondered whether all his heroic qualities and his soldiership might not prove mere imagination when he went into a real battle. I had an uneasy fear that he might cut a poor figure there beside all those clever officers from the Tsar's court.

CATHERINE. A poor figure! Shame on you! The Serbs have Austrian officers who are just as clever as the Russians; but we have beaten them in every battle for all that.

RAINA [laughing and snuggling against her mother] Yes: I was only a prosaic little coward. Oh, to think that it was all true! that Sergius is just as splendid and noble as he looks! that the world is really a glorious world for women who can see its glory and men who can act its romance! What happiness! what unspeakable fulfilment!

They are interrupted by the entry of Louka, a handsome proud girl in a pretty Bulgarian peasant's dress with double apron, so defiant that her servility to Raina is almost insolent. She is afraid of Catherine, but even with her goes as far as she dares.

LOUKA. If you please, madam, all the windows are to be closed and the shutters made fast. They say there may be shooting in the streets. [Raina and Catherine rise together, alarmed]. The Serbs are being chased right back through the pass; and they say they may run into the town. Our cavalry will be after them; and our people will be ready for them, you may be sure, now theyre running away. [She goes out on the balcony, and pulls the outside shutters to; then steps back into the room].

CATHERINE [businesslike, her housekeeping instincts aroused] I must see that everything is made safe downstairs.

RAINA. I wish our people were not so cruel. What glory is there in killing wretched fugitives?

CATHERINE. Cruel! Do you suppose they would hesitate to kill you—or worse?

RAINA [to Louka] Leave the shutters so that I can just close them if I hear any noise.

CATHERINE [authoritatively, turning on her way to the door] Oh no, dear: you must keep them fastened. You would be sure to drop off to sleep and leave them open. Make them fast, Louka.

LOUKA. Yes, madam. [She fastens them].

RAINA. Dont be anxious about me. The moment I hear a shot, I shall blow out the candles and roll myself up in bed with my ears well covered.

CATHERINE. Quite the wisest thing you can do, my love. Goodnight.

RAINA. Goodnight. [Her emotion comes back for a moment]. Wish me joy. [They kiss]. This is the happiest night of my life—if only there are no fugitives.

CATHERINE. Go to bed, dear; and dont think of them. [She goes out].

LOUKA [secretly, to Raina] If you would like the shutters open, just give them a push like this [she pushes them: they open: she pulls them to again]. One of them ought to be bolted at the bottom; but the bolt's gone.

RAINA [with dignity, reproving her] Thanks, Louka; but we must do what we are told. [Louka makes a grimace]. Goodnight.

LOUKA [carelessly] Goodnight. [She goes out, swaggering].

Raina, left alone, takes off her fur cloak and throws it on the ottoman. Then she goes to the chest of drawers, and adores the portrait there with feelings that are beyond all expression. She does not kiss it or press it to her breast, or shew it any mark of bodily affection; but she takes it in her hands and elevates it, like a priestess.

RAINA [looking up at the picture] Oh, I shall never be unworthy of you any more, my soul's hero: never, never, never. [She replaces it reverently. Then she selects a novel from the little pile of books. She turns over the leaves dreamily; finds her page; turns the book inside out at it; and, with a happy sigh, gets into bed and prepares to read herself to sleep. But before abandoning herself to fiction, she raises her eyes once more, thinking of the blessed reality, and murmurs] My hero! my hero! A distant shot breaks the quiet of the night. She starts, listening; and two more shots, much nearer, follow, startling her so that she scrambles out of bed, and hastily blows out the candle on the chest of drawers. Then, putting her fingers in her ears, she runs to the dressing table, blows out the light there, and hurries back to bed in the dark, nothing being visible but the glimmer of the light in the pierced ball before the image, and the starlight seen through the slits at the top of the shutters. The firing breaks out again: there is a startling fusillade quite close at hand. Whilst it is still echoing, the shutters disappear, pulled open from without; and for an instant the rectangle of snowy starlight flashes out with the figure of a man silhouetted in black upon it. The shutters close immediately; and the room is dark again. But the silence is now broken by the sound of panting. Then there is a scratch; and the flame of a match is seen in the middle of the room.

RAINA [crouching on the bed] Who's there? [The match is out instantly]. Who's there? Who is that?

A MAN'S VOICE [in the darkness, subduedly, but threateningly] Sh—sh! Dont call out; or youll be shot. Be good; and no harm will happen to you. [She is heard leaving her bed, and making for the door]. Take care: it's no use trying to run away.

RAINA. But who—

THE VOICE. [warning] Remember: if you raise your voice my revolver will go off. [Commandingly]. Strike a light and let me see you. Do you hear. [Another moment of silence and darkness as she retreats to the chest of drawers. Then she lights a candle; and the mystery is at an end. He is a man of about 35, in a deplorable plight, bespattered with mud and blood and snow, his belt and the strap of his revolver-case keeping together the torn ruins of the blue tunic of a Serbian artillery officer.

All that the candlelight and his unwashed unkempt condition make it possible to discern is that he is of middling stature and undistinguished appearance, with strong neck and shoulders, roundish obstinate looking head covered with short crisp bronze curls, clear quick eyes and good brows and mouth, hopelessly prosaic nose like that of a strong minded baby, trim soldierlike carriage and energetic manner, and with all his wits about him in spite of his desperate predicament: even with a sense of the humour of it, without, however, the least intention of trifling with it or throwing away a chance. Reckoning up what he can guess about Raina: her age, her social position, her character, and the extent to which she is frightened, he continues, more politely but still most determinedly] Excuse my disturbing you; but you recognize my uniform? Serb! If I'm caught I shall be killed. [Menacingly] Do you understand that?

RAINA. Yes.

THE MAN. Well, I dont intend to get killed if I can help it. [Still more formidably] Do you understand that? [He locks the door quickly but quietly].

RAINA [disdainfully] I suppose not. [She draws herself up superbly, and looks him straight in the face, adding, with cutting emphasis] Some soldiers, I know, are afraid to die.

THE MAN [with grim goodhumor] All of them, dear lady, all of them, believe me. It is our duty to live as long as we can. Now, if you raise an alarm—

RAINA [cutting him short] You will shoot me. How do you know that I am afraid to die?

THE MAN [cunningly] Ah; but suppose I dont shoot you, what will happen then? A lot of your cavalry will burst into this pretty room of yours and slaughter me here like a pig; for I'll fight like a demon: they shant get me into the street to amuse themselves with: I know what they are. Are you prepared to receive that sort of company in your present undress? [Raina, suddenly conscious of her nightgown, instinctively shrinks, and gathers it more closely about her neck. He watches her, and adds, pitilessly] Hardly presentable, eh? [She turns to the ottoman. He raises his pistol instantly, and cries] Stop! [She stops]. Where are you going?

RAINA [with dignified patience], Only to get my cloak.

THE MAN [passing swiftly to the ottoman and snatching the cloak] A good idea! I'll keep the cloak; and youll take care that nobody comes in and sees you without it.

This is a better weapon than the revolver: eh? [He throws the pistol down on the ottoman].

RAINA [revolted] It is not the weapon of a gentleman!

THE MAN. It's good enough for a man with only you to stand between him and death. [As they look at one another for a moment, Raina hardly able to believe that even a Serbian officer can be so cynically and selfishly unchivalrous, they are startled by a sharp fusillade in the street. The chill of imminent death hushes the man's voice as he adds] Do you hear? If you are going to bring those blackguards in on me you shall receive them as you are.

Clamor and disturbance. The pursuers in the street batter at the house door, shouting Open the door! Open the door! Wake up, will you! A man servant's voice calls to them angrily from within This is Major Petkoff's house: you cant come in here; but a renewal of the clamor, and a torrent of blows on the door, end with his letting a chain down with a clank, followed by a rush of heavy footsteps and a din of triumphant yells, dominated at last by the voice of Catherine, indignantly addressing an officer with What does this mean, sir? Do you know where you are? The noise subsides suddenly.

LOUKA [outside, knocking at the bedroom door] My lady! my lady! get up quick and open the door. If you dont they will break it down.

The fugitive throws up his head with the gesture of a man who sees that it is all over with him, and drops the manner he has been assuming to intimidate Raina.

THE MAN [sincerely and kindly] No use, dear: I'm done for. [Flinging the cloak to her] Quick! wrap yourself up: theyre coming.

RAINA. Oh, thank you. [She wraps herself up with intense relief].

THE MAN [between his teeth] Dont mention it.

RAINA [anxiously] What will you do?

THE MAN [grimly] The first man in will find out. Keep out of the way; and dont look. It wont last long; but it will not be nice. [He draws his sabre and faces the door, waiting].

RAINA [impulsively] I'll help you. I'll save you.

THE MAN. You cant.

RAINA. I can. I'll hide you. [She drags him towards the window]. Here! behind the curtains.

THE MAN [yielding to her] Theres just half a chance, if you keep your head.

RAINA [drawing the curtain before him] S-sh! [She makes for the ottoman].

THE MAN [putting out his head] Remember—

RAINA [running back to him] Yes?

THE MAN.—nine soldiers out of ten are born fools.

RAINA. Oh! [She draws the curtain angrily before him].

THE MAN [looking out at the other side] If they find me, I promise you a fight: a devil of a fight.

She stamps at him. He disappears hastily. She takes off her cloak, and throws it across the foot of the bed. Then, with a sleepy, disturbed air, she opens the door. Louka enters excitedly.

LOUKA. One of those beasts of Serbs has been seen climbing up the waterpipe to your balcony. Our men want to search for him; and they are so wild and drunk and furious. [She makes for the other side of the room to get as far from the door as possible]. My lady says you are to dress at once, and to—[She sees the revolver lying on the ottoman, and stops, petrified].

RAINA [as if annoyed at being disturbed] They shall not search here. Why have they been let in?

CATHERINE [coming in hastily] Raina, darling: are you safe? Have you seen anyone or heard anything?

RAINA. I heard the shooting. Surely the soldiers will not dare come in here?

CATHERINE. I have found a Russian officer, thank Heaven: he knows Sergius. [Speaking through the door to someone outside] Sir: will you come in now. My daughter will receive you. A young Russian officer, in Bulgarian uniform, enters, sword in hand.

OFFICER [with soft feline politeness and stiff military carriage] Good evening, gracious lady. I am sorry to intrude; but there is a Serb hiding on the balcony. Will you and the gracious lady your mother please to withdraw whilst we search?

RAINA [petulantly] Nonsense, sir: you can see that there is no one on the balcony. [She throws the shutters wide open and stands with her back to the curtain where the man is hidden, pointing to the moonlit balcony. A couple of shots are fired right under the window; and a bullet shatters the glass opposite Raina, who winks and gasps, but stands her ground; whilst Catherine screams, and the officer, with a cry of Take care! rushes to the balcony].

THE OFFICER [on the balcony, shouting savagely down to the street] Cease firing there, you fools: do you hear? Cease firing, damn you! [He glares down for a moment; then turns to Raina, trying to resume his polite manner]. Could anyone have got in without your knowledge? Were you asleep?

RAINA. No: I have not been to bed.

THE OFFICER [impatiently, coming back into the room] Your neighbors have their heads so full of runaway Serbs that they see them everywhere. [Politely] Gracious lady: a thousand pardons.

Goodnight. [Military bow, which Raina returns coldly. Another to Catherine, who follows him out]. Raina closes the shutters. She turns and sees Louka, who has been watching the scene curiously.

RAINA. Dont leave my mother, Louka, until the soldiers go away.

Louka glances at Raina, at the ottoman, at the curtain; then purses her lips secretively, laughs insolently, and goes out. Raina, highly offended by this demonstration, follows her to the door, and shuts it behind her with a slam, locking it violently. The man immediately steps out from behind the curtain, sheathing his sabre. Then, dismissing the danger from his mind in a businesslike way, he comes affably to Raina.

THE MAN. A narrow shave; but a miss is as good as a mile. Dear young lady: your servant to the death. I wish for your sake I had joined the Bulgarian army instead of the other one. I am not a native Serb.

RAINA [haughtily] No: you are one of the Austrians who

set the Serbs oh to rob us of our national liberty, and who officer their army for them. We hate them!

THE MAN. Austrian! not I. Dont hate me, dear young lady. I am a Swiss, fighting merely as a professional soldier. I joined the Serbs because they came first on the road from Switzerland. Be generous: youve beaten us hollow.

RAINA. Have I not been generous?

THE MAN. Noble! Heroic! But I'm not saved yet. This particular rush will soon pass through; but the pursuit will go on all night by fits and starts. I must take my chance to get off in a quiet interval. [Pleasantly] You dont mind my waiting just a minute or two, do you?

RAINA [putting on her most genteel society manner] Oh, not at all. Wont you sit down?

THE MAN. Thanks. [He sits on the foot of the bed].

Raina walks with studied elegance to the ottoman and sits down. Unfortunately she sits on the pistol, and jumps up with a shriek. The man, all nerves, shies like a frightened horse to the other side of the room.

THE MAN [irritably] Dont frighten me like that. What is it?

RAINA. Your revolver! It was staring that officer in the face all the time. What an escape!

THE MAN [vexed at being unnecessarily terrified] Oh, is that all?

RAINA [staring at him rather superciliously as she conceives a poorer and poorer opinion of him, and feels proportionately more and more at her case] I am sorry I frightened you. [She takes up the pistol and hands it to him]. Pray take it to protect yourself against me.

THE MAN [grinning wearily at the sarcasm as he takes the pistol] No use, dear young lady: theres nothing in it. It's not loaded. [He makes a grimace at it, and drops it disparagingly into his revolver case].

RAINA. Load it by all means.

THE MAN. Ive no ammunition. What use are cartridges in battle? I always carry chocolate instead; and I finished the last cake of that hours ago.

RAINA [outraged in her most cherished ideals of manhood] Chocolate! Do you stuff your pockets with sweets—like a schoolboy-even in the field?

THE MAN [grinning] Yes: isnt it contemptible? [Hungrily] I wish I had some now.

RAINA. Allow me. [She sails away scornfully to the chest of drawers, and returns with the box of confectionery in her hand]. I am sorry I have eaten them all except these. [She offers him the box].

THE MAN [ravenously] Youre an angel! [He gobbles the contents]. Creams! Delicious! [He looks anxiously to see whether there are any more. There are none: he can only scrape the box with his fingers and suck them. When that nourishment is exhausted he accepts the inevitable with pathetic goodhumor, and says, with grateful emotion] Bless you, dear lady! You can always tell an old soldier by the inside of his holsters and cartridge boxes. The young ones carry pistols and cartridges: the old ones, grub. Thank you. [He hands back the box. She snatches it contemptuously from him and throws it away. He shies again, as if she had meant to strike him]. Ugh! Dont do things so suddenly, gracious lady. It's mean to revenge yourself because I frightened you just now.

RAINA [loftily] Frighten me! Do you know, sir, that though I am only a woman, I think I am at heart as brave as you.

THE MAN. I should think so. You havnt been under fire for three days as I have. I can stand two days without shewing it much; but no man can stand three days: I'm as nervous as a mouse. [He sits down on the ottoman, and takes his head in his hands]. Would you like to see me cry?

RAINA [alarmed] No.

THE MAN. If you would, all you have to do is to scold me just as if I were a little boy and you my nurse. If I were in camp now, theyd play all sorts of tricks on me.

RAINA [a little moved] I'm sorry. I wont scold you. [Touched by the sympathy in her tone, he raises his head and looks gratefully at her: she immediately draws back and says stiffly] You must excuse me: our soldiers are not like that. [She moves away from the ottoman].

THE MAN. Oh yes they are. There are only two sorts of soldiers: old ones and young ones. Ive served fourteen years: half of your fellows never smelt powder before. Why, how is it that youve just beaten us? Sheer ignorance of the art of war, nothing else. [Indignantly] I never saw anything so unprofessional.

RAINA [ironically] Oh! was it unprofessional to beat you?

THE MAN. Well, come! is it professional to throw a regiment of cavalry on a battery of machine guns, with the dead certainty that if the guns go off not a horse or man will ever get within fifty yards of the fire? I couldnt believe my eyes when I saw it.

RAINA [eagerly turning to him, as all her enthusiasm and her dreams of glory rush back on her] Did you see the great cavalry charge? Oh, tell me about it. Describe it to me.

THE MAN. You never saw a cavalry charge, did you?

RAINA. How could I?

THE MAN. Ah, perhaps not. No: of course not! Well, it's a funny sight. It's like slinging a handful of peas against a window pane: first one comes; then two or three close behind him; and then all the rest in a lump.

RAINA [her eyes dilating as she raises her clasped hands ecstatically] Yes, first One! the bravest of the brave!

THE MAN [prosaically] Hm! you should see the poor devil pulling at his horse.

RAINA. Why should he pull at his horse?

THE MAN [impatient of so stupid a question] It's running away with him, of course: do you suppose the fellow wants to get there before the others and be killed? Then they all come. You can tell the young ones by their wildness and their slashing. The old ones come bunched up under the number one guard: they know that theyre mere projectiles, and that it's no use trying to fight. The wounds are mostly broken knees, from the horses cannoning together.

RAINA. Ugh! But I dont believe the first man is a coward. I know he is a hero!

THE MAN [goodhumoredly] Thats what youd have said if youd seen the first man in the charge today.

RAINA [breathless, forgiving him everything] Ah, I knew it! Tell me. Tell me about him.

THE MAN. He did it like an operatic tenor. A regular handsome fellow, with flashing eyes and lovely moustache, shouting his war-cry and charging like Don Quixote at the windmills. We did laugh.

RAINA. You dared to laugh!

THE MAN. Yes; but when the sergeant ran up as white as a sheet, and told us theyd sent us the wrong ammunition, and that we couldnt fire a round for the next ten minutes, we laughed at the other side of our mouths. I never felt so sick in my life; though Ive been in one or two very tight places. And I hadnt even a revolver cartridge: only chocolate. We'd no bayonets: nothing. Of course, they just cut us to bits. And there was Don Quixote flourishing like a drum major, thinking he'd done the cleverest thing ever known, whereas he ought to be courtmartialled for it. Of all the fools ever let loose on a field of battle, that man must be the very maddest. He and his regiment simply committed suicide; only the pistol missed fire: thats all.

RAINA [deeply wounded, but steadfastly loyal to her ideals] Indeed! Would you know him again if you saw him?

THE MAN. Shall I ever forget him!

She again goes to the chest of drawers. He watches her with a vague hope that she may have something more for him to eat. She takes the portrait from its stand and brings it to him.

RAINA. That is a photograph of the gentleman—the patriot and hero—to whom I am betrothed.

THE MAN [recognizing it with a shock] I'm really very sorry. [Looking at her] Was it fair to lead me on? [He looks at the portrait again] Yes: thats Don Quixote: not a doubt of it. [He stifles a laugh].

RAINA [quickly] Why do you laugh?

THE MAN [apologetic, but still greatly tickled] I didnt laugh, I assure you. At least I didnt mean to. But when I think of him charging the windmills and imagining he was doing the finest thing—[He chokes with suppressed laughter].

RAINA [sternly] Give me back the portrait, sir.

THE MAN [with sincere remorse] Of course. Certainly. I'm really very sorry. [He hands her the picture. She deliberately kisses it and looks him straight in the face before returning to the chest of drawers to replace it. He follows her, apologizing]. Perhaps I'm quite wrong, you know: no doubt I am. Most likely he had got wind of the cartridge business somehow, and knew it was a safe job.

RAINA. That is to say, he was a pretender and a coward! You did not dare say that before.

THE MAN [with a comic gesture of despair] It's no use, dear lady: I cant make you see it from the professional point of view. [As he turns away to get back to the ottoman, a couple of distant shots threaten renewed trouble].

RAINA [sternly, as she sees him listening to the shots] So much the better for you!

THE MAN [turning] How?

RAINA. You are my enemy; and you are at my mercy. What would I do if I were a professional soldier?

THE MAN. Ah, true, dear young lady: youre always right. I know how good youve been to me: to my last hour I shall remember those three chocolate creams. It was unsoldierly; but it was angelic.

RAINA [coldly] Thank you. And now I will do a soldierly thing. You cannot stay here after what you have just said about my future husband; but I will go out on the balcony and see whether it is safe for you to climb down into the street. [She turns to the window].

THE MAN [changing countenance] Down that waterpipe! Stop! Wait! I cant! I darent! The very thought of it makes me giddy. I came up it fast enough with death behind me. But to face it now in cold blood—! [He sinks on the ottoman]. It's no use: I give up: I'm beaten.

Give the alarm. [He drops his head on his hands in the deepest dejection].

RAINA [disarmed by pity] Come: dont be disheartened.

She stoops over him almost maternally: he shakes his head]. Oh, you are a very poor soldier: a chocolate cream soldier! Come, cheer up! it takes less courage to climb down than to face capture: remember that.

THE MAN [dreamily, lulled by her voice] No: capture only means death; and death is sleep: oh, sleep, sleep, sleep, undisturbed sleep! Climbing down the pipe means doing something—exerting myself—thinking! Death ten times over first.

RAINA [softly and wonderingly, catching the rhythm of his weariness] Are you as sleepy as that?

THE MAN. Ive not had two hours undisturbed sleep since I joined. I havnt closed my eyes for forty-eight hours.

RAINA [at her wit's end] But what am I to do with you?

THE MAN [staggering up, roused by her desperation] Of course. I must do something. [He shakes himself; pulls himself together; and speaks with rallied vigour and courage]. You see, sleep or no sleep, hunger or no hunger, tired or not tired, you can always do a thing when you know it must be done. Well, that pipe must be got down: [he hits himself on the chest] do you hear that, you chocolate cream soldier? [He turns to the window].

RAINA [anxiously] But if you fall?

THE MAN. I shall sleep as if the stones were a feather bed. Goodbye. [He makes boldly for the window; and his hand is on the shutter when there is a terrible burst of firing in the street beneath].

RAINA [rushing to him] Stop! [She seizes him recklessly, and pulls him quite round]. Theyll kill you.

THE MAN [coolly, but attentively] Never mind: this sort of thing is all in my day's work. I'm bound to take my chance. [Decisively] Now do what I tell you. Put out the candle; so that they shant see the light when I open the shutters. And keep away from the window, whatever you do. If they see me theyre sure to have a shot at me.

RAINA [clinging to him] Theyre sure to see you: it's bright moonlight. I'll save you. Oh, how can you be so indifferent! You want me to save you, dont you?

THE MAN. I really dont want to be troublesome. She shakes him in her impatience]. I am not indifferent, dear young lady, I assure you. But how is it to be done?

RAINA. Come away from the window. [She takes him firmly back to the middle of the room. The moment she releases him he turns mechanically towards the window again. She seizes him and turns him back, exclaiming] Please! [He becomes motionless, like a hypnotized rabbit, his fatigue gaining fast on him. She releases him, and addresses him patronizingly]. Now listen. You must trust to our hospitality. You do not yet know in whose house you are. I am a Petkoff.

THE MAN. A pet what?

RAINA [rather indignantly] I mean that I belong to the family of the Petkoffs, the richest and best known in our country.

THE MAN. Oh yes, of course. I beg your pardon. The Petkoffs, to be sure. How stupid of me!

RAINA. You know you never heard of them until this moment. How can you stoop to pretend!

THE MAN. Forgive me: I'm too tired to think; and the change of subject was too much for me. Dont scold me.

RAINA. I forgot. It might make you cry. [He nods, quite seriously. She pouts and then resumes her patronizing tone]. I must tell you that my father holds the highest command of any Bulgarian in our army. He is [proudly] a Major.

THE MAN [pretending to be deeply impressed] A Major! Bless me! Think of that!

RAINA. You shewed great ignorance in thinking that it was necessary to climb up to the balcony because ours is the only private house that has two rows of windows. There is a flight of stairs inside to get up and down by.

THE MAN, Stairs! How grand! You live in great luxury indeed, dear young lady.

RAINA. Do you know what a library is?

THE MAN. A library? A roomful of books?

RAINA. Yes. We have one, the only one in Bulgaria.

THE MAN. Actually a real library! I should like to see that.

RAINA [affectedly] I tell you these things to shew you that you are not in the house of ignorant country folk who would kill you the moment they saw your Serbian uniform, but among civilized people. We go to Bucharest every year for the opera season; and I have spent a whole month in Vienna.

THE MAN. I saw that, dear young lady. I saw at once that you knew the world.

RAINA. Have you ever seen the opera of Ernani?

THE MAN. Is that the one with the devil in it in red velvet, and a soldiers' chorus?

RAINA [contemptuously] No!

THE MAN [stifling a heavy sigh of weariness] Then I dont know it.

RAINA. I thought you might have remembered the great scene where Ernani, flying from his foes just as you are tonight, takes refuge in the castle of his bitterest enemy, an old Castilian noble. The noble refuses to give him up. His guest is sacred to him.

THE MAN [quickly, waking up a little] Have your people got that notion?

RAINA [with dignity] My mother and I can understand that notion, as you call it. And if instead of threatening me with your pistol as you did you had simply thrown yourself as a fugitive on our hospitality, you would have been as safe as in your father's house.

THE MAN. Quite sure?

RAINA [turning her back on him in disgust] Oh, it is useless to try to make y o u understand.

THE MAN. Dont be angry: you see how awkward it would be for me if there was any mistake. My father is a very hospitable man: he keeps six hotels; but I couldnt trust him as far as that. What about your father?

RAINA. He is away at Slivnitza fighting for his country. I answer for your safety. There is my hand in pledge of it. Will that reassure you? [She offers him her hand].

THE MAN [looking dubiously at his own hand] Better not touch my hand, clear young lady. I must have a wash first.

RAINA [touched] That is very nice of you. I see that you are a gentleman.

THE MAN [puzzled] Eh? RAINA. You must not think I am surprised. Bulgarians of really good standing—people in our position—wash their hands nearly every day. So you see I can appreciate your delicacy. You may take my hand. [She offers it again].

THE MAN [kissing it with his hands behind his back] Thanks, gracious young lady: I feel safe at last. And now would you mind breaking the news to your mother? I had better not stay here secretly longer than is necessary.

RAINA. If you will be so good as to keep perfectly still whilst I am away.

THE MAN. Certainly. [He sits down on the ottoman].

Raina goes to the bed and wraps herself in the fur cloak. His eyes close. She goes to the door. Turning for a last look at him, she sees that he is dropping off to sleep.

RAINA [at the door] You are not going asleep, are you? [He murmurs inarticulately: she runs to him and shakes him]. Do you hear? Wake up: you are falling asleep.

THE MAN. Eh? Falling aslee—? Oh no: not the least in the world: I was only thinking. It's all right: I'm wide awake.

RAINA [severely] Will you please stand up while I am away. [He rises reluctantly]. All the time, mind.

THE MAN [standing unsteadily] Certainly. Certainly: you may depend on me.

Raina looks doubtfully at him. He smiles weakly. She goes reluctantly, turning again at the door, and almost catching him in the act of yawning. She goes out.

THE MAN [drowsily] Sleep, sleep, sleep, sleep, slee—[The words trail off into a murmur. He wakes again with a shock on the point of falling]. Where am I? Thats what I want to know: where am I? Must keep awake.Nothing keeps me awake except danger: remember that: [intently] danger, danger, danger, dan-[trailing off again: another shock] Wheres danger? Mus' find it. [He starts off vaguely round the room in search of it]. What am I looking for? Sleep—danger—dont know. [He stumbles against the bed]. Ah yes: now I know. All right now. I'm to go to bed, but not to sleep. Be sure not to sleep, because of danger. Not to lie down either, only sit down. [He sits on the bed. A blissful expression comes into his face]. Ah! [With a happy sigh he sinks back at full length; lifts his boots into the bed with a final effort; and falls fast asleep instantly].

Catherine comes in, followed by Raina.

RAINA [looking at the ottoman] He's gone! I left him here.

CATHERINE. Here! Then he must have climbed down from the—

RAINA [seeing him] Oh! [She points].

CATHERINE [scandalized] Well! [She strides to the bed, Raina following until she is opposite her on the other side]. He's fast asleep. The brute!

RAINA [anxiously] Sh!

CATHERINE [shaking him] Sir! [Shaking him again, harder] Sir!! [Vehemently, shaking very hard] Sir!!!

RAINA [catching her arm] Dont, mamma: the poor darling is worn out. Let him sleep.

CATHERINE [letting him go, and turning amazed to Raina] The poor darling! Raina!!! [She looks sternly at her daughter].

The man sleeps profoundly.

ACT II

The sixth of March, 1886. In the garden of Major Petkoff's house. It is a fine spring morning: the garden looks fresh and pretty. Beyond the paling the tops of a couple of minarets can be seen, shewing that there is a valley there, with the little town in it. A few miles further the Balkan mountains rise and shut in the landscape. Looking towards them from within the garden, the side of the house is seen on the left, with a garden door reached by a little flight of steps. On the right the stable yard, with its gateway, encroaches on the garden. There are fruit bushes along the paling and house, covered with washing spread out to dry. A path runs by the house, and rises by two steps at the corner, where it turns out of sight. In the middle, a small table, with two bent wood chairs at it, is laid for breakfast with Turkish coffee pot, cups, rolls, etc.; but the cups have been used and the bread broken. There is a wooden garden seat against the wall on the right. Louka, smoking a cigaret, is standing between the table and the house, turning her back with angry disdain on a man servant who is lecturing her. He is a middle-aged man of cool temperament and low but clear and keen intelligence, with the complacency of the servant who values himself on his rank in servitude, and the imperturbability of the accurate calculator who has no illusions. He wears a white Bulgarian costume: jacket with embroidered border, sash, wide knickerbockers, and decorated gaiters. His head is shaved up to the crown, giving him a high Japanese forehead. His name is Nicola.

NICOLA. Be warned in time, Louka: mend your manners. I know the mistress. She is so grand that she never dreams that any servant could dare be disrespectful to her; but if she once suspects that you are defying her, out you go.

LOUKA. I do defy her. I will defy her. What do I care for her?

NICOLA. If you quarrel with the family, I never can marry you. It's the same as if you quarrelled with me!

LOUKA. You take her part against me, do you?

NICOLA [sedately] I shall always be dependent on the good will of the family. When I leave their service and start a shop in Sofia, their custom will be half my capital: their bad word would ruin me.

LOUKA. You have no spirit. I should like to catch them saying a word against me!

NICOLA [pityingly] I should have expected more sense from you, Louka. But youre young: youre young!

LOUKA. Yes; and you like me the better for it, dont you? But I know some family secrets they wouldnt care to have told, young as I am. Let them quarrel with me if they dare!

NICOLA [with compassionate superiority] Do you know what they would do if they heard you talk like that?

LOUKA. What could they do?

NICOLA. Discharge you for untruthfulness. Who would believe any stories you told after that? Who would give you another situation? Who in this house would dare be seen speaking to you ever again? How long would your father be left on his little farm? [She impatiently throws away the end of her cigaret, and stamps on it]. Child: you dont know the power such high people have over the like of you and me when we try to rise out of our poverty against them. [He goes close to her and lowers his voice]. Look at me, ten years in their service. Do you think I know no secrets? I know things about the mistress that she wouldnt have the master know for a thousand levas. I know things about him that she wouldnt let him hear the last of for six months if I blabbed them to her. I know things about Raina that would break off her match with Sergius if—

LOUKA [turning on him quickly] How do you know? I never told you!

NICOLA [opening his eyes cunningly] So thats your little secret, is it? I thought it might be something like that. Well, you take my advice and be respectful; and make the mistress feel that no matter what you know or dont know, she can depend on you to hold your tongue and serve the family faithfully. Thats what they like; and thats how youll make most out of them.

LOUKA [with searching scorn] You have the soul of a servant, Nicola.

NICOLA [complacently] Yes: thats the secret of success in service.

A loud knocking with a whip handle on a wooden door is heard from the stable yard.

MALE VOICE OUTSIDE. Hollo! Hollo there!

Nicola!

LOUKA. Master! back from the war!

NICOLA [quickly] My word for it, Louka, the war's over. Off with you and get some fresh coffee. [He runs out into the stable yard].

LOUKA [as she collects the coffee pot and cups on the tray, and carries it into the house] Youll never put the soul of a servant into me. Major Petkoff comes from the stable yard, followed by Nicola. He is a cheerful, excitable, insignificant, unpolished man of about 50, naturally unambitious except as to his income and his importance in local society, but just now greatly pleased with the military rank which the war has thrust on him as a man of consequence in his town. The fever of plucky patriotism which the Serbian attack roused in all the Bulgarians has pulled him through the war; but he is obviously glad to be home again.

PETKOFF [pointing to the table with his whip] Breakfast out here, eh?

NICOLA. Yes, sir. The mistress and Miss Raina have just gone in.

PETKOFF [sitting down and taking a roll] Go in and say Ive come; and get me some fresh coffee.

NICOLA. It's coming, sir. [He goes to the house door. Louka, with fresh coffee, a clean cup, and a brandy bottle on her tray, meets him]. Have you told the mistress?

LOUKA. Yes: she's coming.

Nicola goes into the house. Louka brings the coffee to the table.

PETKOFF. Well: the Serbs havnt run away with you, have they?

LOUKA. No, sir.

PETKOFF. Thats right. Have you brought me some cognac?

LOUKA [putting the bottle on the table] Here, sir.

PETKOFF. Thats right. [He pours some into his coffee].

Catherine, who, having at this early hour made only a very perfunctory toilet, wears a Bulgarian apron over a once brilliant but now half worn-out dressing gown, and a colored handkerchief tied over her thick black hair, comes from the house with Turkish slippers on her bare feet, looking astonishingly handsome and stately under all the circumstances. Louka goes into the house.

CATHERINE. My dear Paul: what a surprise for us! [She stoops over the back of his chair to kiss him]. Have they brought you fresh coffee?

PETKOFF. Yes: Louka's been looking after me. The war's over. The treaty was signed three days ago at Bucharest; and the decree for our army to demobilize was issued yesterday.

CATHERINE [springing erect, with flashing eyes] Paul: have you let the Austrians force you to make peace?

PETKOFF [submissively] My dear: they didnt consult me. What could I do? [She sits down and turns away from him]. But of course we saw to it that the treaty was an honorable one. It declares peace—

CATHERINE [outraged] Peace!

PETKOFF [appeasing her]—but not friendly relations: remember that. They wanted to put that in; but I insisted on its being struck out. What more could I do?

CATHERINE. You could have annexed Serbia and made Prince Alexander Emperor of the Balkans. Thats what I would have done.

PETKOFF. I dont doubt it in the least, my dear. But I should have had to subdue the whole Austrian Empire first; and that would have kept me too long away from you. I missed you greatly.

CATHERINE [relenting] Ah! [She stretches her hand affectionately across the table to squeeze his].

PETKOFF. And how have you been, my dear?

CATHERINE. Oh, my usual sore throats: thats all.

PETKOFF [with conviction] That comes from washing your neck every day. Ive often told you so.

CATHERINE. Nonsense, Paul!

PETKOFF [over his coffee and cigaret] I dont believe in going too far with these modern customs. All this washing cant be good for the health: it's not natural.

There was an Englishman at Philippopolis who used to wet himself all over with cold water every morning when he got up.

Disgusting! It all comes from the English: their climate makes them so dirty that they have to be perpetually washing themselves. Look at my father! he never had a bath in his life; and he lived to be ninety-eight, the healthiest man in Bulgaria. I dont mind a good wash once a week to keep up my position; but once a day is carrying the thing to a ridiculous extreme.

CATHERINE. You are a barbarian at heart still, Paul. I hope you behaved yourself before all those Russian officers.

PETKOFF. I did my best. I took care to let them know that we have a library.

CATHERINE. Ah; but you didnt tell them that we have an electric bell in it? I have had one put up.

PETKOFF. Whats an electric bell?

CATHERINE. You touch a button: something tinkles in the kitchen; and then Nicola comes up.

PETKOFF. Why not shout for him?

CATHERINE. Civilized people never shout for their servants. Ive learnt that while you were away.

PETKOFF. Well, I'll tell you something Ive learnt too. Civilized people dont hang out their washing to dry where visitors can see it; so youd better have all that [indicating the clothes on the bushes] put somewhere else.

CATHERINE. Oh, thats absurd, Paul: I dont believe really refined people notice such things.

SERGIUS [knocking at the stable gates] Gate, Nicola!

PETKOFF. Theres Sergius. [Shouting] Hollo, Nicola!

CATHERINE. Oh, dont shout, Paul: it really isnt nice.

PETKOFF. Bosh! [He shouts louder than before] Nicola!

NICOLA [appearing at the house door] Yes, sir.

PETKOFF. Are you deaf? Dont you hear Major Saranoff knocking? Bring him round this way. [He pronounces the name with the stress on the second syllable: Sarahnoff].

NICOLA. Yes, major. [He goes into the stable yard].

PETKOFF. You must talk to him, my dear, until Raina takes him off our hands. He bores my life out about our not promoting him. Over my head, if you please.

CATHERINE. He certainly ought to be promoted when he marries Raina. Besides, the country should insist on having at least one native general.

PETKOFF. Yes; so that he could throw away whole brigades instead of regiments. It's no use, my dear: he hasnt the slightest chance of promotion until we're quite sure that the peace will be a lasting one.

NICOLA [at the gate, announcing] Major Sergius Saranoff! [He goes into the house and returns presently with a third chair, which he places at the table. He then withdraws].

Major Sergius Saranoff, the original of the portrait in Raina's room, is a tall romantically handsome man, with the physical hardihood, the high spirit, and the susceptible imagination of an untamed mountaineer chieftain. But his remarkable personal distinction is of a characteristically civilized type. The ridges of his eyebrows, curving with an interrogative twist round the projections at the outer corners; his jealously observant eye; his nose, thin, keen, and apprehensive in spite of the pugnacious high bridge and large nostril; his assertive chin would not be out of place in a Parisian salon, shewing that the clever imaginative barbarian has an acute critical faculty which has been thrown into intense activity by the arrival of western civilization in the Balkans. The result is precisely what the advent of nineteenth century thought first produced in England: to wit, Byronism. By his brooding on the perpetual failure, not only of others, but of himself, to live up to his ideals; by his consequent cynical scorn for humanity; by his jejune credulity as to the absolute validity of his concepts and the unworthiness of the world in disregarding them; by his wincings and mockeries under the sting of the petty disillusions which every hour spent among men brings to his sensitive observation, he has acquired the half tragic, half ironic air, the mysterious moodiness, the suggestion of a strange and terrible history that has left nothing but undying remorse, by which Childe Harold fascinated the grandmothers of his English contemporaries. It is clear that here or nowhere is Raina's ideal hero. Catherine is hardly less enthusiastic about him than her daughter, and much less reserved in shewing her enthusiasm. As he enters from the stable gate, she rises effusively to greet him. Petkoff is distinctly less disposed to make a fuss about him.

PETKOFF. Here already, Sergius! Glad to see you.

CATHERINE. My dear Sergius! [She holds out both her hands].

SERGIUS [kissing them with scrupulous gallantry] My dear mother, if I may call you so.

PETKOFF [drily] Mother-in-law, Sergius: mother in law! Sit down; and have some coffee.

SERGIUS. Thank you: none for me. [He gets away from the table with a certain distaste for Petkoff's enjoyment of it, and posts himself with conscious dignity against the rail of the steps leading to the house].

CATHERINE. You look superb. The campaign has improved you, Sergius. Everybody here is mad about you. We were all wild with enthusiasm about that magnificent cavalry charge.

SERGIUS [with grave irony] Madam: it was the cradle and the grave of my military reputation.

CATHERINE. How so?

SERGIUS. I won the battle the wrong way when our worthy Russian generals were losing it the right way. In short, I upset their plans, and wounded their self-esteem. Two Cossack colonels had their regiments routed on the most correct principles of scientific warfare. Two major-generals got killed strictly according to military etiquette. The two colonels are now major-generals; and I am still a simple major.

CATHERINE. You shall not remain so, Sergius. The women are on your side; and they will see that justice is done you.

SERGIUS. It is too late. I have only waited for the peace to send in my resignation.

PETKOFF [dropping his cup in his amazement] Your resignation!

CATHERINE. Oh, you must withdraw it!

SERGIUS [with resolute measured emphasis, folding his arms] I never withdraw.

PETKOFF [vexed] Now who could have supposed you were going to do such a thing?

SERGIUS [with fire] Everyone that knew me. But enough of myself and my affairs. How is Raina; and where is Raina?

RAINA [suddenly coming round the corner of the house and standing at the top of the steps in the path] Raina is here.

She makes a charming picture as they turn to look at her. She wears an underdress of pale green silk, draped with an overdress of thin ecru canvas embroidered with gold. She is crowned with a dainty eastern cap of gold tinsel. Sergius goes impulsively to meet her. Posing regally, she presents her hand: he drops chivalrously on one knee and kisses it.

PETKOFF [aside to Catherine, beaming with parental pride] Pretty, isnt it? She always appears at the right moment.

CATHERINE [impatiently] Yes: she listens for it. It is an abominable habit.

Sergius leads Raina forward with splendid gallantry. When they arrive at the table, she turns to him with a bend of the head: he bows; and thus they separate, he coming to his place, and she going behind her father's chair.

RAINA [stooping and kissing her father] Dear father! Welcome home!

PETKOFF [patting her cheek] My little pet girl. [He kisses her. She goes to the chair left by Nicola for Sergius, and sits down].

CATHERINE. And so youre no longer a soldier, Sergius.

SERGIUS. I am no longer a soldier. Soldiering, my dear madam, is the coward's art of attacking mercilessly when you are strong, and keeping out of harm's way when you are weak. That is the whole secret of successful fighting. Get your enemy at a disadvantage; and never, on any account, fight him on equal terms.

PETKOFF. They wouldnt let us make a fair stand-up fight of it. However, I suppose soldiering has to be a trade like any other trade.

SERGIUS. Precisely. But I have no ambition to shine as a tradesman; so I have taken the advice of that bagman of a captain that settled the exchange of prisoners with us at Pirot, and given it up.

PETKOFF. What! that Swiss fellow? Sergius: Ive often thought of that exchange since. He over-reached us about those horses.

SERGIUS. Of course he over-reached us. His father was a hotel and livery stable keeper; and he owed his first step to his knowledge of horse-dealing. [With mock enthusiasm] Ah, he was a soldier: every inch a soldier! If only I had bought the horses for my regiment instead of foolishly leading it into danger, I should have been a field-marshal now!

CATHERINE. A Swiss? What was he doing in the Serbian army?

PETKOFF. A volunteer, of course: keen on picking up his profession. [Chuckling] We shouldnt have been able to begin fighting if these foreigners hadnt shewn us how to do it: we knew nothing about it; and neither did the Serbs. Egad, there'd have been no war without them!

RAINA. Are there many Swiss officers in the Serbian Army?

PETKOFF. No. All Austrians, just as our officers were all Russians. This was the only Swiss I came across. I'll never trust a Swiss again. He humbugged us into giving him fifty ablebodied men for two hundred worn out chargers. They werent even eatable!

SERGIUS. We were two children in the hands of that consummate soldier, Major: simply two innocent little children.

RAINA. What was he like?

CATHERINE. Oh, Raina, what a silly question!

SERGIUS. He was like a commercial traveller in uniform. Bourgeois to his boots!

PETKOFF [grinning] Sergius: tell Catherine that queer story his friend told us about how he escaped after Slivnitza. You remember. About his being hid by two women.

SERGIUS [with bitter irony] Oh yes: quite a romance! He was serving in the very battery I so unprofessionally charged. Being a thorough soldier, he ran away like the rest of them, with our cavalry at his heels. To escape their sabres he climbed a waterpipe and made his way into the bedroom of a young Bulgarian lady.

The young lady was enchanted by his persuasive commercial traveller's manners. She very modestly entertained him for an hour or so, and then called in her mother lest her conduct should appear unmaidenly. The old lady was equally fascinated; and the fugitive was sent on his way in the morning, disguised in an old coat belonging to the master of the house, who was away at the war.

RAINA [rising with marked stateliness] Your life in the camp has made you coarse, Sergius. I did not think you would have repeated such a story before me. [She turns away coldly].

CATHERINE [also rising] She is right, Sergius. If such women exist, we should be spared the knowledge of them.

PETKOFF. Pooh! nonsense! what does it matter?

SERGIUS [ashamed] No, Petkoff: I was wrong. [To Raina, with earnest humility] I beg your pardon. I have behaved abominably. Forgive me, Raina. [She bows reservedly]. And you too, madam. [Catherine bows graciously and sits down. He proceeds solemnly, again addressing Raina] The glimpses I have had of the seamy side of life during the last few months have made me cynical; but I should not have brought my cynicism here; least of all into your presence, Raina. I—[Here, turning to the others, he is evidently going to begin a long speech when the Major interrupts him].

PETKOFF. Stuff and nonsense, Sergius! Thats quite enough fuss about nothing: a soldier's daughter should be able to stand up without flinching to a little strong conversation. [He rises]. Come: it's time for us to get to business. We have to make up our minds how those three regiments are to get back to Philippopolis: theres no forage for them on the Sofia route. [He goes towards the house]. Come along. [Sergius is about to follow him when Catherine rises and intervenes].

CATHERINE. Oh, Paul, cant you spare Sergius for a few moments? Raina has hardly seen him yet. Perhaps I can help you to settle about the regiments.

SERGIUS [protesting] My dear madam, impossible: you—

CATHERINE [stopping him playfully] You stay here, my dear Sergius: theres no hurry. I have a word or two to say to Paul. [Sergius instantly bows and steps back]. Now, dear [taking Petkoff's arm]: come and see the electric bell.

PETKOFF. Oh, very well, very well.

They go into the house together affectionately. Sergius, left alone with Raina, looks anxiously at her, fearing that she is still offended. She smiles, and stretches out her arms to him.

SERGIUS [hastening to her] Am I forgiven?

RAINA [placing her hands on his shoulders as she looks up at him with admiration and worship]

My hero! My king!

SERGIUS. My queen! [He kisses her on the forehead].

RAINA. How I have envied you, Sergius! You have been out in the world, on the field of battle, able to prove yourself there worthy of any woman in the world; whilst I have had to sit at home inactive—dreaming—useless—doing nothing that could give me the right to call myself worthy of any man.

SERGIUS. Dearest: all my deeds have been yours. You inspired me. I have gone through the war like a knight in a tournament with his lady looking down at him!

RAINA. And you have never been absent from my thoughts for a moment. [Very solemnly] Sergius: I think we two have found the higher love. When I think of you, I feel that I could never do a base deed, or think an ignoble thought.

SERGIUS. My lady and my saint! [He clasps her reverently].

RAINA [returning his embrace] My lord and my—

SERGIUS. Sh—sh! Let me be the worshipper, dear. You little know how unworthy even the best man is of a girl's pure passion!

RAINA. I trust you. I love you. You will never disappoint me, Sergius. [Louka is heard singing within the house. They quickly release each other]. I cant pretend to talk indifferently before her: my heart is too full. [Louka comes from the house with her tray. She goes to the table, and begins to clear it, with her back turned to them]. I will get my hat; and then we can go out until lunch time. Wouldnt you like that?

SERGIUS. Be quick. If you are away five minutes, it will seem five hours. [Raina runs to the top of the steps, and turns there to exchange looks with him and wave him a kiss with both hands. He looks after her with emotion for a moment; then turns slowly away, his face radiant with the loftiest exaltation.

The movement shifts his field of vision, into the corner of which there now comes the tail of Louka's double apron. His attention is arrested at once. He takes a stealthy look at her, and begins to twirl his moustache mischievously, with his left hand akimbo on his hip.

Finally, striking the ground with his heels in something of a cavalry swagger, he strolls over to the other side of the table, opposite her, and says] Louka: do you know what the higher love is?

LOUKA [astonished] No, sir.

SERGIUS. Very fatiguing thing to keep up for any length of time, Louka. One feels the need of some relief after it.

LOUKA [innocently] Perhaps you would like some coffee, sir? [She stretches her hand across the table for the coffee pot].

SERGIUS [taking her hand] Thank you, Louka.

LOUKA [pretending to pull] Oh, sir, you know I didnt mean that. I'm surprised at you!

SERGIUS [coming clear of the table and drawing her with him] I am surprised at myself, Louka. What would Sergius, the hero of Slivnitza, say if he saw me now?

What would Sergius, the apostle of the higher love, say if he saw me now?

What would the half dozen Sergiuses who keep popping in and out of this handsome figure of mine say if they caught us here? [Letting go her hand and slipping his arm dexterously round her waist] Do you consider my figure handsome, Louka?

LOUKA. Let me go, sir. I shall be disgraced. [She struggles: he holds her inexorably]. Oh, will you let go?

SERGIUS [looking straight into her eyes] No.

LOUKA. Then stand back where we cant be seen. Have you no common sense?

SERGIUS. Ah! thats reasonable. [He takes her into the stableyard gateway, where they are hidden from the house].

LOUKA [plaintively] I may have been seen from the windows: Miss Raina is sure to be spying about after you.

SERGIUS [stung: letting her go] Take care, Louka. I may be worthless enough to betray the higher love; but do not you insult it.

LOUKA [demurely] Not for the world, sir, I'm sure. May I go on with my work, please, now?

SERGIUS [again putting his arm round her] You are a provoking little witch, Louka. If you were in love with me, would you spy out of windows on me?

LOUKA. Well, you see, sir, since you say you are half a

dozen different gentlemen all at once, I should have a great deal to look after.

SERGIUS [charmed] Witty as well as pretty. [He tries to kiss her].

LOUKA [avoiding him] No: I dont want your kisses. Gentlefolk are all alike: you making love to me behind Miss Raina's back; and she doing the same behind yours.

SERGIUS [recoiling a step] Louka!

LOUKA. It shews how little you really care.

SERGIUS [dropping his familiarity, and speaking with freezing politeness] If our conversation is to continue, Louka, you will please remember that a gentleman does not discuss the conduct of the lady he is engaged to with her maid.

LOUKA. It's so hard to know what a gentleman considers right. I thought from your trying to kiss me that you had given up being so particular.

SERGIUS [turning from her and striking his forehead as he comes back into the garden from the gateway] Devil! devil!

LOUKA. Ha! ha! I expect one of the six of you is very like me, sir; though I am only Miss Raina's maid. [She goes back to her work at the table, taking no further notice of him].

SERGIUS [speaking to himself] Which of the six is the real man? thats the question that torments me. One of them is a hero, another a buffoon, another a humbug, another perhaps a bit of a blackguard. [He pauses, and looks furtively at Louka as he adds, with deep bitterness] And one, at least, is a coward: jealous, like all cowards. [He goes to the table]. Louka.

LOUKA. Yes?

SERGIUS. Who is my rival?

LOUKA. You shall never get that out of me, for love or money.

SERGIUS. Why?

LOUKA. Never mind why. Besides, you would tell that I told you; and I should lose my place.

SERGIUS [holding out his right hand in affirmation] No! on the honor of a—[He checks himself; and his hand drops, nerveless, as he concludes sardonically]—of a man capable of be having as I have been behaving for the last five minutes. Who is he?

LOUKA. I dont know. I never saw him. I only heard his voice through the door of her room.

SERGIUS. Damnation! How dare you?

LOUKA [retreating] Oh, I mean no harm: youve no right to take up my words like that. The mistress knows all about it. And I tell you that if that gentleman ever comes here again, Miss Raina will marry him, whether he likes it or not. I know the difference between the sort of manner you and she put on before one another and the real manner.

Sergius shivers as if she had stabbed him. Then, setting his face like iron, he strides grimly to her, and grips her above the elbows with both hands.

SERGIUS. Now listen you to me.

LOUKA [wincing] Not so tight: youre hurting me.

SERGIUS. That doesnt matter. You have stained my honor by making me a party to your eavesdropping. And you have betrayed your mistress.

LOUKA [writhing] Please—

SERGIUS. That shews that you are an abominable little clod of common clay, with the soul of a servant. [He lets her go as if she were an unclean thing, and turns away, dusting his hands of her, to the bench by the wall, where he sits down with averted head, meditating gloomily].

LOUKA [whimpering angrily with her hands up her sleeves, feeling her bruised arms] You know how to hurt with your tongue as well as with your hands. But I dont care, now Ive found out that whatever clay I'm made of, youre made of the same.

As for her, she's a liar; and her fine airs are a cheat; and I'm worth six of her. [She shakes the pain off hardily; tosses her head; and sets to work to put the things on the tray].

He looks doubtfully at her. She finishes packing the tray, and laps the cloth over the edges, so as to carry all out together. As she stoops to lift it, he rises.

SERGIUS. Louka! [She stops and looks defiantly at him]. A gentleman has no right to hurt a woman under any circumstances. [With profound humility, uncovering his head] I beg your pardon.

LOUKA. That sort of apology may satisfy a lady. Of what use is it to a servant?

SERGIUS [rudely crossed in his chivalry, throws it off with a bitter laugh, and says slightingly] Oh! you wish to be paid for the hurt? [He puts on his shako, and takes some money from his pocket].

LOUKA [her eyes filling with tears in spite of herself] No: I want my hurt made well.

SERGIUS [sobered by her tone] How?

She rolls up her left sleeve; clasps her arm with the thumb and fingers of her right hand; and looks down at the bruise. Then she raises her head and looks straight at him. Finally, with a superb gesture, she presents her arm to be kissed. Amazed, he looks at her; at the arm; at her again; hesitates; and then, with shuddering intensity, exclaims Never! and gets away as far as possible from her.

Her arm drops. Without a word, and with unaffected dignity, she takes her tray, and is approaching the house when Raina returns, wearing a hat and jacket in the height of the Vienna fashion of the previous year, 1885. Louka makes way proudly for her, and then goes into the house.

RAINA. I'm ready. Whats the matter? [Gaily] Have you been flirting with Louka?

SERGIUS [hastily] No, no. How can you think such a thing?

RAINA [ashamed of herself] Forgive me, dear: it was only a jest. I am so happy today.

He goes quickly to her, and kisses her hand remorsefully. Catherine comes out and calls to them from the top of the steps.

CATHERINE [coming down to them] I am sorry to disturb you, children; but Paul is distracted over those three regiments. He doesnt know how to send them to Philippopolis; and he objects to every suggestion of mine. You must go and help him, Sergius. He is in the library.

RAINA [disappointed] But we are just going out for a walk.

SERGIUS. I shall not be long. Wait for me just five minutes. [He runs up the steps to the door].

RAINA [following him to the foot of the steps and looking up at him with timid coquetry] I shall go round and wait in full view of the library windows. Be sure you draw father's attention to me. If you are a moment longer than five minutes, I shall go in and fetch you, regiments or no regiments.

SERGIUS [laughing] Very well. [He goes in].

Raina watches him until he is out of her sight. Then, with a perceptible relaxation of manner, she begins to pace up and down the garden in a brown study.

CATHERINE. Imagine their meeting that

Swiss and hearing the whole story! The very first thing your father asked for was the old coat we sent him off in. A nice mess you have got us into!

RAINA [gazing thoughtfully at the gravel as she walks] The little beast!

CATHERINE. Little beast! What little beast?

RAINA. To go and tell! Oh, if I had him here, I'd cram him with chocolate creams til he couldnt ever speak again!

CATHERINE. Dont talk such stuff. Tell me the truth, Raina. How long was he in your room before you came to me?

RAINA [whisking round and recommencing her march in the opposite direction] Oh, I forget.

CATHERINE. You cannot forget! Did he really climb up after the soldiers were gone; or was he there when that officer searched the room?

RAINA. No. Yes: I think he must have been there then.

CATHERINE. You think! Oh, Raina! Raina! Will anything ever make you straightforward? If Sergius finds out, it will be all over between you.

RAINA [with cool impertinence] Oh, I know Sergius is your pet. I sometimes wish you could marry him instead of me. You would just suit him. You would pet him, and spoil him, and mother him to perfection.

CATHERINE [opening her eyes very widely indeed] Well, upon my word!

RAINA [capriciously: half to herself] I always feel a longing to do or say something dreadful to him—to shock his propriety—to scandalize the five senses out of him. [To

Catherine, perversely] I dont care whether he finds out about the chocolate cream soldier or not. I half hope he may. [She again turns and strolls flippantly away up the path to the corner of the house].

CATHERINE. And what should I be able to say to your father, pray?

RAINA [over her shoulder, from the top of the two steps] Oh, poor father! As if he could help himself! [She turns the corner and passes out of sight].

CATHERINE [looking after her, her fingers itching] Oh, if you were only ten years younger! [Louka comes from the house with a salver, which she carries hanging down by her side]. Well?

LOUKA. Theres a gentleman just called, madam. A Serbian officer.

CATHERINE [flaming] A Serb! And how dare he— [checking herself bitterly] Oh, I forgot. We are at peace now. I suppose we shall have them calling every day to pay their compliments.

Well: if he is an officer why dont you tell your master? He is in the library with Major Saranoff. Why do you come to me?

LOUKA. But he asks for you, madam. And I dont think he knows who you are: he said the lady of the house. He gave me this little ticket for you. [She takes a card out of her bosom; puts it on the salver; and offers it to Catherine].

CATHERINE [reading] "CaptainBluntschli"? Thats a German name.

LOUKA. Swiss, madam, I think.

CATHERINE [with a bound that makes Louka jump back] Swiss! What is he like?

LOUKA [timidly] He has a big carpet bag, madam.

CATHERINE. Oh Heavens! he's come to return the coat. Send him away: say we're not at home: ask him to leave his address and I'll write to him.

Oh stop: that will never do. Wait! [She throws herself into a chair to think it out. Louka waits]. The master and Major Saranoff are busy in the library, arnt they?

LOUKA. Yes, madam.

CATHERINE [decisively] Bring the gentleman out here at once. [Peremptorily] And be very polite to him. Dont delay. Here [impatiently snatching the salver from her]: leave that here; and go straight back to him.

LOUKA. Yes, madam [going].

CATHERINE. Louka!

LOUKA [stopping] Yes, madam.

CATHERINE. Is the library door shut?

LOUKA. I think so, madam.

CATHERINE. If not, shut it as you pass through.

LOUKA. Yes, madam [going].

CATHERINE. Stop! [Louka stops]. He will have to go that way [indicating the gate of the stable yard]. Tell Nicola to bring his bag here after him. Dont forget.

LOUKA [surprised] His bag?

CATHERINE. Yes: here: as soon as possible. [Vehemently] Be quick! [Louka runs into the house. Catherine snatches her apron off and throws it behind a bush. She then takes up the salver and uses it as a mirror, with the result that the handkerchief tied round her head follows the apron. A touch to her hair and a shake to her dressing gown make her presentable]. Oh, how? how? how can a man be such a fool! Such a

moment to select! [Louka appears at the door of the house, announcing Captain Bluntschli. She stands aside at the top of the steps to let him pass before she goes in again. He is the man of the midnight adventure in Raina's room, clean, well brushed, smartly uniformed, and out of trouble, but still unmistakeably the same man. The moment Louka's back is turned, Catherine swoops on him with impetuous, urgent, coaxing appeal]. Captain Bluntschli: I am very glad to see you; but you must leave this house at once. [He raises his eyebrows]. My husband has just returned with my future son-in-law; and they know nothing. If they did, the consequences would be terrible. You are a foreigner: you do not feel our national animosities as we do. We still hate the Serbs: the effect of the peace on my husband has been to make him feel like a lion baulked of his prey. If he discovers our secret, he will never forgive me; and my daughter's life will hardly be safe. Will you, like the chivalrous gentleman and soldier you are, leave at once before he finds you here?

BLUNTSCHLI [disappointed, but philosophical] At once, gracious lady. I only came to thank you and return the coat you lent me. If you will allow me to take it out of my bag and leave it with your servant as I pass out, I need detain you no further. [He turns to go into the house].

CATHERINE [catching him by the sleeve] Oh, you must not think of going back that way. [Coaxing him across to the stable gates] This is the shortest way out. Many thanks. So glad to have been of service to you. Goodbye.

BLUNTSCHLI. But my bag?

CATHERINE. It shall be sent on. You will leave me your address.

BLUNTSCHLI. True. Allow me. [He takes out his card-case, and stops to write his address, keeping Catherine in an agony of impatience. As he hands her the card, Petkoff, hatless, rushes from the house in a flutter of hospitality, followed by Sergius].

PETKOFF [as he hurries down the steps] My dear Captain Bluntschli—

CATHERINE. Oh Heavens! [She sinks on the seat against the wall].

PETKOFF [too preoccupied to notice her as he shakes Bluntschli's hand heartily] Those stupid people of mine thought I was out here, instead of in the—haw!—library [he cannot mention the library without betraying how proud he is of it]. I saw you through the window. I was wondering why you didnt come in. Saranoff is with me: you remember him, dont you?

SERGIUS [saluting humorously, and then offering his hand with great charm of manner] Welcome, our friend the enemy!

PETKOFF. No longer the enemy, happily. [Rather anxiously] I hope youve called as a friend, and not about horses or prisoners.

CATHERINE. Oh, quite as a friend, Paul. I was just asking Captain Bluntschli to stay to lunch; but he declares he must go at once.

SERGIUS [sardonically] Impossible, Bluntschli. We want you here badly. We have to send on three cavalry regiments to Philippopolis; and we dont in the least know how to do it.

BLUTSCHLI [suddenly attentive and businesslike] Philippopolis? The forage is the trouble, I suppose.

PETKOFF [eagerly] Yes: thats it. [To Sergius] He sees the whole thing at once.

BLUNTSCHLI. I think I can shew you how to manage that.

SERGIUS. Invaluable man! Come along! [Towering over Bluntschli, he puts his hand on his shoulder and takes him to the steps, Petkoff following].

Raina comes from the house as Bluntschli puts his foot on the first step.

RAINA. Oh! The chocolate cream soldier!

Bluntschli stands rigid. Sergius, amazed, looks at Raina, then at Petkoff, who looks back at him and then at his wife.

CATHERINE [with commanding presence of mind] My dear Raina, dont you see that we have a guest here? Captain Bluntschli: one of our new Serbian friends.

Raina bows: Bluntschli bows.

RAINA. How silly of me! [She comes down into the centre of the group, between Bluntschli and Petkoff]. I made a beautiful ornament this morning for the ice pudding; and that stupid Nicola has just put down a pile of plates on it and spoilt it. [To Bluntschli, winningly] I hope you didnt think that you were the chocolate cream soldier, Captain Bluntschli.

BLUNTSCHLI [laughing] I assure you I did. [Stealing a whimsical glance at her] Your explanation was a relief.

PETKOFF [suspiciously, to Raina] And since when, pray, have you taken to cooking?

CATHERINE. Oh, whilst you were away. It is her latest fancy.

PETKOFF [testily] And has Nicola taken to drinking? He used to be careful enough. First he shews Captain Bluntschli out here when he knew quite well I was in the library; and then he goes downstairs and breaks Raina's chocolate soldier. He must—[Nicola appears at the top of the steps with the bag. He descends; places it respectfully before Bluntschli; and waits for further orders. General amazement. Nicola, unconscious of the effect he is producing, looks perfectly satisfied with himself. When Petkoff recovers his power of speech, he breaks out at him with] Are you mad, Nicola?

NICOLA [taken aback] Sir?

PETKOFF. What have you brought that for?

NICOLA. My lady's orders, major. Louka told me that—

CATHERINE [interrupting him] My orders! Why should I order you to bring Captain Bluntschli's luggage out here? What are you thinking of, Nicola?

NICOLA [after a moment's bewilderment, picking up the bag as he addresses Bluntschli with the very perfection of servile discretion] I beg your pardon, captain, I am sure. [To Catherine] My fault, madam: I hope youll overlook it. [He bows, and is going to the steps with the bag, when Petkoff addresses him angrily].

PETKOFF. Youd better go and slam that bag, too, down on Miss Raina's ice pudding! [This is too much for Nicola. The bag drops from his hand almost on his master's toes, eliciting a roar of] Begone, you butter-fingered donkey.

NICOLA [snatching up the bag, and escaping into the house] Yes, major.

CATHERINE. Oh, never mind, Paul: dont be angry.

PETKOFF [blustering] Scoundrel! He's got out of hand while I was away. I'll teach him. Infernal blackguard! The sack next Saturday! I'll clear out the whole establishment—[He is stifled by the caresses of his wife and daughter, who hang round his neck, petting him].

CATHERINE

RAINA together Now, now, now, it

Wow, wow, wow:

mustnt be angry. He meant

not on your first day at home.

no harm. Be good to please

I'll make another ice pudding.

me, dear. Sh-sh-sh-sh!

Tch-ch-ch!

PETKOFF [yielding] Oh well, never mind. Come, Bluntschli: lets have no more nonsense about going away. You know very well youre not going back to Switzerland yet. Until you do go back youll stay with us.

RAINA. Oh, do, Captain Bluntschli.

PETKOFF [to Catherine] Now, Catherine: it's of you he's afraid. Press him; and he'll stay.

CATHERINE. Of course I shall be only too delighted if [appealingly] Captain Bluntschli really wishes to stay. He knows my wishes.

BLUNTSCHLI [in his driest military manner] I am at madam's orders.

SERGIUS [cordially] That settles it!

PETKOFF [heartily] Of course!

RAINA. You see you must stay.

BLUNTSCHLI [smiling] Well, if I must, I must.

Gesture of despair from Catherine.

ACT III

In the library after lunch. It is not much of a library. Its literary equipment consists of a single fixed shelf stocked with old paper covered novels, broken backed, coffee stained, torn and thumbed; and a couple of little hanging shelves with a few gift books on them: the rest of the wall space being occupied by trophies of war and the chase. But it is a most comfortable sitting room. A row of three large windows shews a mountain panorama, just now seen in one of its friendliest aspects in the mellowing afternoon light. In the corner next the right hand window a square earthenware stove, a perfect tower of glistening pottery, rises nearly to the ceiling and guarantees plenty of warmth. The ottoman is like that in Raina's room, and similarly placed; and the window seats are luxurious with decorated cushions. There is one object, however, hopelessly out of keeping with its surroundings. This is a small kitchen table, much the worse for wear, fitted as a writing table with an old canister full of pens, an eggcup filled with ink, and a deplorable scrap of heavily used pink blotting paper. At the side of this table, which stands to the left of anyone facing the window, Bluntschli is hard at work with a couple of maps before him, writing orders. At the head of it sits Sergius, who is supposed to be also at work, but is actually gnawing the feather of a pen, and contemplating Bluntschli's quick, sure, businesslike progress with a mixture of envious irritation at his own incapacity and awestruck wonder at an ability which seems to him almost miraculous, though its prosaic character forbids him to esteem it.

The Major is comfortably established on the ottoman, with a newspaper in his hand and the tube of his hookah within easy reach. Catherine sits at the stove, with her back to them, embroidering. Raina, reclining on the divan, is gazing in a daydream out at the Balkan landscape, with a neglected novel in her lap.

The door is on the same side as the stove, farther from the window. The button of the electric bell is at the opposite side, behind Bluntschli.

PETKOFF [looking up from his paper to watch how they are getting on at the table] Are you sure I cant help you in any way, Bluntschli?

BLUNTSCHLI [without interrupting his writing or looking up] Quite sure, thank you. Saranoff and I will manage it.

SERGIUS [grimly] Yes: we'll manage it. He finds out what to do; draws up the orders; and I sign em. Division of labour! [Bluntschli passes him a paper]. Another one? Thank you. [He plants the paper squarely before him; sets his chair carefully parallel to it; and signs with his cheek on his elbow and his protruded tongue following the movements of his pen]. This hand is more accustomed to the sword than to the pen.

PETKOFF. It's very good of you, Bluntschli: it is indeed, to let yourself be put upon in this way. Now are you quite sure I can do nothing?

CATHERINE [in a low warning tone] You can stop interrupting, Paul.

PETKOFF [starting and looking round at her] Eh? Oh! Quite right, my love: quite right. [He takes his newspaper up again, but presently lets it drop]. Ah, you havnt been campaigning, Catherine: you dont know how pleasant it is for us to sit here, after a good lunch, with nothing to do but enjoy ourselves. Theres only one thing I want to make me thoroughly comfortable.

CATHERINE. What is that?

PETKOFF. My old coat. I'm not at home in this one: I feel as if I were on parade.

CATHERINE. My dear Paul, how absurd you are about that old coat! It must be hanging in the blue closet where you left it.

PETKOFF. My dear Catherine, I tell you Ive looked there. Am I to believe my own eyes or not? [Catherine rises and crosses the room to press the button of the electric bell]. What are you shewing off that bell for? [She looks at him majestically, and silently resumes her chair and her needlework]. My dear: if you think the obstinacy of your sex can make a coat out of two old dressing gowns of Raina's, your waterproof, and my mackintosh, youre mistaken. Thats exactly what the blue closet contains at present.

Nicola presents himself.

CATHERINE. Nicola: go to the blue closet and bring your master's old coat here: the braided one he wears in the house.

NICOLA. Yes, madame. [He goes out].

PETKOFF. Catherine.

CATHERINE. Yes, Paul?

PETKOFF. I bet you any piece of jewellery you like to order from Sofia against a week's housekeeping money that the coat isnt there.

CATHERINE. Done, Paul!

PETKOFF [excited by the prospect of a gamble] Come: heres an opportunity for some sport. Wholl bet on it? Bluntschli: I'll give you six to one.

BLUNTSCHLI [imperturbably] It would be robbing you, major. Madame is sure to be right. [Without looking up, he passes another batch of papers to Sergius].

SERGIUS [also excited] Bravo, Switzerland! Major: I bet my best charger against an Arab mare for Raina that Nicola finds the coat in the blue closet.

PETKOFF [eagerly] Your best char—

CATHERINE [hastily interrupting him] Dont be foolish, Paul. An Arabian mare will cost you 50,000 levas.

RAINA [suddenly coming out of her picturesque revery] Really, mother, if you are going to take the jewellery, I dont see why you should grudge me my Arab.

Nicola comes back with the coat, and brings it to Petkoff, who can hardly believe his eyes.

CATHERINE. Where was it, Nicola?

NICOLA. Hanging in the blue closet, madame.

PETKOFF. Well, I am d—

CATHERINE [stopping him] Paul!

PETKOFF. I could have sworn it wasnt there. Age is beginning to tell on me. I'm getting hallucinations. [To Nicola] Here: help me to change. Excuse me, Bluntschli. [He begins changing coats, Nicola acting as valet]. Remember: I didnt take that bet of yours, Sergius.

Youd better give Raina that Arab steed yourself, since youve roused her expectations. Eh, Raina? [He looks round at her; but she is again rapt in the landscape. With a little gush of parental affection and pride, he points her out to them, and says] She's dreaming, as usual.

SERGIUS. Assuredly she shall not be the loser.

PETKOFF. So much the better for her. I shant come off so cheaply, I expect. [The change is now complete. Nicola goes out with the discarded coat]. Ah, now I feel at home at last. [He sits down and takes his newspaper with a grunt of relief].

BLUNTSCHLI [to Sergius, handing a paper] Thats the last order.

PETKOFF [jumping up] What! Finished?

BLUNTSCHLI. Finished.

PETKOFF [with childlike envy] Havnt you anything for me to sign?

BLUNTSCHLI. Not necessary. His signature will do.

PETKOFF [inflating his chest and thumping it] Ah well, I think weve done a thundering good day's work. Can I do anything more?

BLUNTSCHLI. You had better both see the fellows that

are to take these. [Sergius rises] Pack them off at once; and shew them that Ive marked on the orders the time they should hand them in by. Tell them that if they stop to drink or tell stories—if theyre five minutes late, theyll have the skin taken off their backs.

SERGIUS [stiffening indignantly] I'll say so. [He strides to the door]. And if one of them is man enough to spit in my face for insulting him, I'll buy his discharge and give him a pension. [He goes out].

BLUNTSCHLI [confidentially] Just see that he talks to them properly, major, will you?

PETKOFF [officiously] Quite right, Bluntschli, quite right. I'll see to it. [He goes to the door importantly, but hesitates on the threshold]. By the bye, Catherine, you may as well come too. Theyll be far more frightened of you than of me.

CATHERINE [putting down her embroidery] I daresay I had better. You would only splutter at them. [She goes out, Petkoff holding the door for her and following her].

BLUNTSCHLI. What an army! They make cannons out of cherry trees; and the officers send for their wives to keep discipline! [He begins to fold and docket the papers].

Raina, who has risen from the divan, marches slowly down the room with her hands clasped behind her, and looks mischievously at him.

RAINA. You look ever so much nicer than when we last met. [He looks up, surprised]. What have you done to yourself?

BLUNTSCHLI. Washed; brushed; good night's sleep and breakfast. Thats all.

RAINA. Did you get back safely that morning?

BLUNTSCHLI. Quite, thanks.

RAINA. Were they angry with you for running away from Sergius's charge?

BLUNTSCHLI [grinning] No: they were glad; because theyd all just run away themselves.

RAINA [going to the table, and leaning over it towards him] It must have made a lovely story for them: all that about me and my room.

BLUNTSCHLI. Capital story. But I only told it to one of them: a particular friend.

RAINA. On whose discretion you could absolutely rely?

BLUNTSCHLI. Absolutely.

RAINA. Hm! He told it all to my father and Sergius the day you exchanged the prisoners.

[She turns away and strolls carelessly across to the other side of the room].

*BLUNTSCHLI*4 [deeply concerned, and half incredulous] No! You dont mean that, do you?

RAINA [turning, with sudden earnestness] I do indeed. But they dont know that it was in this house you took refuge. If Sergius knew, he would challenge you and kill you in a duel.

BLUNTSCHLI. Bless me! then dont tell him.

RAINA. Please be serious, Captain Bluntschli. Can you not realize what it is to me to deceive him? I want to be quite perfect with Sergius: no meanness, no smallness, no deceit. My relation to him is the one really beautiful and noble part of my life. I hope you can understand that.

BLUNTSCHLI [sceptically] You mean that you wouldnt like him to find out that the story about the ice pudding was a—a—a—You know.

RAINA [wincing] Ah, dont talk of it in that flippant way. I lied: I know it.

But I did it to save your life. He would have killed you. That was the second time I ever uttered a falsehood. [Bluntschli rises quickly and looks doubtfully and somewhat severely at her]. Do you remember the first time?

BLUNTSCHLI. I! No. Was I present?

RAINA. Yes; and I told the officer who was searching for you that you were not present.

BLUNTSCHLI. True. I should have remembered it.

RAINA [greatly encouraged] Ah, it is natural that you should forget it first. It cost you nothing: it cost me a lie! A lie!!

She sits down on the ottoman, looking straight before her with her hands clasped round her knee. Bluntschli, quite touched, goes to the ottoman with a particularly reassuring and considerate air, and sits down beside her.

BLUNTSCHLI. My dear young lady, dont let this worry

you. Remember: I'm a soldier. Now what are the two things that happen to a soldier so often that he comes to think nothing of them? One is hearing people tell lies [Raina recoils]: the other is getting his life saved in all sorts of ways by all sorts of people.

RAINA [rising in indignant protest] And so he becomes a creature incapable of faith and of gratitude.

BLUNTSCHLI [making a wry face] Do you like gratitude? I dont. If pity is akin to love, gratitude is akin to the other thing.

RAINA. Gratitude! [Turning on him] If you are incapable of gratitude you are incapable of any noble sentiment. Even animals are grateful.

Oh, I see now exactly what you think of me! You were not surprised to hear me lie. To you it was something I probably did every day! every hour!! That is how men think of women. [She paces the room tragically].

BLUNTSCHLI [dubiously] Theres reason in everything. You said youd told only two lies in your whole life. Dear young lady: isnt that rather a short allowance? I'm quite a straightforward man myself; but it wouldnt last me a whole morning.

RAINA [staring haughtily at him] Do you know, sir, that you are insulting me?

BLUNTSCHLI. I cant help it. When you strike that noble attitude and speak in that thrilling voice, I admire you; but I find it impossible to believe a single word you say.

RAINA [superbly] Captain Bluntschli!

BLUNTSCHLI [unmoved] Yes?

RAINA [standing over him, as if she could not believe her senses] Do you mean what you said just now? Do you know what you said just now?

BLUNTSCHLI. I do.

RAINA [gasping] I! I!!! [She points to herself incredulously, meaning "I, Raina Petkoff, tell lies!" He meets her gaze unflinchingly. She suddenly sits down beside him, and adds, with a complete change of manner from the heroic to a babyish familiarity] How did you find me out?

BLUNTSCHLI [promptly] Instinct, dear young lady. Instinct, and experience of the world.

RAINA [wonderingly] Do you know, you are the first man I ever met who did not take me seriously?

BLUNTSCHLI. You mean, dont you, that I am the first man that has ever taken you quite seriously?

RAINA. Yes: I suppose I do mean that. [Cosily, quite at her ease with him] How strange it is to be talked to in such a way! You know, Ive always gone on like that.

BLUNTSCHLI. You mean the—?

RAINA. I mean the noble attitude and the thrilling voice. [They laugh together]. I did it when I was a tiny child to my nurse. She believed in it. I do it before my parents. They believe in it. I do it before Sergius. He believes in it.

BLUNTSCHLI. Yes: he's a little in that line himself, isnt he?

RAINA [startled] Oh! Do you think so?

BLUNTSCHLI. You know him better than I do.

RAINA. I wonder—I wonder is he? If I thought that—! [Discouraged] Ah, well: what does it matter? I suppose, now youve found me out, you despise me.

BLUNTSCHLI [warmly, rising] No, my dear young lady, no, no, no a thousand times. It's part of your youth: part of your charm. I'm like all the rest of them: the nurse, your parents, Sergius: I'm your infatuated admirer.

RAINA [pleased] Really?

BLUNTSCHLI [slapping his breast smartly with his hand, German fashion] Hand aufs Herz! Really and truly.

RAINA [very happy] But what did you think of me for giving you my portrait?

BLUNTSCHLI [astonished] Your portrait! You never gave me your portrait.

RAINA [quickly] Do you mean to say you never got it?

BLUNTSCHLI. No. [He sits down beside her, with renewed interest, and says, with some complacency] When did you send it to me?

RAINA [indignantly] I did not send it to you. [She turns her head away, and adds, reluctantly] It was in the pocket of that coat.

BLUNTSCHLI [pursing his lips and rounding his eyes] Oh-o-oh! I never found it. It must be there still.

RAINA [springing up] There still! for my father to find the first time he puts his hand in his pocket! Oh, how could you be so stupid?

BLUNTSCHLI [rising also] It doesnt matter: I suppose it's only a photograph: how can he tell who it was intended for? Tell him he put it there himself.

RAINA [bitterly] Yes: that is so clever! isnt it? [Distractedly] Oh! what shall I do?

BLUNTSCHLI. Ah, I see. You wrote something on it. That was rash.

RAINA [vexed almost to tears] Oh, to have done such a thing for you, who care no more—except to laugh at me—oh! Are you sure nobody has touched it?

BLUNTSCHLI. Well, I cant be quite sure. You see, I couldnt carry it about with me all the time: one cant take much luggage on active service.

RAINA. What did you do with it?

BLUNTSCHLI. When I got through to Pirot I had to put it in safe keeping somehow. I thought of the railway cloak room; but thats the surest place to get looted in modern warfare. So I pawned it.

RAINA. Pawned it!!!

BLUNTSCHLI. I know it doesnt sound nice; but it was much the safest plan. I redeemed it the day before yesterday. Heaven only knows whether the pawnbroker cleared out the pockets or not.

RAINA [furious: throwing the words right into his face] You have a low shopkeeping mind. You think of things that would never come into a gentleman's head.

BLUNTSCHLI [phlegmatically] Thats the Swiss national character, dear lady. [He returns to the table].

RAINA. Oh, I wish I had never met you. [She flounces away, and sits at the window fuming]. Louka comes in with a heap of letters and telegrams on her salver, and crosses, with her bold free gait, to the table. Her left sleeve is looped up to the shoulder with a brooch, shewing her naked arm, with a broad gilt bracelet covering the bruise.

LOUKA [to Bluntschli] For you. [She empties the salver

with a fling on to the table]. The messenger is waiting. [She is determined not to be civil to an enemy, even if she must bring him his letters].

BLUNTSCHLI [to Raina] Will you excuse me: the last postal delivery that reached me was three weeks ago. These are the subsequent accumulations. Four telegrams: a week old. [He opens one]. Oho! Bad news!

RAINA [rising and advancing a little remorsefully] Bad news?

BLUNTSCHLI. My father's dead. [He looks at the telegram with his lips pursed, musing on the unexpected change in his arrangements. Louka crosses herself hastily].

RAINA. Oh, how very sad!

BLUNTSCHLI. Yes: I shall have to start for home in an hour. He has left a lot of big hotels behind him to be looked after. [He takes up a fat letter in a long blue envelope]. Here's a whacking letter from the family solicitor. [He pulls out the enclosures and glances over them]. Great Heavens! Seventy! Two hundred! [In a crescendo of dismay] Four hundred! Four thousand!! Nine thousand six hundred!!! What on earth am I to do with them all?

RAINA [timidly] Nine thousand hotels?

BLUNTSCHLI Hotels! nonsense. If you only knew! Oh, it's too ridiculous! Excuse me: I must give my fellow orders about starting. [He leaves the room hastily, with the documents in his hand].

LOUKA [knowing instinctively that she can annoy Raina by disparaging Bluntschli] He has not much heart, that Swiss. He has not a word of grief for his poor father.

RAINA [bitterly] Grief! A man who has been doing nothing but killing people for years! What does he care? What does any soldier care? [She goes to the door, restraining her tears with difficulty].

LOUKA. Major Saranoff has been fighting too; and he has plenty of heart left. [Raina, at the door, draws herself up haughtily and goes out]. Aha! I thought you wouldnt get much feeling out of your soldier. [She is following Raina when Nicola enters with an armful of logs for the stove].

NICOLA [grinning amorously at her] Ive been trying all the afternoon to get a minute alone with you, my girl. [His countenance changes as he notices her arm]. Why, what fashion is that of wearing your sleeve, child?

LOUKA [proudly] My own fashion.

NICOLA. Indeed! If the mistress catches you, she'll talk to you. [He puts the logs down, and seats himself comfortably on the ottoman].

LOUKA. Is that any reason why you should take it on yourself to talk to me?

NICOLA. Come! dont be so contrairy with me. Ive some good news for you. [She sits down beside him. He takes out some paper money. Louka, with an eager gleam in her eyes, tries to snatch it; but he shifts it quickly to his left hand, out of her reach]. See! a twenty leva bill! Sergius gave me that, out of pure swagger. A

fool and his money are soon parted. Theres ten levas more. The Swiss gave me that for backing up the mistress's and Raina's lies about him. He's no fool, he isnt. You should have heard old Catherine downstairs as polite as you please to me, telling me not to mind the Major being a little impatient; for they knew what a good servant I was—after making a fool and a liar of me before them all! The twenty will go to our savings; and you shall have the ten to spend if youll only talk to me so as to remind me I'm a human being. I get tired of being a servant occasionally.

LOUKA. Yes: sell your manhood for 30 levas, and buy me for 10! [Rising scornfully] Keep your money. You were born to be a servant. I was not. When you set up your shop you will only be everybody's servant instead of somebody's servant. [She goes moodily to the table and seats herself regally in Sergius's chair].

NICOLA [picking up his logs, and going to the stove] Ah, wait til you see. We shall have our evenings to ourselves; and I shall be master in my own house, I promise you. [He throws the logs down and kneels at the stove].

LOUKA. You shall never be master in mine.

NICOLA [turning, still on his knees, and squatting down

rather forlornly on his calves, daunted by her implacable disdain] You have a great ambition in you, Louka. Remember: if any luck comes to you, it was I that made a woman of you.

LOUKA. You!

NICOLA [scrambling up and going at her] Yes, me. Who was it made you give up wearing a couple of pounds of false black hair on your head and reddening your lips and cheeks like any other Bulgarian girl? I did. Who taught you to trim your nails, and keep your hands clean, and be dainty about yourself, like a fine Russian lady? Me: do you hear that? me! [She tosses her head defiantly; and he turns away, adding, more coolly] Ive often thought that if Raina were out of the way, and you just a little less of a fool and Sergius just a little more of one, you might come to be one of my grandest customers, instead of only being my wife and costing me money.

LOUKA. I believe you would rather be my servant than my husband. You would make more out of me. Oh, I know that soul of yours.

NICOLA [going closer to her for greater emphasis] Never you mind my soul; but just listen to my advice. If you want to be a lady, your present behavior to me wont do at all, unless when we're alone. It's too sharp and impudent; and impudence is a sort of familiarity: it shews affection for me. And dont you try being high and mighty with me, either. Youre like all country girls: you think it's genteel to treat a servant the way I treat a stableboy. Thats only your ignorance; and dont you forget it. And dont be so ready to defy everybody. Act as if you expected to have your own way, not as if you expected to be ordered about. The way to get on as a lady is the same as the way to get on as a servant: youve got to know your place: thats the secret of it. And you may depend on me to know my place if you get promoted. Think over it, my girl. I'll stand by you: one servant should always stand by another.

LOUKA [rising impatiently] Oh, I must behave in my own way. You take all the courage out of me with your cold-blooded wisdom. Go and put those logs on the fire: thats the sort of thing you understand.

Before Nicola can retort, Sergius comes in. He checks himself a moment on seeing Louka; then goes to the stove.

SERGIUS [to Nicola] I am not in the way of your work, I hope.

NICOLA [in a smooth, elderly manner] Oh no, sir: thank you kindly. I was only speaking to this foolish girl about her habit of running up here to the library whenever she gets a chance, to look at the books. Thats the worst of her education, sir: it gives her habits above her station. [To Louka] Make that table tidy, Louka, for the Major. [He goes out sedately].

Louka, without looking at Sergius, pretends to arrange the papers on the table. He crosses slowly to her, and studies the arrangement of her sleeve reflectively.

SERGIUS. Let me see: is there a mark there? [He turns up the bracelet and sees the bruise made by his grasp. She stands motionless, not looking at him: fascinated, but on her guard]. Ffff! Does it hurt?

LOUKA. Yes.

SERGIUS. Shall I cure it?

LOUKA [instantly withdrawing herself proudly, but still not looking at him] No. You cannot cure it now.

SERGIUS [masterfully] Quite sure? [He makes a movement as if to take her in his arms].

LOUKA. Dont trifle with me, please. An officer should not trifle with a servant.

SERGIUS [indicating the bruise with a merciless stroke of his forefinger] That was no trifle, Louka.

LOUKA [flinching; then looking at him for the first time] Are you sorry?

SERGIUS [with measured emphasis, folding his arms] I am never sorry.

LOUKA [wistfully] I wish I could believe a man could be as unlike a woman as that. I wonder are you really a brave man?

SERGIUS [unaffectedly, relaxing his attitude] Yes: I am a brave man. My heart jumped like a woman's at the first shot; but in the charge I found that I was brave. Yes: that at least is real about me.

LOUKA. Did you find in the charge that the men whose fathers are poor like mine were any less brave than the men who are rich like you.

SERGIUS [with bitter levity] Not a bit. They all slashed and cursed and yelled like heroes. Psha! the courage to rage and kill is cheap. I have an English bull terrier who has as much of that sort of courage as the whole Bulgarian nation, and the whole Russian nation at its back. But he lets my groom thrash him, all the same. Thats your soldier all over! No, Louka: your poor men can cut throats; but they are afraid of their officers; they put up with insults and blows; they stand by and see one another punished like children: aye, and help to do it when they are ordered. And the officers!!! Well [with a short harsh laugh] I am an officer. Oh, [fervently] give me the man who will defy to the death any power on earth or in heaven that sets itself up against his own will and conscience: he alone is the brave man.

LOUKA. How easy it is to talk! Men never seem to me to grow up: they all have schoolboy's ideas. You dont know what true courage is.

SERGIUS [ironically] Indeed! I am willing to be instructed. [He sits on the ottoman, sprawling magnificently].

LOUKA. Look at me! how much am I allowed to have my own will? I have to get your room ready for you: to sweep and dust, to fetch and carry. How could that degrade me if it did not degrade you to have it done for you? But [with subdued passion] if I were Empress of Russia, above everyone in the world, then!! Ah then, though according to you I could shew no courage at all, you should see, you should see.

SERGIUS. What would you do, most noble Empress?

LOUKA. I would marry the man I loved, which no other queen in Europe has the courage to do. If I loved you, though you would be as far beneath me as I am beneath you, I would dare to be the equal of my inferior. Would you dare as much if you loved me? No: if you felt the beginnings of love for me you would not let it grow. You would not dare: you would marry a rich man's daughter because you would be afraid of what other people would say of you.

SERGIUS [bounding up] You lie: it is not so, by all the stars! If I loved you, and I were the Czar himself, I would set you on the throne by my side. You know that I love another woman, a woman as high above you as heaven is above earth. And you are jealous of her.

LOUKA. I have no reason to be. She will never marry you now. The man I told you of has come back. She will marry the Swiss.

SERGIUS [recoiling] The Swiss!

LOUKA. A man worth ten of you. Then you can come to me; and I will refuse you. You are not good enough for me. [She turns to the door].

SERGIUS [springing after her and catching her fiercely in his arms] I will kill the Swiss; and afterwards I will do as I please with you.

LOUKA [in his arms, passive and steadfast] The Swiss will kill you, perhaps. He has beaten you in love. He may beat you in war.

SERGIUS [tormentedly] Do you think I believe that she—she! whose worst thoughts are higher than your best ones, is capable of trifling with another man behind my back?

LOUKA. Do you think she would believe the Swiss if he told her now that I am in your arms?

SERGIUS [releasing her in despair] Damnation! Oh, damnation! Mockery! mockery everywhere! everything I think is mocked by everything I do. [He strikes himself frantically on the breast]. Coward! liar! fool! Shall I kill myself like a man, or live and pretend to laugh at myself? [She again turns to go]. Louka! [She stops near the door]. Remember: you belong to me.

LOUKA [turning] What does that mean? An insult?

SERGIUS [commandingly] It means that you love me, and that I have had you here in my arms, and will perhaps have you there again.

Whether that is an insult I neither know nor care: take it as you please. But [vehemently] I will not be a coward and a trifler. If I choose to love you, I dare marry you, in spite of all Bulgaria. If these hands ever touch you again, they shall touch my affianced bride.

LOUKA. We shall see whether you dare keep your word. And take care. I will not wait long.

SERGIUS [again folding his arms and standing motionless in the middle of the room] Yes: we shall see. And you shall wait my pleasure. Bluntschli, much preoccupied, with his papers still in his hand, enters, leaving the door open for Louka to go out. He goes across to the table, glancing at her as he passes. Sergius, without altering his resolute attitude, watches him steadily. Louka goes out, leaving the door open.

BLUNTSCHLI [absently, sitting at the table as before, and putting down his papers] Thats a remarkable looking young woman.

SERGIUS [gravely, without moving] Captain Bluntschli.

BLUNTSCHLI. Eh?

SERGIUS. You have deceived me. You are my rival. I brook no rivals. At six o'clock I shall be in the drilling-ground on the Klissoura road, alone, on horseback, with my sabre. Do you understand?

BLUNTSCHLI [staring, but sitting quite at his ease] Oh, thank you: thats a cavalry man's proposal. I'm in the artillery; and I have the choice of weapons. If I go, I shall take a machine gun. And there shall be no mistake about the cartridges this time.

SERGIUS [flushing, but with deadly coldness] Take care, sir. It is not our custom in Bulgaria to allow invitations of that kind to be trifled with.

BLUNTSCHLI [warmly] Pooh! dont talk to me about Bulgaria. You dont know what fighting is. But have it your own way. Bring your sabre along. I'll meet you.

SERGIUS [fiercely delighted to find his opponent a man of spirit] Well said, Switzer. Shall I lend you my best horse?

BLUNTSCHLI. No: damn your horse! thank you all the same, my dear fellow. [Raina comes in, and hears the next sentence]. I shall fight you on foot. Horseback's too dangerous: I dont want to kill you if I can help it.

RAINA [hurrying forward anxiously] I have heard what Captain Bluntschli said, Sergius. You are going to fight. Why? [Sergius turns away in silence, and goes to the stove, where he stands watching her as she continues, to Bluntschli] What about?

BLUNTSCHLI. I dont know: he hasnt told me. Better not interfere, dear young lady. No harm will be done: Ive often acted as sword instructor. He wont be able to touch me; and I'll not hurt him. It will save explanations. In the morning I shall be off home; and youll never see me or hear of me again. You and he will then make it up and live happily ever after.

RAINA [turning away deeply hurt, almost with a sob in her voice] I never said I wanted to see you again.

SERGIUS [striding forward] Ha! That is a confession.

RAINA [haughtily] What do you mean?

SERGIUS. You love that man!

RAINA [scandalized] Sergius!

SERGIUS. You allow him to make love to you behind my back, just as you treat me as your affianced husband behind his. Bluntschli: you knew our relations; and you deceived me. It is for that that I call you to account, not for having received favors I never enjoyed.

BLUNTSCHLI [jumping up indignantly] Stuff! Rubbish! I have received no favors. Why, the young lady doesnt even know whether I'm married or not.

RAINA [forgetting herself] Oh! [*Collapsing on the ottoman*] Are you?

SERGIUS. You see the young lady's concern, Captain Bluntschli. Denial is useless. You have enjoyed the privilege of being received in her own room, late at night—

BLUNTSCHLI [interrupting him pepperily] Yes, you blockhead! she received me with a pistol at her head. Your cavalry were at my heels. I'd have blown out her brains if she'd uttered a cry.

SERGIUS [taken aback] Bluntschli! Raina: is this true?

RAINA [rising in wrathful majesty] Oh, how dare you, how dare you?

BLUNTSCHLI. Apologize, man: apologize. [He resumes his seat at the table].

SERGIUS [with the old measured emphasis, folding his arms] I never apologize!

RAINA [passionately] This is the doing of that friend of yours, Captain Bluntschli. It is he who is spreading this horrible story about me. [She walks about excitedly].

BLUNTSCHLI. No: he's dead. Burnt alive.

RAINA [stopping, shocked] Burnt alive!

BLUNTSCHLI. Shot in the hip in a woodyard.

Couldnt drag himself out. Your fellows' shells set the timber on fire and burnt him, with half a dozen other poor devils in the same predicament.

RAINA. How horrible!

SERGIUS. And how ridiculous! Oh, war! war! the dream of patriots and heroes! A fraud, Bluntschli. A hollow sham, like love.

RAINA [outraged] Like love! You say that before me!

BLUNTSCHLI. Come, Saranoff: that matter is explained.

SERGIUS. A hollow sham, I say. Would you have come back here if nothing had passed between you except at the muzzle of your pistol? Raina is mistaken about your friend who was burnt. He was not my informant.

RAINA. Who then? [Suddenly guessing the truth] Ah, Louka! my maid! my servant! You were with her this morning all that time after—after—Oh, what sort of god is this I have been worshipping! [He meets her gaze with sardonic enjoyment of her disenchantment. Angered all the more, she goes closer to him, and says, in a lower, intenser tone] Do you know that I looked out of the window as I went upstairs, to have another sight of my hero; and I saw something I did not understand then. I know now that you were making love to her.

SERGIUS [with grim humour] You saw that?

RAINA. Only too well. [She turns away, and throws herself on the divan under the centre window, quite overcome].

SERGIUS [cynically] Raina: our romance is shattered. Life's a farce.

BLUNTSCHLI [to Raina, whimsically] You see: he's found himself out now.

SERGIUS [going to him] Bluntschli: I have allowed you to call me a blockhead. You may now call me a coward as well. I refuse to fight you. Do you know why?

BLUNTSCHLI. No; but it doesnt matter. I didnt ask the reason when you cried on; and I dont ask the reason now that you cry off. I'm a professional soldier: I fight when I have to, and am very glad to get out of it when I havnt to. Youre only an amateur: you think fighting's an amusement.

SERGIUS [sitting down at the table, nose to nose with him] You shall hear the reason all the same, my professional. The reason is that it takes two men—real men—men of heart, blood and honor—to make a genuine combat. I could no more fight with you than I could make love to an ugly woman. Youve no magnetism: youre not a man: youre a machine.

BLUNTSCHLI [apologetically] Quite true, quite true. I always was that sort of chap. I'm very sorry.

SERGIUS. Psha!

BLUNTSCHLI. But now that youve found that life isnt a farce, but something quite sensible and serious, what further obstacle is there to your happiness?

RAINA [rising] You are very solicitous about my happiness and his. Do you forget his new love—Louka? It is not you that he must fight now, but his rival, Nicola.

SERGIUS. Rival!! [bounding half across the room].

RAINA. Dont you know that theyre engaged?

SERGIUS. Nicola! Are fresh abysses opening? Nicola!!

RAINA [sarcastically] A shocking sacrifice, isnt it? Such beauty! such intellect! such modesty! wasted on a middle-aged servant man. Really, Sergius, you cannot stand by and allow such a thing. It would be unworthy of your chivalry.

SERGIUS [losing all self-control] Viper! Viper! [He rushes to and fro, raging].

BLUNTSCHLI. Look here, Saranoff: youre getting the worst of this.

RAINA [getting angrier] Do you realize what he has done, Captain Bluntschli? He has set this girl as a spy on us; and her reward is that he makes love to her.

SERGIUS. False! Monstrous!

RAINA. Monstrous! [Confronting him] Do you deny that she told you about Captain Bluntschli being in my room?

SERGIUS. No; but—

RAINA [interrupting] Do you deny that you were making love to her when she told you?

SERGIUS. No; but I tell you—

RAINA [cutting him short contemptuously] It is unnecessary to tell us anything more. That is quite enough for us.

[She turns away from him and sweeps majestically back to the window].

BLUNTSCHLI [quietly, as Sergius, in an agony of mortification, sinks on the ottoman, clutching his averted head between his fists] I told you you were getting the worst of it, Saranoff.

SERGIUS. Tiger cat!

RAINA [running excitedly to Bluntschli] You hear this man calling me names, Captain Bluntschli?

BLUNTSCHLI. What else can he do, dear lady? He must defend himself somehow. Come [very persuasively]: dont quarrel. What good does it do?

Raina, with a gasp, sits down on the ottoman, and after a vain effort to look vexedly at Bluntschli, falls a victim to her sense of humour, and actually leans back babyishly against the writhing shoulder of Sergius.

SERGIUS. Engaged to Nicola! Ha! ha! Ah well, Bluntschli, you are right to take this huge imposture of a world coolly.

RAINA [quaintly to Bluntschli, with an intuitive guess at his state of mind] I daresay you think us a couple of grown-up babies, dont you?

SERGIUS [grinning savagely] He does: he does. Swiss civilization nursetending Bulgarian barbarism, eh?

BLUNTSCHLI [blushing] Not at all, I assure you. I'm only very glad to get you two quieted. There! there! let's be pleasant and talk it over in a friendly way. Where is this other young lady?

RAINA. Listening at the door, probably.

SERGIUS [shivering as if a bullet had struck him, and speaking with quiet but deep indignation] I will prove that that, at least, is a calumny. [He goes with dignity to the door and opens it. A yell of fury bursts from him as he looks out. He darts into the passage, and returns dragging in Louka, whom he flings violently against the table, exclaiming] Judge her, Bluntschli. You, the cool impartial man: judge the eavesdropper.

Louka stands her ground, proud and silent.

BLUNTSCHLI [shaking his head] I musnt judge her. I once listened myself outside a tent when there was a mutiny brewing. It's all a question of the degree of provocation. My life was at stake.

LOUKA. My love was at stake. I am not ashamed.

RAINA [contemptuously] Your love! Your curiosity, you mean.

LOUKA [facing her and retorting her contempt with interest] My love, stronger than anything you can feel, even for your chocolate cream soldier.

SERGIUS [with quick suspicion, to Louka] What does that mean?

LOUKA [fiercely] It means—

SERGIUS [interrupting her slightingly] Oh, I remember: the ice pudding. A paltry taunt, girl!

Major Petkoff enters, in his shirtsleeves.

PETKOFF. Excuse my shirtsleeves, gentlemen. Raina: somebody has been wearing that coat of mine: I'll swear it. Somebody with a differently shaped back. It's all burst open at the sleeve. Your mother is mending it. I wish she'd make haste: I shall catch cold. [He looks wore attentively at them]. Is anything the matter?

RAINA. No. [She sits down at the stove, with a tranquil air].

SERGIUS. Oh no. [He sits down at the end of the table, as at first].

BLUNTSCHLI [who is already seated] Nothing. Nothing.

PETKOFF [sitting down on the ottoman in his old place] Thats all right. [He notices Louka]. Anything the matter, Louka?

LOUKA. No, sir.

PETKOFF [genially] Thats all right. [He sneezes]. Go and ask your mistress for my coat, like a good girl, will you?

Nicola enters with the coat. Louka makes a pretence of having business in the room by taking the little table with the hookah away to the wall near the windows.

RAINA [rising quickly as she sees the coat on Nicola's arm] Here it is, papa. Give it to me, Nicola; and do you put some more wood on the fire. [She takes the coat, and brings it to the Major, who stands up to put it on. Nicola attends to the fire].

PETKOFF [to Raina, teasing her affectionately] Aha! Going to be very good to poor old papa just for one day after his return from the wars, eh?

RAINA [with solemn reproach] Ah, how can you say that to me, father?

PETKOFF. Well, well, only a joke, little one. Come: give me a kiss. [She kisses him]. Now give me the coat.

RAINA. No: I am going to put it on for you. Turn your back. [He turns his back and feels behind him with his arms for the sleeves. She dexterously takes the photograph from the pocket and throws it on the table before Bluntschli, who covers it with a sheet of paper under the very nose of Sergius, who looks on amazed, with his suspicions roused in the highest degree. She then helps Petkoff on with his coat]. There, dear! Now are you comfortable?

PETKOFF. Quite, little love. Thanks. [He sits down; and Raina returns to her seat near the stove]. Oh, by the bye, Ive found something funny. Whats the meaning of this? [He puts his hand into the picked pocket]. Eh? Hallo! [He tries the other pocket]. Well, I could have sworn—! [Much puzzled, he tries the breast pocket]. I wonder—[trying the original pocket]. Where can it—? [He rises, exclaiming] Your mother's taken it!

RAINA [very red] Taken what?

PETKOFF. Your photograph, with the inscription: "Raina, to her Chocolate Cream Soldier: a Souvenir." Now you know theres something more in this than meets the eye; and I'm going to find it out. [Shouting] Nicola!

NICOLA [coming to him] Sir!

PETKOFF. Did you spoil any pastry of Miss Raina's this morning?

NICOLA. You heard Miss Raina say that I did, sir.

PETKOFF. I know that, you idiot. Was it true?

NICOLA. I am sure Miss Raina is incapable of saying anything that is not true, sir.

PETKOFF. Are you? Then I'm not. [Turning to the others] Come: do you think I dont see it all? [He goes to Sergius, and slaps him on the shoulder]. Sergius: youre the chocolate cream soldier, arnt you?

SERGIUS [starting up] I! A chocolate cream soldier! Certainly not.

PETKOFF. Not! [He looks at them. They are all very serious and very conscious]. Do you mean to tell me that Raina sends things like that to other men?

SERGIUS [enigmatically] The world is not such an innocent place as we used to think, Petkoff.

BLUNTSCHLI [rising] It's all right, Major. I'm the chocolate cream soldier. [Petkoff and Sergius are equally astonished]. The gracious young lady saved my life by giving me chocolate creams when I was starving: shall I ever forget their flavour! My late friend Stolz told you the story at Pirot. I was the fugitive.

PETKOFF. You! [He gasps]. Sergius: do you remember how these two women went on this morning when we mentioned it? [Sergius smiles cynically. Petkoff confronts Raina severely]. Youre a nice young woman, arnt you?

RAINA [bitterly] Major Saranoff has changed his mind. And when I wrote that on the photograph, I did not know that Captain Bluntschli was married.

BLUNTSCHLI [startled into vehement protest] I'm not married.

RAINA [with deep reproach] You said you were.

BLUNTSCHLI. I did not. I positively did not. I never was married in my life.

PETKOFF [exasperated] Raina: will you kindly inform me, if I am not asking too much, which of these gentlemen you are engaged to?

RAINA. To neither of them. This young lady [introducing Louka, who faces them all proudly] is the object of Major Saranoff's affections at present.

PETKOFF. Louka! Are you mad, Sergius? Why, this girl's engaged to Nicola.

NICOLA. I beg your pardon, sir. There is a mistake. Louka is not engaged to me.

PETKOFF. Not engaged to you, you scoundrel! Why, you had twenty-five levas from me on the day of your betrothal; and she had that gilt bracelet from Miss Raina.

NICOLA [with cool unction] We gave it out so, sir. But it was only to give Louka protection. She had a soul above her station; and I have been no more than her confidential servant. I intend, as you know, sir, to set up a shop later on in Sofia; and I look forward to her custom and recommendation should she marry into the nobility. [He goes out with impressive discretion, leaving them all staring after him].

PETKOFF [breaking the silence] Well, I am-hm!

SERGIUS. This is either the finest heroism or the most crawling baseness. Which is it, Bluntschli?

BLUNTSCHLI. Never mind whether it's heroism or baseness. Nicola's the ablest man Ive met in Bulgaria. I'll make him manager of a hotel if he can speak French and German.

LOUKA [suddenly breaking out at Sergius] I have been insulted by everyone here. You set them the example. You owe me an apology.

Sergius, like a repeating clock of which the spring has been touched, immediately begins to fold his arms.

BLUNTSCHLI [before he can speak] It's no use. He never apologizes.

LOUKA. Not to you, his equal and his enemy. To me, his poor servant, he will not refuse to apologize.

SERGIUS [approvingly] You are right. [He bends his knee in his grandest manner] Forgive me.

LOUKA. I forgive you. [She timidly gives him her hand, which he kisses]. That touch makes me your affianced wife.

SERGIUS [springing up] Ah! I forgot that.

LOUKA [coldly] You can withdraw if you like.

SERGIUS. Withdraw! Never! You belong to me. [He puts his arm about her].

Catherine comes in and finds Louka in Sergius's arms, with all the rest gazing at them in bewildered astonishment.

CATHERINE. What does this mean?

Sergius releases Louka.

PETKOFF. Well, my dear, it appears that Sergius is going to marry Louka instead of Raina. [She is about to break out indignantly at him: he stops her by exclaiming testily] Dont blame me: Ive nothing to do with it. [He retreats to the stove].

CATHERINE. Marry Louka! Sergius: you are bound by your word to us!

SERGIUS [folding his arms] Nothing binds me.

BLUNTSCHLI [much pleased by this piece of common sense] Saranoff: your hand. My congratulations. These heroics of yours have their practical side after all. [To Louka] Gracious young lady: the best wishes of a good Republican! [He kisses her hand, to Raina's great disgust, and returns to his seat].

CATHERINE. Louka: you have been telling stories.

LOUKA. I have done Raina no harm.

CATHERINE. [haughtily] Raina!

Raina, equally indignant, almost snorts at the liberty.

LOUKA. I have a right to call her Raina: she calls me Louka. I told Major Saranoff she would never marry him if the Swiss gentleman came back.

BLUNTSCHLI [rising, much surprised] Hallo!

LOUKA [turning to Raina] I thought you were fonder of him than of Sergius. You know best whether I was right.

BLUNTSCHLI. What nonsense! I assure you, my dear Major, my dear Madame, the gracious young lady simply saved my life, nothing else. She never cared two straws for me. Why, bless my heart and soul, look at the young lady and look at me. She, rich, young, beautiful, with her imagination full of fairy princes and noble natures and cavalry charges and goodness knows what! And I, a commonplace Swiss soldier who hardly knows what a decent life is after fifteen years of barracks and battles: a vagabond, a man who has spoiled all his chances in life through an incurably romantic disposition, a man—

SERGIUS [starting as if a needle had pricked him and interrupting Bluntschli in incredulous amazement] Excuse me, Bluntschli: what did you say had spoiled your chances in life?

BLUNTSCHLI [promptly] An incurably romantic

disposition. I ran away from home twice when I was a boy. I went into the army instead of into my father's business. I climbed the balcony of this house when a man of sense would have dived into the nearest cellar. I came sneaking back here to have another look at the young lady when any other man of my age would have sent the coat back—

PETKOFF. My coat!

BLUNTSCHLI.—yes: thats the coat I mean-would have sent it back and gone quietly home. Do you suppose I am the sort of fellow a young girl falls in love with? Why, look at our ages! I'm thirty-four: I dont suppose the young lady is much over seventeen. [This estimate produces a marked sensation, all the rest turning and staring at one another. He proceeds innocently] All that adventure which was life or death to me, was only a schoolgirl's game to her—chocolate creams and hide and seek. Heres the proof! [He takes the photograph from the table]. Now, I ask you, would a woman who took the affair seriously have sent me this and written on it "Raina, to her Chocolate Cream Soldier: a Souvenir"? [He exhibits the photograph triumphantly, as if it settled the matter beyond all possibility of refutation].

PETKOFF. Thats what I was looking for. How the deuce did it get there? [He comes from the stove to look at it, and sits down on the ottoman].

BLUNTSCHLI [to Raina, complacently] I have put everything right, I hope, gracious young lady.

RAINA [going to the table to face him] I quite agree with your account of yourself. You are a romantic idiot. [Bluntschli is unspeakably taken aback]. Next time, I hope you will know the difference between a schoolgirl of seventeen and a woman of twenty-three.

BLUNTSCHLI [stupefied] Twenty-three!

Raina snaps the photograph contemptuously from his hand; tears it up; throws the pieces in his face; and sweeps back to her former place.

SERGIUS [with grim enjoyment of his rival's

discomfiture] Bluntschli: my one last belief is gone. Your sagacity is a fraud, like everything else. You have less sense than even I!

BLUNTSCHLI [overwhelmed] Twenty-three! Twenty-three!! [He considers]. Hm! [Swiftly making up his mind and coming to his host] In that case, Major Petkoff, I beg to propose formally to become a suitor for your daughter's hand, in place of Major Saranoff retired.

RAINA. You dare!

BLUNTSCHLI. If you were twenty-three when you said those things to me this afternoon, I shall take them seriously.

CATHERINE [loftily polite] I doubt, sir, whether you quite realize either my daughter's position or that of Major Sergius Saranoff, whose place you propose to take. The Petkoffs and the Saranoffs are known as the richest and most important families in the country. Our position is almost historical: we can go back for twenty years.

PETKOFF. Oh, never mind that, Catherine. [To Bluntschli] We should be most happy, Bluntschli, if it were only a question of your position; but hang it, you know, Raina is accustomed to a very comfortable establishment. Sergius keeps twenty horses.

BLUNTSCHLI. But who wants twenty horses? We're not going to keep a circus.

CATHERINE [severely] My daughter, sir, is accustomed to a first-rate stable.

RAINA. Hush, mother: youre making me ridiculous.

BLUNTSCHLI. Oh well, if it comes to a question of an establishment, here goes! [He darts impetuously to the table; seizes the papers in the blue envelope; and turns to Sergius]. How many horses did you say?

SERGIUS. Twenty, noble Switzer.

BLUNTSCHLI. I have two hundred horses. [They are amazed]. How many carriages?

SERGIUS. Three.

BLUNTSCHLI. I have seventy. Twenty-four of them will hold twelve inside, besides two on the box, without counting the driver and conductor. How many tablecloths have you?

SERGIUS. How the deuce do I know?

BLUNTSCHLI. Have you four thousand?

SERGIUS. No.

BLUNTSCHLI. I have. I have nine thousand six hundred pairs of sheets and blankets, with two thousand four hundred eider-down quilts. I have ten thousand knives and forks, and the same quantity of dessert spoons. I have three hundred servants. I have six palatial establishments, besides two livery stables, a tea gardens, and a private house. I have four medals for distinguished services; I have the rank of an officer and the standing of a gentleman; and I have three native languages. Shew me any man in Bulgariathat can offer as much!

PETKOFF [with childish awe] Are you Emperor of Switzerland?

BLUNTSCHLI. My rank is the highest known in Switzerland: I am a free citizen.

CATHERINE. Then, Captain Bluntschli, since you are my daughter's choice—

RAINA [mutinously] He's not.

CATHERINE [ignoring her]—I shall not stand in the way of her happiness. [Petkoff is about to speak] That is Major Petkoff's feeling also.

PETKOFF. Oh, I shall be only too glad. Two hundred horses! Whew!

SERGIUS. What says the lady?

RAINA [pretending to sulk] The lady says that he can keep his tablecloths and his omnibuses. I am not here to be sold to the highest bidder. [She turns her back on him].

BLUNTSCHLI. I wont take that answer. I appealed to you as a fugitive, a beggar, and a starving man. You accepted me. You gave me your hand to kiss, your bed to sleep in, and your roof to shelter me.

RAINA. I did not give them to the Emperor of Switzerland.

BLUNTSCHLI. Thats just what I say. [He catches her by the shoulders and turns her faceto-face with him]. Now tell us whom you did give them to.

RAINA [succumbing with a shy smile] To my chocolate cream soldier.

BLUNTSCHLI [with a boyish laugh of delight] Thatll do. Thank you. [He looks at his watch and suddenly becomes businesslike]. Time's up, Major. Youve managed those regiments so well that youre sure to be asked to get rid of some of the infantry of the Timok division. Send them home by way of Lom Palanka. Saranoff: dont get married until I come back: I shall be here punctually at five in the evening on Tuesday fortnight. Gracious ladies [his heels click] good evening. [He makes them a military bow, and goes].

SERGIUS. What a man! Is he a man?

Chapter 9

Study Questions

Q. Analyse the Social Context of Arms and the Man" by George Bernard Shaw

Or

Q. Discuss the political and social context of Arms and the Man

George Bernard Shaw wrote Arms and the Man in 1893 during the Victorian era when most plays were lighter dramas or comedies in the vein of The Importance of Being Earnest, which was a play about manners and other Victorian conventions. Still, in many ways, Arms and the Man, despite some of its themes, is a perfect example of Victorian literature. The play opened to the British public in 1894 to mixed reviews and was one of the plays included in the Plays Pleasant Volume which included a few of Shaw's other, less popular works including "You Never Can Tell." What is most interesting about *Arms and the Man* is that, although it is a comedy, it deals with several political and social themes covertly. Ideas such as the idealism behind war and the romanticism of love are attacked through satire and even more importantly, issues of class are brought to the forefront. Shaw was an avid socialist and had a number of beliefs about class that are appropriate to the historical situation in Europe. At the time the play was performed, Britain was experiencing a number of significant social and political changes as issues of class were coming to the forefront of national debates.

Q. Critically comment on the Shaw's Arms and the Man

Or

Q. Discuss military heroism in Arms and the Man by Shaw

Arms and the Man is one of Shaw's earliest plays. It was first produced in London in 1894. Then It was published in the volume ",*Plays Pleasant*" in 1898.

It is true that this play is a comedy, but it is also about war and about soldiers' real values. Actually it is a parody of military heroism, showing the contrast between realistic and romantic morality. The setting of the play is in a small town near a mountain pass in the Balkans. The story focuses not only on the romance between the young people of the play, but also the ideals that men carry with them during war times. Actually if we read the passage titled "*The soldier*" we notice how the Swiss officer Bluntschli, who fights for money rather than ideals, destroys the conception of war Raina always held. In the same way, when the first world war was declared, the men who go to fight carried with them the same romantic ideas of the "glories" of war that Raina and her mother Catherine carry with them at the start of the play. The author of this play wants to show principally the reality of fear and of war, that is not based on ideals; in conclusion we can say that Shaw's aim was the improvement of society of the time that was under the control of Victorian values and institutions

Q. Write a short note on the Literature of George Bernard Shaw

Or

Q. Discuss Shaw's plays as layered with opinions and social commentary

Oftentimes in literature an author will use his works as a means for the expression of views. It then becomes the job of the reader to find those views and make an attempt to understand them. George Bernard Shaw is a playwright who layered his plays with opinions and social commentary. It is these views that present themselves after a close reading in which the reader feels he has read more than a play. In his classic work Man and Superman Shaw attempts to further his opinions both sublimely and forthrightly. Though many do not appreciate his attempts and criticize his works, the legacy of Shavian writing lives on.

To the everyday reader the play Man and Superman is a

dry love story with an interesting third act. To those well versed in Shavian script, it is more than that, much more. The outset of the play contains the most important lines for this is where first impressions are made. Shaw believed that an impression of his characters should hold true throughout the work. The play opens with the upper class Englishman, Roebuck Ramsden, ordering his maid around. With this Shaw already begins to show the class dichotomy he hates so much. On the surface the most important character is the one who never speaks, Mr. Whitefield, the deceased father of Ann Whitefield, the woman who must be married. Ann becomes the vessel Shaw uses to demonstrate his views on the struggle between sexes. She teases poor Octavius or Tavy as the others call him. The pen name Tavy stems from Ann's referring to him as Ricky Ticky Tavy, in a sensually sly, almost devious manner because she knows he loves her. This love Octavius has for Ann becomes a main argument in the play because much of the character interaction branches from this.

The real story begins with the death of Ann's father and the reading of his will where a shocking revelation is learned. Mr. Whitefield has named the regale elderly Ramsden as well as the radical youthful Jack Tanner to be the guardian of his two daughters. It comes as a great surprise to all (except Ann) that Tanner has been named a suitor because he has such radical social views. In fact, the mention of his book The Revolutionist's Handbook brings disgust and shock to the room it was uttered in. A guardian for Ann is crucial because she holds the wishes of her father up so high. So high that she becomes a slave to them. This power over Ann is thus transferred to her two new guardians.

The next two acts seem somewhat insignificant to the story, but not to the cause of Shaw. The second act demonstrates how desperately in love with Ann Octavius is and the growing realization that he can't have her. It is here that we also begin to see Ann trying to manipulate the reluctant Jack Tanner into marrying her. It is also here that a subplot is formed with Violet and her secret husband Hector. When Violet announces that she is married but won't disclose to whom, a row ensues. It isn't until later that everyone finds out that the husband is Hector, a friend, and not some disrespectful stranger. Shaw uses this subplot to further demonstrate his distaste for classes because it is Hector's rich father that is preventing Hector from admitting that he is the husband.

Hector and Jack go for a joyride in their cars along with the others in the cast. The third act takes place after Tanner and his chauffer ran away from Ann and the passengers in her car. The reason he fled was because Straker, his chauffer, had pointed out that Ann intended to make Tanner her husband and not Octavius. His fleeing brings the play to its most famous and sometimes misunderstood scene, "Don Juan in Hell". Jack Tanner meets a group of brigands led by Mendoza who steal from the rich by disabling their cars. Jack listens to Mendoza's stories about life and his social grievances and stays the night with him and his "army." The dream sequence that ensues is that of Don Juan in hell who encounters the devil, the woman he loved and her father. It is here that Shaw criticizes religion and the government the most. Mendoza and Tanner think little of their dream, but to the reader it speaks volumes of the ideas Shaw is trying to express.

The fourth and final act of the play is more down to earth and answers most of the questions raised throughout the work. It is in this act that we learn that Ann has been playing with Octavius' emotions and has been trying to get Jack Tanner to marry her all along. It was she that chose Jack to be her guardian as the best way to get him to marry her. This is also the act where Hector fesses up to being Violet's husband resulting in a quarrel with his father. Much like the other confrontations in the play this one ends with a conciliatory action, in a way that shows Shaw despises drawn out fighting. The predictable ending of Jack Tanner wedding Ann leads some to think this a simple comedy, but it is much more than that. The interactions each character has were Shavian ways of mocking society and life itself. Each act holds its own when placed under a microscope, and that's the way Shaw wanted it. Critics such as Louis Kronenberger who feel Shaw to be little more than a garrulous writer condemn much of his antics in writing. However, even Kronenberger admits to the genius that the nefarious third act in hell holds.

Bernard Shaw uses character interactions as his main container when spreading his ideas in his plays. There are many interactions in Man and Superman with each one proving a different point of view of Shaw's, or multiple views of his. There are essentially two themes in this play. One deals with the struggle of the sexes and the other deals with the struggles in society. The predominate theme is that of the sexes because Shaw goes out of his way to mock marriage and the power of both men and women. The struggle of the sexes can be broken down in its simplest terms by the fact that without women there is no life, and without men there is no value. Shaw writes of the "life force" in his play as a qualifier for marriage. That the sole purpose in a woman's life is to find a husband and create more children, this is the only way life can go on. Shaw's close-minded view of the man's role in life is that men make life worth living. It is the role of man to teach his children the ways of the world and make that world suitable for living. It is the men that make all the decisions in life, and fight for freedoms they cherish. In Shaw's case he wants nothing else but the end of democracy and the start of socialism where all new children can live together equally.

Shaw writes Jack Tanner as he would himself in this play. In a work of literature there is always a character that embodies the spirit of the author. It is a natural occurrence for an author to put himself in his work. Throughout Man and Superman Ann's function is to get a husband, never is it spoken, "would you like to get married?" or "if you choose to marry." It is written, as "I must get married." Indeed she must because Shaw realizes that at this time in history it is vital for a woman to have a mate. She can do nothing else but breed and comfort her husband. In act II line 74 Tanner says it best with "...what other work has she in life but to get a husband? It is a woman's business to get married as soon as possible, and a man's to keep unmarried as long as he can."

What Shaw tries to express that is sometimes lost on critics is the presence of the "life force" and what it does to both sexes. This "force" drives the two together, in fact Tanner mentions the force as Ann slowly weakens him into marrying her. Shaw writes the battle for marriage as a battle for freedom and individuality. To the last line in the play Jack won't give up his freedom, but the life force proves too strong and he succumbs to it.

It is this period in the play where he runs away, argues and does everything in his power to stay single that Tanner is being forced to learn why superman is needed. Superman in the sense that the next generation needs to be able to combat the evils of democracy, but these "warriors" can only come about from the marriage of a woman like Ann and a man like Tanner. It takes a man with radical ideas and a woman with shrewd ideals to produce a child worthy of a battle for society. Shaw errs in this play though. He writes with great verbosity the objection Tanner has to getting married and writes pages to demonstrate the determination of Ann to show the need for "supermen" but does not solve the problem. He only writes it to break the verbiage of democracy and get the idea out in the minds of his readers. There is no blue print for how it's done, only that the need is there and waiting for the compliant few. This here is the arrogance that many critics come to hate in Shaw. He is a man of a million ideas with no way to make the flourish.

The feeling of the need for a marriage is ever present but not that of a want for a marriage because Shaw wanted it that way. If he had wanted a romance with sparks flying he would have allowed Ann to marry Octavius. In fact he goes as far to say through Ann that a compassionate man like Octavius never marries (Act IV line 303). This lack of emotion between Ann and Jack Tanner is Shaw's way of mocking marriage that there is no need for it other than that of the life force it gives. That marriage picks you; you don't pick marriage.

To say that Shaw wrote devoid of emotion is an unfair assessment of the play, his romantic writings lacked spark but there is emotion where it is needed. Bruce R. Park stated that Shakespeare showed love and Shaw showed ideas. After reading a Shavian writing this would appear true, where Shakespeare excelled in love Shaw surpassed in opinions. The majority of the third act in hell is jam packed with emotion. It is here that Man and Superman earns its tragic in tragic comedy. It would have been literary suicide for Shaw to incorporate the sometimes mystifying "Don Juan in hell scene" if he didn't want it to mean something. All strange things must hold some idealistic standing otherwise they wouldn't be strange. It is here that Shaw attacks his main targets of religion, marriage, democracy and the deception of society.

The interaction between Don Juan and the Devil is just as important as that of Ann and Jack Tanner. Due to the fact that Tanner dreams up this sequence and is said to be Don Juan in his dream we can now parallel the two characters. After juxtaposing Don Juan and Tanner it becomes apparent that Shaw is using Don Juan as a vessel for his revolutionary ideas. He becomes a rebel against God and is transformed into a saint and thus an idealist, it is he who becomes and predicts a superman who is God defying. It can be said that Don Juan is Tanner not bound by earthly obligations, in fact Shaw makes it a point to write Don Juan opposite from his normal stereotype as a womanizer and even goes so far as to mock those in hell who do look for sexual satisfaction. Don Juan embodies everything Shaw feels his superman is to be. He holds the ideals of libertine such as Tanner but owes nothing to the life force that would ground him to earth. However, it is this life force that stops a great man like Tanner, that ultimately chooses who will become a superman. Don Juan states that evolution strives to make god-like men, but only those men seen fit by the life force, which Shaw considers himself as a chosen one.

The satire Shaw uses in this section is great for not only does he write that hell is a place that can be enjoyed but also that he was brought there due to a duel over a woman. It took a less than noble death and a trip to hell to make him into what is needed to overcome the failure of democracy. Shaw writes Don Juan as the opposite of the womanizer he is commonly referred to for a comical effect and to make the dream sequence all that more unreal. His sexual drive is taken away because the ecstasy two people bring each other is basically impersonal and thus leads to conflict. Shaw is avoiding this conflict and adding a vital character trait of unselfishness needed to combat society and become a superman. It is the interaction between Don Juan and the Devil that Shaw uses to advance his ideals in the play. It seems to be a fascinating conversation but in actuality it is didactic in the eyes of Bernard Shaw.

The relationship Don Juan has with the Devil can be seen as neither negative nor positive, however, the relationship with Ann and Octavius is another story. From the first scene of the play the audience realizes that Octavius is meant to have his heart broken. The shrewd character of Ann only teases Octavius to become someone that can be called less than a man. Shaw uses this negative influence of Ann on Octavius to demonstrate the power women have and to show the fact that the life force is the only factor that can truly create a marriage. It can also be said that the dead father of Ann had and still has a negative influence on his daughter. He runs her life even from beyond the grave because she honored every wish he had. Tanner has to confront her several times to get her to live her own life, not knowing that this is exactly what she wants to hear from her future husband. Octavius and Tanner are at opposite ends of the spectrum and Shaw uses this to demonstrate how the misunderstood radical is the one who is chosen by the life force to thrive over the failed democracy. Roebuck Ramsden has a positive influence on Ann and the others but is seen as an outdated person. He is the idealistic liberal that is made the butt of Shaw's jokes. No information is given to him and it seems as if the younger more shrew cast members take advantage of him. However, all have much respect for the man and wouldn't dare dishonor him. Despite the fact that Tanner and Ramsden dislike each other immensely they hold a great deal of respect for one another and they both stand strongly by their beliefs. Much like Octavius and Tanner are polar on romance, Ramsden and Tanner are opposites on the matter of government. Bernard

Shaw uses personal feelings as a means for ironic amusement as a fact of life; much of the satire in Man and Superman is done this way. The relationships and conflicts we see are nothing more than ironic twists with a message used by Shaw to get a laugh by the educated few. Perhaps that is the problem with Bernard Shaw that his humour and themes are written so only he and those like him can understand them. If he had written in a more universal tone possibly he would be praised more today than he is. Despite all this, the points are made and a Shavian style survives.

After reading Shaw's Man and Superman several themes are apparent. However, there are two main themes that can be combined into one grievance with society, the superiority of man and the fallacy of democracy. Eric Bently wrote in his book The Life of The Drama that Shaw didn't just want to show us his ideas but he wanted to make us understand through the relationships between the characters. These relationships are where one can find the clues to the themes in the play. Though Ann ultimately gets what she wants in a marriage with Jack, it is his decision in the end. Throughout the play we see the dominance of men, it's not as visible as in other literature but it is ever present. There is an air present that every decision must be approved by a male and that there are different levels of superiority. These levels go as deep as heaven and hell with Don Juan and his former lover. Don Juan's former lover needs his accompaniment even in the afterlife but even her father turns her down. Shaw is making the point with the third act taking place in hell that on earth men are bound by rules but in the afterlife is where true freedom can take place. This theme is ever present because we see the moral and social obligations that each character has, Hector to his father, Ann to her father, and even Straker to Jack Tanner. On earth there is always an obligation to someone, but Shaw makes the point that in hell there is nothing to worry about but you.

The different levels of superiority are a major theme that can be taken away from Man and Superman. The play brings the rebellion Shaw has in conflict with flesh and blood reality to where he balances the ideals of philosophical moralist against the neutrality of the natural historian. Shaw uses the relationships between the characters to promote this theme and when looked at even deeper it becomes a commentary on society. Shaw is an avid socialist who constantly argues with current dogma and criticizes civilized society calling it "one huge Bourgeoisie". In the play Shaw attempts to demonstrate the lack of social awareness that people have and the corruption that results due to it. This is how the morass of man due to woman can be compared with that of society. Robert Brustein wrote that Man and Superman is like heaven and hell, similar in function but very different in ideology. It is this quest for supermen that Shaw wants to portray. These are the people who will champion his cause and it will only come about though the limitations and actions seen in Man and Superman.

The style of George Bernard Shaw is that of many different writers. He is someone who has been influenced greatly by a variety of people, both in his diction and in his views. This becomes the focal point of many pejorative critics of the man. They denounce him for his unoriginal ideas and trite styles. Shaw didn't write for acclaim, however. He seldom cared what others felt or said about his writing, as long as he got his point across that was good enough. It becomes apparent why so many critics disapprove of him when one looks at the list of contributors to his work. They range from Schopenhauer, Nietzsche, Butler, Marx, Ruskin, Morris, Caryle and Wagner to Ibsen, Chokhov and even Jesus. During the time period of his life people as radical as these were feared and thus shunned by society. A number of people on that list are great reformers and socialists.

Today we have the term Shavian when discussing the radical type of literature produced by Bernard Shaw. The simple definition of Shavian would be to describe his style of writing, but the real meaning as J. Percy Smith put it is that Shavian means to vigorously object to doctrine. That is exactly what he does in Man and Superman; he attacks marriage, government and religion, subtlety and very powerfully. When a man writes in the public eye and is considered a radical he is oftentimes misunderstood. Shaw never wanted to destroy religion or see it removed from the fabric of society. No, he wanted to affirm religion, that it is needed and available. Though hypocritical in many ways it should persist. Shaw would write letters to Tolstoy for his opinion on his writings. In a letter about Man and Superman Tolstoy replied to Shaw that it was obvious that Shaw recognized that God has definite aims. Shaw never wanted to proclaim himself an atheist because he made it apparent in his works that there was a God and this God had power.

Possibly the reason Shaw received a bad reputation from many critics was because of his attitudes, not solely his writings. In a statement made after the conclusion of one of his plays Shaw compared himself to Shakespeare and stated he was better than him. This arrogant socialist went up against one of the most loved authors in history and expected to exit with a clean reputation. Shaw hated Shakespeare; he hated everything he stood for and every way he wrote. Though there was always respect for the man, Shaw despised the man. He may have hated Shakespeare but he was no better, writes Harold Bloom. After reading Man and Superman and other Shavian writings that statement holds true. However, as stated earlier, Shakespeare was a master of romance and love on paper, but his works had little political substance. Shaw wrote for purpose not praise that is why he hated the use of allegory. The comedy Shaw used was dry social wit that might be offensive to some. Shaw felt that allegory took advantage of people's ignorance, where its only use was for a laugh and nothing else. How Shakespeare made allegory his own and part of his style lies at the root of the conflict between Shaw and Shakespeare.

Each one of Bernard Shaw's plays has a character with radical beliefs that are misread. Shaw did this to place himself in his works. There is always a shattered or an oppressor like Jack Tanner whose birth stems from his author. This is a style all Shaw's own yet it is not uncommon for an author to write himself into a play. It is certainly no surprise that the activists in his plays are the ones who bear a relation to Shaw. It should be stated though that Shaw did not hide the fact he used ideas of many extremists. In the foreword to Man and Superman Shaw writes that he owes the work to the men Bunyan, Hogarith and Turner. Never does he pretend to be original like many critics blast him for doing. It seems that Shaw writes his plays with influence from a triplet of contributors. Man and Superman is said to be a change in Shavian writing from his previous plays, such as Candida, that got their influence from Ibsen, Becque and Brieux. It is no wonder Shaw admired Marx after reading Man and Superman because one would believe Jack Tanner to embody the spirits of that man and the comparison can even be made that Tanner's The Revolutionist's Handbook is similar in theory to that of the Communist manifesto. There are many philosophers and radicals that Shaw got his ideas from, but he does not deserve scorn for it. This proves his willingness to read others views and adopt them as his own. The criticism still remains though. Shaw saw himself as an "advanced thinker" and this attitude is what turns off many people about him. The feeling that his views are better than others creates conflict in his work when read by someone of a more conservative stance. Eric Bentley writes that Shaw was more of an old fashion thinker, that his brand of an "advanced thinker" is closer to those advanced thinkers of Nietzsche's time not today's.

Hopefully the idea that Man and Superman was written for the purpose of sending a message is apparent. This play is highly political in nature for it holds a number of grievances with common institutions in England and the world. Coupled with the fact that Shaw brought the ideas of many ideological thinkers into this work there becomes an overwhelming feeling that this is more than a dry love story. The third act holds the "Don Juan in hell" scene that many refer to as a play in itself. This "play" holds more of the political commentary than found throughout the real play. It is here that Shaw writes how democracy will fail and that there needs to be a strong few to pick the country up after its demise. The institution of marriage that Shaw continually attacks in Man and Superman is in fact more than just an attack on that institution. It is an attack on what the government has created through that institution.

Marriage has become something forced upon the two due to a life force. Some critics feel this life force is a biological thinking; in fact many hold this belief. However, others feel the life force is a term used for the state. There are so many more benefits that await a couple who marry that it seems that the government is endorsing marriage and condemning bachelorhood. Like that of so many things in literature the symbolism is in the eyes of the beholder. In Man and Superman the political beliefs pressed upon the reader can be interpreted a number of ways. Some interpretations Shaw never intended to be thought, but others he is adamant about sharing. One thing he wanted in writing this and his other plays was to stir controversy. He wanted his work to be more than a simple one-tier comedy. Shaw loved to spark controversy because he had so many opposing views and that is what he strived for in writing one of his most famous works, Man and Superman.

Literature can be seen as a barometer of the times, it holds the views and opinions dear to each author. George Bernard Shaw was a writer who did not care what waves he made, because he wanted that turbulence. In his classic work Man and Superman Shaw used character interactions to voice his objections to common institutions. There is more to this play than a love story and a son's struggle for his father's approval. It is this approval that each character strives to achieve that introduces conflict into the plot. Shaw uses the conflict he created to further his cause and lay the blueprint for what he feels is needed in a superman to combat the doomed democracy.

Chapter 10

Bernard Shaw: The Critic

It appears a point of some mystery to the present writer that Bernard Shaw should have been so long unrecognised and almost in beggary. I should have thought his talent was of the ringing and arresting sort; such as even editors and publishers would have sense enough to seize. Yet it is quite certain that he almost starved in London for many years,writing occasional columns for an advertisement or words for a picture. And it is equally certain (it is proved by twenty anecdotes, but no one who knows Shaw needs any anecdotes to prove it) that in those days of desperation he again and again threw up chances and flung back good bargains which did not suit his unique and erratic sense of honour. The fame of having first offered Shaw to the public upon a platform worthy of him belongs, like many other public services, to Mr. William Archer.

I say it seems odd that such a writer should not be appreciated in a flash; but upon this point there is evidently a real difference of opinion, and it constitutes for me the strangest difficulty of the subject. I hear many people complain that Bernard Shaw deliberately mystifies them. I cannot imagine what they mean; it seems to me that he deliberately insults them. His language, especially on moral questions, is generally as straight and solid as that of a bargee and far less ornate and symbolic than that of a hansom-cabman. The prosperous English

Philistine complains that Mr. Shaw is making a fool of him. Whereas Mr. Shaw is not in the least making a fool of him; Mr. Shaw is, with laborious lucidity, calling him a fool. G. B. S. calls a landlord a thief; and the landlord, instead of denying or resenting it, says, "Ah, that fellow hides his meaning so cleverly that one can never make out what he means, it is all so fine spun and fantastical." G. B. S. calls a

statesman a liar to his face, and the statesman cries in a kind of ecstasy, "Ah, what quaint, intricate and half-tangled trains of thought!

Ah, what elusive and many-coloured mysteries of half-meaning!" I think it is always quite plain what Mr. Shaw means, even when he is joking, and it generally means that the people he is talking to ought to howl aloud for their sins. But the average representative of them undoubtedly treats the Shavian meaning as tricky and complex, when it is really direct and offensive. He always accuses Shaw of pulling his leg, at the exact moment when Shaw is pulling his nose.

This prompt and pungent style he learnt in the open, upon political tubs and platforms; and he is very legitimately proud of it. He boasts ofbeing a demagogue; "The cart and the trumpet for me," he says, withadmirable good sense. Everyone will remember the effective appearance of Cyrano de Bergerac in the first act of the fine play of that name; when instead of leaping in by any hackneyed door or window, he suddenly springs upon a chair above the crowd that has so far kept him invisible; "les bras croises, le feutre en bataille, la moustache herissee, le nez terrible." I will not go so far as to say that when Bernard Shaw sprang upon a chair or tub in Trafalgar Square he had the hat in battle, or even that he had the nose terrible. But just as we see Cyrano best when he thus leaps above the crowd, I think we may take this moment of Shaw stepping on his little platform to see him clearly as he then was, and even as he has largely not ceased to be. I, at least, have only known him in his middle age; yet I think I can see him, younger yet only a little more alert, with hair more red but with face yet paler, as he first stood up upon some cart or barrow in the tossing glare of the gas.

The first fact that one realises about Shaw (independent of all one has read and often contradicting it) is his voice. Primarily it is the voice of an Irishman, and then something of the voice of a musician. It possibly explains much of his career; a man may be permitted to say so many impudent things with so pleasant an intonation. But the voice is not only Irish and agreeable, it is also frank and as it were inviting conference. This goes with a style and gesture which can only be described as at once very casual and very emphatic. He assumes that bodily supremacy which goes with oratory, but he assumes it with almost ostentatious carelessness; he throws back the head, but loosely and laughingly. He is at once swaggering and yet shrugging his shoulders, as if to drop from them the mantle of the orator which he has confidently assumed. Lastly, no man ever used voice or gesture better for the purpose of expressing certainty; no man can say "I tell Mr. Jones he is totally wrong" with more air of unforced and even casual conviction. This particular play of feature or pitch of voice, at once didactic and yet not uncomrade-like, must be counted a very important fact, especially in connection with the period when that voice was first heard. It must be remembered that Shaw emerged as a wit in a sort of secondary age of wits; one of those stale interludes of prematurely old young men, which separate the serious epochs of history. Oscar Wilde was its god; but he was somewhat more mystical, not to say monstrous, than the average of its dried and decorous impudence. The two survivals of that time, as far as I know, are Mr. Max Beerbohm and Mr. Graham Robertson; two most charming people; but the air they had to live in was the devil. One of its notes was an artificial reticence of speech, which waited till it could plant the perfect epigram. Its typical products were far too conceited to lay down the law. Now when people heard that Bernard Shaw was witty, as he most certainly was, when they heard his mots repeated like those of Whistler or Wilde, when they heard things like "the Seven deadly Virtues" or "Who was Hall Caine?" they expected another of these silent sarcastic dandies who went about with one epigram, patient and poisonous, like a bee with his one sting. And when they saw and heard the new humorist they found no fixed sneer, no frock coat, no green carnation, no silent Savoy Restaurant good manners, no fear of looking a fool, no particular notion of looking a gentleman. They found a talkative Irishman with a kind voice and a brown coat; open gestures and an evident desire to make people really agree with him. He had his own kind of affectations no doubt, and his own kind of tricks of debate; but he broke, and, thank God, forever the spell of the little man with the single eye glass who had frozen both faith and fun at so many tea-tables. Shaw's humane voice and hearty manner were so obviously more the things of a great man than the hard, gem-like brilliancy of Wilde or the careful ill-temper of Whistler. He brought in a breezier sort of insolence; the single eye-glass fled before the single eye.

Added to the effect of the amiable dogmatic voice and lean, loose swaggering figure, is that of the face with which so many caricaturists have fantastically delighted themselves, the Mephistophelean face with the fierce tufted eyebrows and forked red beard. Yet those caricaturists in their natural delight in coming upon so striking a face, have somewhat misrepresented it, making it merely Satanic; whereas its actual expression has quite as much benevolence as mockery. By this time his costume has become a part of his personality; one has come to think of the reddish brown Jaeger suit as if it were a sort of reddish brown fur, and were, like the hair and eyebrows, a part of the animal; yet there are those who claim to remember a Bernard Shaw of yet more awful aspect before Jaeger came to his assistance; a Bernard Shaw in a dilapidated frock-coat and some sort of straw hat. I can hardly believe it; the man is so much of a piece, and must always have dressed appropriately. In any case his brown woollen clothes, at once artistic and hygienic, completed the appeal for which he stood; which might be defined as an eccentric healthy-mindedness. But something of the vagueness and equivocation of his first fame is probably due to the different functions which he performed in the contemporary world of art.

He began by writing novels. They are not much read, and indeed not imperatively worth reading, with the one exception of the crude and magnificent Cashel Byron's Profession. Mr. William Archer, in the course of his kindly efforts on behalf of his young Irish friend, sent this book to Samoa, for the opinion of the most elvish and yet efficient of modern critics. Stevenson summed up much of Shaw even from that fragment when he spoke of a romantic griffin roaring with laughter at the nature of his own quest. He also added the not wholly unjustified postscript: "I say, Archer,—my God, what women!"

The fiction was largely dropped; but when he began work he felt his way by the avenues of three arts. He was an art critic, a dramatic critic, and a musical critic; and in all three, it need hardly be said, he fought for the newest style and the most revolutionary school. He wrote on all these as he would have written on anything; but it was, I fancy, about the music that he cared most.

It may often be remarked that mathematicians love and understand music more than they love or understand poetry. Bernard Shaw is in much the same condition; indeed, in attempting to do justice to Shakespeare's poetry, he always calls it "word music." It is not difficult to explain this special attachment of the mere logician to music. The logician, like every other man on earth, must have sentiment and romance in his existence; in every man's life, indeed, which can be called a life at all, sentiment is the most solid thing. But if the extreme logician turns for his emotions to poetry, he is exasperated and bewildered by discovering that the words of his own trade are used in an entirely different meaning. He conceives that he understands the word "visible," and then finds Milton applying it to darkness, in which nothing is visible. He supposes that he understands the word "hide," and then finds

Shelley talking of a poet hidden in the light. He has reason to believe that he understands the common word "hung"; and then William Shakespeare, Esquire, of Stratford-on-Avon, gravely assures him that the tops of the tall sea waves were hung with deafening clamours on the slippery clouds. That is why the common arithmetician prefers music to poetry. Words are his scientific instruments. It irritates him that they should be anyone else's musical instruments. He is willing to see men juggling, but not men juggling with his own private tools and possessions—his terms. It is then that he turns with an utter relief to music. Here are all the same fascination and inspiration, all the same purity and plunging force as in poetry; but not requiring any verbal confession that light conceals things or that darkness can be seen in the dark. Music is mere beauty; it is beauty in the abstract, beauty in solution. It is a shapeless and liquid element of beauty, in which a man may really float, not indeed affirming the truth, but not denying it.

Bernard Shaw, as I have already said, is infinitely far above all such mere mathematicians and pedantic reasoners; still his feeling is partly the same. He adores music because it cannot deal with romantic terms either in their right or their wrong sense. Music can be romantic without reminding him of Shakespeare and Walter Scott, with whom he has had personal quarrels. Music can be Catholic without reminding him verbally of the Catholic Church, which he has never seen, and is sure he does not like. Bernard Shaw can agree with Wagner, the musician, because he speaks without words; if it had been Wagner the man he would certainly have had words with him. Therefore I would suggest that Shaw's love of music (which is so fundamental that it must be mentioned early, if not first, in his story) may itself be considered in the first case as the imaginative safety-valve of the rationalistic Irishman.

This much may be said conjecturally over the present signature; but more must not be said. Bernard Shaw understands music so much better than I do that it is just possible that he is, in that tongue and atmosphere, all that he is not elsewhere. While he is writing with a pen I know his limitations as much as I admire his genius; and I know it is true to say that he does not appreciate romance. But while he is playing on the piano he may be cocking a feather, drawing a sword or draining a flagon for all I know. While he is speaking I am sure that there are some things he does not understand. But while he is listening (at the Queen's Hall) he may understand everything, including God and me. Upon this part of him I am a reverent agnostic; it is well to have some such dark continent in the character of a man of whom one writes. It preserves two very important things—modesty in the biographer and mystery in the biography.

For the purpose of our present generalisation it is only

necessary to say that Shaw, as a musical critic, summed himself up as "The Perfect Wagnerite"; he threw himself into subtle and yet trenchant eulogy of that revolutionary voice in music. It was the same with the other arts. As he was a Perfect Wagnerite in music, so he was a Perfect Whistlerite in painting; so above all he was a Perfect Ibsenite in drama. And with this we enter that part of his career with which this book is more specially concerned. When Mr. William Archer got him established as dramatic critic of the Saturday Review, he became for the first time "a star of the stage"; a shooting star and sometimes a destroying comet. On the day of that appointment opened one of the very few exhilarating and honest battles that broke the silence of the slow and cynical collapse of the nineteenth century. Bernard Shaw the demagogue had got his cart and his trumpet; and was resolved to make them like the car of destiny and the trumpet of judgment. He had not the servility of the ordinary rebel, who is content to go on rebelling against kings and priests, because such rebellion is as old and as established as any priests or kings. He cast about him for something to attack which was not merely powerful or placid, but was unattacked. After a little quite sincere reflection, he found it. He would not be content to be a common atheist; he wished to blaspheme something in which even atheists believed. He was not satisfied with being revolutionary; there were so many revolutionists. He wanted to pick out some prominent institution which had been irrationally and instinctively accepted by the most violent and profane; something of which Mr. Foote would speak as respectfully on the front page of the Freethinker as Mr. St. Loe Strachey on the front page of the Spectator. He found the thing; he found the great unassailed English institution—Shakespeare.

But Shaw's attack on Shakespeare, though exaggerated for the fun of the thing, was not by any means the mere folly or firework paradox that has been supposed. He meant what he said; what was called his levity was merely the laughter of a man who enjoyed saying what he meant—an occupation which is indeed one of the greatest larks in life. Moreover, it can honestly be said that Shaw did good by shaking the mere idolatry of Him of Avon. That idolatry was bad for England; it buttressed our perilous self-complacency by making us think that we alone had, not merely a great poet, but the one poet above criticism. It was bad for literature; it made a minute model out of work that was really a hasty and faulty masterpiece. And it was bad for religion and morals that there should be so huge a terrestrial idol, that we should put such utter and unreasoning trust in any child of man. It is true that it was largely through Shaw's own defects that he beheld the defects of Shakespeare. But it needed someone equally prosaic to resist what was perilous in the charm of such poetry; it may not be altogether a mistake to send a deaf man to destroy the rock of the sirens.

This attitude of Shaw illustrates of course all three of the divisions or aspects to which the reader's attention has been drawn. It was partly the attitude of the Irishman objecting to the Englishman turning his mere artistic taste into a religion; especially when it was a taste merely taught him by his aunts and uncles. In Shaw's opinion (one might say) the English do not really enjoy Shakespeare or even admire Shakespeare; one can only say, in the strong colloquialism, that they swear by Shakespeare. He is a mere god; a thing to be invoked. And Shaw's whole business was to set up the things which were to be sworn by as things to be sworn at. It was partly again the revolutionist in pursuit of pure novelty, hating primarily the oppression of the past, almost hating history itself. For Bernard Shaw the prophets were to be stoned after, and not before, men had built their sepulchres. There was a Yankee smartness in the man which was irritated at the idea of being dominated by a person dead for three hundred years; like Mark Twain, he wanted a fresher corpse.

These two motives there were, but they were small compared with the other. It was the third part of him, the Puritan, that was really at war with Shakespeare. He denounced that playwright almost exactly as any contemporary Puritan coming out of a conventicle in a steeple-crowned hat and stiff bands might have denounced the playwright coming out of the stage door of the old Globe Theatre. This is not a mere fancy; it is philosophically true. A legend has run round the newspapers that Bernard Shaw offered himself as a better writer than Shakespeare. This is false and quite unjust; Bernard Shaw never said anything of the kind. The writer whom he did say was better than Shakespeare was not himself, but Bunyan. And he justified it by attributing to Bunyan a virile acceptance of life as a high and harsh adventure, while in Shakespeare he saw nothing but profligate pessimism, the vanitas vanitatum of a disappointed voluptuary. According to this view Shakespeare was always saying, "Out, out, brief candle," because his was only a ballroom candle; while Bunyan was seeking to light such a candle as by God's grace should never be put out.

It is odd that Bernard Shaw's chief error or insensibility should have been the instrument of his noblest affirmation. The denunciation of Shakespeare was a mere misunderstanding. But the denunciation of Shakespeare's pessimism was the most splendidly understanding of all his utterances. This is the greatest thing in Shaw, a serious optimism—even a tragic optimism. Life is a thing too glorious to be enjoyed. To be is an exacting and exhausting business; the trumpet though inspiring is terrible. Nothing that he ever wrote is so noble as his simple reference to the sturdy man who stepped up to the Keeper of the Book of Life and said, "Put down my name, Sir." It is true that Shaw called this heroic philosophy by wrong names and buttressed it with false metaphysics; that was the weakness of the age. The temporary decline of theology had involved the neglect of philosophy and all fine thinking; and Bernard Shaw had to find shaky justifications in Schopenhauer for the sons of God shouting for joy. He called it the Will to Live—a phrase invented by Prussian professors who would like to exist, but can't. Afterwards he asked people to worship the Life-Force; as if one could worship a hyphen. But though he covered it with crude new names (which are now fortunately crumbling everywhere like bad mortar) he was on the side of the good old cause; the oldest and the best of all causes, the cause of creation against destruction, the cause of yes against no, the cause of the seed against the stony earth and the star against the abyss.

His misunderstanding of Shakespeare arose largely from the fact that he is a Puritan, while Shakespeare was spiritually a Catholic. The former is always screwing himself up to see truth; the latter is often content that truth is there. The Puritan is only strong enough to stiffen; the Catholic is strong enough to relax. Shaw, I think, has entirely misunderstood the pessimistic passages of Shakespeare. They are flying moods which a man with a fixed faith can afford to entertain. That all is vanity, that life is dust and love is ashes, these are frivolities, these are jokes that a Catholic can afford to utter. He knows well enough that there is a life that is not dust and a love that is not ashes. But just as he may let himself go more than the Puritan in the matter of enjoyment, so he may let himself go more than the Puritan in the matter of melancholy. The sad exuberances of Hamlet are merely like the glad exuberances of Falstaff. This is not conjecture; it is the text of Shakespeare. In the very act of uttering his pessimism, Hamlet admits that it is a mood and not the truth. Heaven is a heavenly thing, only to him it seems a foul congregation of vapours. Man is the paragon of animals, only to him he seems a quintessence of dust. Hamlet is quite the reverse of a sceptic. He is a man whose strong intellect believes much more than his weak temperament can make vivid to him. But this power of knowing a thing without feeling it, this power of believing a thing without experiencing it, this is an old Catholic complexity, and the Puritan has never understood it. Shakespeare confesses his moods (mostly by the mouths of villains and failures), but he never sets up his moods against his mind. His cry of vanitas vanitatum is itself only a harmless vanity. Readers may not agree with my calling him Catholic with a big C; but they will hardly complain of my calling him catholic with a small one. And that is here the principal point.

Shakespeare was not in any sense a pessimist; he was, if anything, an optimist so universal as to be able to enjoy even pessimism. And this is exactly where he differs from the

Puritan. The true Puritan is not squeamish: the true Puritan is free to say "Damn it!" But the Catholic Elizabethan was free (on passing provocation) to say "Damn it all!" It need hardly be explained that Bernard Shaw added to his negative case of a dramatist to be depreciated a corresponding affirmative case of a dramatist to be exalted and advanced. He was not content with so remote a comparison as that between Shakespeare and Bunyan. In his vivacious weekly articles in the Saturday Review, the real comparison upon which everything turned was the comparison between Shakespeare and Ibsen. He early threw himself with all possible eagerness into the public disputes about the great Scandinavian; and though there was no doubt whatever about which side he supported, there was much that was individual in the line he took. It is not our business here to explore that extinct volcano. You may say that anti-Ibsenism is dead, or you may say that Ibsen is dead; in any case, that controversy is dead, and death, as the Roman poet says, can alone confess of what small atoms we are made. The opponents of Ibsen largely exhibited the permanent qualities of the populace; that is, their instincts were right and their reasons wrong.

They made the complete controversial mistake of calling Ibsen a pessimist; whereas, indeed, his chief weakness is a rather childish confidence in mere nature and freedom, and a blindness (either of experience or of culture) in the matter of original sin. In this sense Ibsen is not so much a pessimist as a highly crude kind of optimist.

Nevertheless the man in the street was right in his fundamental instinct, as he always is. Ibsen, in his pale northern style, is an optimist; but for all that he is a depressing person. The optimism of Ibsen is less comforting than the pessimism of Dante; just as a Norwegian sunrise, however splendid, is colder than a southern night. But on the side of those who fought for Ibsen there was also a disagreement, and perhaps also a mistake. The vague army of "the advanced" (an army which advances in all directions) were united in feeling that they ought to be the friends of Ibsen because he also was advancing somewhere somehow. But they were also seriously impressed by Flaubert, by Oscar Wilde and all the rest who told them that a work of art was in another universe from ethics and social good. Therefore many, I think most, of the Ibsenites praised the Ibsen plays merely as choses vues, aesthetic affirmations of what can be without any reference to what ought to be. Mr. William Archer himself inclined to this view, though his strong sagacity kept him in a haze of healthy doubt on the subject. Mr. Walkley certainly took this view. But this view Mr. George Bernard Shaw abruptly and violently refused to take.

With the full Puritan combination of passion and precision he informed everybody that Ibsen was not artistic, but moral; that his dramas were didactic, that all great art was didactic, that Ibsen was strongly on the side of some of his characters and strongly against others, that there was preaching and public spirit in the work of good dramatists; and that if this were not so, dramatists and all other artists would be mere panders of intellectual debauchery, to be locked up as the Puritans locked up the stage players. No one can understand Bernard Shaw who does not give full value to this early revolt of his on behalf of ethics against the ruling school of l'art pour l'art. It is interesting because it is connected with other ambitions in the man, especially with that which has made him somewhat vainer of being a Parish Councillor than of being one of the most popular dramatists in Europe. But its chief interest is again to be referred to our stratification of the psychology; it is the lover of true things rebelling for once against merely new things; it is the Puritan suddenly refusing to be the mere Progressive.

But this attitude obviously laid on the ethical lover of Ibsen a not inconsiderable obligation. If the new drama had an ethical purpose, what was it? and if Ibsen was a moral teacher, what the deuce was he teaching? Answers to this question, answers of manifold brilliancy and promise, were scattered through all the dramatic criticisms of those years on the Saturday Review. But even Bernard Shaw grew tired after a time of discussing Ibsen only in connection with the current pantomime or the latest musical comedy. It was felt that so much sincerity and fertility of explanation justified a concentrated attack; and in 1891 appeared the brilliant book called The Quintessence of Ibsenism, which some have declared to be merely the quintessence of Shaw. However this may be, it was in fact and profession the quintessence of Shaw's theory of the morality or propaganda of Ibsen.

The book itself is much longer than the book that I am writing; and as is only right in so spirited an apologist, every paragraph is provocative. I could write an essay on every sentence which I accept and three essays on every sentence which I deny. Bernard Shaw himself is a master of compression; he can put a conception more compactly than any other man alive. It is therefore rather difficult to compress his compression; one feels as if one were trying to extract a beef essence from Bovril. But the shortest form in which I can state the idea of The Quintessence of Ibsenism is that it is the idea of distrusting ideals, which are universal, in comparison with facts, which are miscellaneous.

The man whom he attacks throughout he calls "The Idealist"; that is the man who permits himself to be mainly moved by a moral generalisation. "Actions," he says, "are to be judged by their effect on happiness, and not by their conformity to any ideal." As we have already seen, there is a certain inconsistency here; for while Shaw had always chucked all ideals overboard the one he had chucked first was the ideal of happiness. Passing this however for the present, we may mark the above as the most satisfying summary. If I tell a lie I am not to blame myself for having violated the ideal of truth, but only for having perhaps got myself into a mess and made things worse than they were before. If I have broken my word I need not feel (as my fathers did) that I have broken something inside of me, as one who breaks a blood vessel. It all depends on whether I have broken up something outside me; as one who breaks up an evening party. If I shoot my father the only question is whether I have made him happy. I must not admit the idealistic conception that the mere shooting of my father might possibly make me unhappy. We are to judge of every individual case as it arises, apparently without any social summary or moral ready-reckoner at all. "The Golden Rule is that there is no Golden Rule." We must not say that it is right to keep promises, but that it may be right to keep this promise. Essentially it is anarchy; nor is it very easy to see how a state could be very comfortable which was Socialist in all its public morality and Anarchist in all its private. But if it is anarchy, it is anarchy without any of the abandon and exuberance of anarchy. It is a worried and conscientious anarchy; an anarchy of painful delicacy and even caution. For it refuses to trust in traditional experiments or plainly trodden tracks; every case must be considered anew from the beginning, and yet considered with the most wide-eyed care for human welfare; every man must act as if he were the first man made. Briefly, we must always be worrying about what is best for our children, and we must not take one hint or rule of thumb from our fathers. Some think that this anarchism would make a man tread down mighty cities in his madness. I think it would make a man walk down the street as if he were walking on egg-shells. I do not think this experiment in opportunism would end in frantic license; I think it would end in frozen timidity.

If a man was forbidden to solve moral problems by moral science or the help of mankind, his course would be quite easy—he would not solve the problems. The world instead of being a knot so tangled as to need unravelling, would simply become a piece of clockwork too complicated to be touched. I cannot think that this untutored worry was what Ibsen meant; I have my doubts as to whether it was what Shaw meant; but I do not think that it can be substantially doubted that it was what he said.

In any case it can be asserted that the general aim of the work was to exalt the immediate conclusions of practice against the general conclusions of theory. Shaw objected to the solution of every problem in a play being by its nature a general solution, applicable to all other such problems. He disliked the entrance of a universal justice at the end of the last act; treading down all the personal ultimatums and all the varied certainties of men. He disliked the god from the machine—because he was from a machine. But even without the machine he tended to dislike the god; because a god is more general than a man. His enemies have accused Shaw of being anti-domestic, a shaker of the roof-tree. But in this sense Shaw may be called almost madly domestic. He wishes each private problem to be settled in private, without reference to sociological ethics. And the only objection to this kind of gigantic casuistry is that the theatre is really too small to discuss it. It would not be fair to play David and Goliath on a stage too small to admit Goliath. And it is not fair to discuss private morality on a stage too small to admit the enormous presence of public morality; that character which has not appeared in a play since the Middle Ages; whose name is Everyman and whose honour we have all in our keeping.

Chapter 11

Bernard Shaw: The Dramatist

No one who was alive at the time and interested in such matters will ever forget the first acting of Arms and the Man. It was applauded by that indescribable element in all of us which rejoices to see the genuine thing prevail against the plausible; that element which rejoices that even its enemies are alive. Apart from the problems raised in the play, the very form of it was an attractive and forcible innovation. Classic plays which were wholly heroic, comic plays which were wholly and even heartlessly ironical, were common enough. Commonest of all in this particular time was the play that began playfully, with plenty of comic business, and was gradually sobered by sentiment until it ended on a note of romance or even of pathos. A commonplace little officer, the butt of the mess, becomes by the last act as high and hopeless a lover as Dante. Or a vulgar and violent pork-butcher remembers his own youth before the curtain goes down. The first thing that Bernard Shaw did when he stepped before the footlights was to reverse this process. He resolved to build a play not on pathos, but on bathos. The officer should be heroic first and then everyone should laugh at him; the curtain should go up on a man remembering his youth, and he should only reveal himself as a violent pork-butcher when someone interrupted him with an order for pork. This merely technical originality is indicated in the very title of the play. The Arma Virumque of Virgil is a mounting and ascending phrase, the man is more than his weapons. The Latin line suggests a superb procession which should bring on to the stage the brazen and resounding armour, the shield and shattering axe, but end with the hero himself, taller and more terrible because unarmed.

The technical effect of Shaw's scheme is like the same scene, in which a crowd should carry even more gigantic shapes of shield and helmet, but when the horns and howls were at their highest, should end with the figure of Little Tich. The name itself is meant to be a bathos; arms—and the man. It is well to begin with the superficial; and this is the superficial effectiveness of Shaw; the brilliancy of bathos. But of course the vitality and value of his plays does not lie merely in this; any more than the value of Swinburne lies in alliteration or the value of Hood in puns. This is not his message; but it is his method; it is his style. The first taste we had of it was in this play of Arms and the Man; but even at the very first it was evident that there was much more in the play than that. Among other things there was one thing not unimportant; there was savage sincerity. Indeed, only a ferociously sincere person can produce such effective flippancies on a matter like war; just as only a strong man could juggle with cannon balls. It is all very well to use the word "fool" as synonymous with "jester"; but daily experience shows that it is generally the solemn and silent man who is the fool. It is all very well to accuse Mr. Shaw of standing on his head; but if you stand on your head you must have a hard and solid head to stand on. In Arms and the Man the bathos of form was strictly the incarnation of a strong satire in the idea. The play opens in an atmosphere of military melodrama; the dashing officer of cavalry going off to death in an attitude, the lovely heroine left in tearful rapture; the brass band, the noise of guns and the red fire. Into all this enters Bluntschli, the little sturdy crop-haired Swiss professional soldier, a man without a country but with a trade. He tells the army-adoring heroine frankly that she is a humbug; and she, after a moment's reflection, appears to agree with him. The play is like nearly all Shaw's plays, the dialogue of a conversion. By the end of it the young lady has lost all her military illusions and admires this mercenary soldier not because he faces guns, but because he faces facts.

This was a fitting entrance for Shaw to his didactic drama;

because the commonplace courage which he respects in Bluntschli was the one virtue which he was destined to praise throughout. We can best see how the play symbolises and summarises Bernard Shaw if we compare it with some other attack by modern humanitarians upon war. Shaw has many of the actual opinions of Tolstoy. Like Tolstoy he tells men, with coarse innocence, that romantic war is only butchery and that romantic love is only lust.

But Tolstoy objects to these things because they are real; he really wishes to abolish them. Shaw only objects to them in so far as they are ideal; that is in so far as they are idealised. Shaw objects not so much to war as to the attractiveness of war. He does not so much dislike love as the love of love. Before the temple of Mars, Tolstoy stands and thunders, "There shall be no wars"; Bernard Shaw merely murmurs, "Wars if you must; but for God's sake, not war songs." Before the temple of Venus, Tolstoy cries terribly, "Come out of it!"; Shaw is quite content to say, "Do not be taken in by it." Tolstoy seems really to propose that high passion and patriotic valour should be destroyed. Shaw is more moderate; and only asks that they should be desecrated. Upon this note, both about sex and conflict, he was destined to dwell through much of his work with the most wonderful variations of witty adventure and intellectual surprise. It may be doubted perhaps whether this realism in love and war is quite so sensible as it looks. Securus judicat orbis terrarum; the world is wiser than the moderns. The world has kept sentimentalities simply because they are the most practical things in the world. They alone make men do things. The world does not encourage a quite rational lover, simply because a perfectly rational lover would never get married. The world does not encourage a perfectly rational army, because a perfectly rational army would run away. The brain of Bernard Shaw was like a wedge in the literal sense. Its sharpest end was always in front; and it split our society from end to end the moment it had entrance at all. As I have said he was long unheard of; but he had not the tragedy of many authors, who were heard of long before they were heard. When you had read any Shaw you read all Shaw. When you had seen one of his plays you waited for more. And when he brought them out in volume form, you did what is repugnant to any literary man—you bought a book.

The dramatic volume with which Shaw dazzled the public was called, Plays, Pleasant and Unpleasant. I think the most striking and typical thing about it was that he did not know very clearly which plays were unpleasant and which were pleasant. "Pleasant" is a word which is almost unmeaning to Bernard Shaw. Except, as I suppose, in music (where I cannot follow him), relish and receptivity are things that simply do not appear. He has the best of tongues and the worst of palates. With the possible exception of Mrs. Warren's Profession (which was at least unpleasant in the sense of being forbidden) I can see no particular reason why any of the seven plays should be held specially to please or displease. First in fame and contemporary importance came the reprint of Arms and the Man, of which I have already spoken. Over all the rest towered unquestionably the two figures of Mrs. Warren and of Candida.

They were neither of them pleasant, except as all good art is pleasant. They were neither of them really unpleasant except as all truth is unpleasant. But they did represent the author's normal preference and his principal fear; and those two sculptured giantesses largely upheld his fame. I fancy that the author rather dislikes Candida because it is so generally liked. I give my own feeling for what it is worth (a foolish phrase), but I think that there were only two moments when this powerful writer was truly, in the ancient and popular sense, inspired; that is, breathing from a bigger self and telling more truth than he knew. One is that scene in a later play where after the secrets and revenges of Egypt have rioted and rotted all round him, the colossal sanity of Caesar is suddenly acclaimed with swords. The other is that great last scene in Candida where the wife, stung into final speech, declared her purpose of remaining with the strong man because he is the weak man. The wife is asked to decide between two men, one a strenuous self-confident popular preacher, her husband, the other a wild and weak young poet, logically futile and physically timid, her lover; and she chooses the former because he has more weakness and more need of her. Even among the plain and ringing paradoxes of the Shaw play this is one of the best reversals or turnovers ever effected. A paradoxical writer like Bernard Shaw is perpetually and tiresomely told that he stands on his head. But all romance and all religion consist in making the whole universe stand on its head. That reversal is the whole idea of virtue; that the last shall be first and the first last. Considered as a pure piece of Shaw therefore, the thing is of the best. But it is also something much better than Shaw. The writer touches certain realities commonly outside his scope; especially the reality of the normal wife's attitude to the normal husband, an attitude which is not romantic but which is yet quite quixotic; which is insanely unselfish and yet quite cynically clear-sighted. It involves human sacrifice without in the least involving idolatry.

The truth is that in this place Bernard Shaw comes within an inch of expressing something that is not properly expressed anywhere else; the idea of marriage. Marriage is not a mere chain upon love as the anarchists say; nor is it a mere crown upon love as the sentimentalists say. Marriage is a fact, an actual human relation like that of motherhood which has certain human habits and loyalties, except in a few monstrous cases where it is turned to torture by special insanity and sin. A marriage is neither an ecstasy nor a slavery; it is a commonwealth; it is a separate working and fighting thing like a nation. Kings and diplomatists talk of "forming alliances" when they make weddings; but indeed every wedding is primarily an alliance. The family is a fact even when it is not an agreeable fact, and a man is part of his wife even when he wishes he wasn't. The twain are one flesh—yes, even when they are not one spirit. Man is duplex. Man is a quadruped. Of this ancient and essential relation there are certain emotional results, which are subtle, like all the growths of nature. And one of them is the attitude of the wife to the husband, whom she regards at once as the strongest and most helpless of human figures. She regards him in some strange fashion at once as a warrior who must make his way and as an infant who is sure to lose his way. The man has emotions which exactly correspond; sometimes looking down at his wife and sometimes up at her; for marriage is like a splendid game of see-saw. Whatever else it is, it is not comradeship. This living, ancestral bond (not of love or fear, but strictly of marriage) has been twice expressed splendidly in literature. The man's incurable sense of the mother in his lawful wife was uttered by Browning in one of his two or three truly shattering lines of genius, when he makes the execrable Guido fall back finally upon the fact of marriage and the wife whom he has trodden like mire:

"Christ! Maria! God,
Pompilia, will you let them murder me?"

And the woman's witness to the same fact has been best expressed by Bernard Shaw in this great scene where she remains with the great stalwart successful public man because he is really too little to run alone.

There are one or two errors in the play; and they are all due to the primary error of despising the mental attitude of romance, which is the only key to real human conduct. For instance, the love making of the young poet is all wrong. He is supposed to be a romantic and amorous boy; and therefore the dramatist tries to make him talk turgidly, about seeking for "an archangel with purple wings" who shall be worthy of his lady. But a lad in love would never talk in this mock heroic style; there is no period at which the young male is more sensitive and serious and afraid of looking a fool. This is a blunder; but there is another much bigger and blacker. It is completely and disastrously false to the whole nature of falling in love to make the young Eugene complain of the cruelty which makes Candida defile her fair hands with domestic duties.

No boy in love with a beautiful woman would ever feel disgusted when she peeled potatoes or trimmed lamps. He would like her to be domestic. He would simply feel that the potatoes had become poetical and the lamps gained an extra light. This may be irrational; but we are not talking of rationality, but of the psychology of first love. It may be very unfair to women that the toil and triviality of potato peeling should be seen through a glamour of romance; but the glamour is quite as certain a fact as the potatoes. It may be a bad thing in sociology that men should deify domesticity in girls as something dainty and magical; but all men do. Personally I do not think it a bad thing at all; but that is another argument. The argument here is that Bernard Shaw, in aiming at mere realism, makes a big mistake in reality. Misled by his great heresy of looking at emotions from the outside, he makes Eugene a cold-blooded prig at the very moment when he is trying, for his own dramatic purposes, to make him a hot-blooded lover. He makes the young lover an idealistic theoriser about the very things about which he really would have been a sort of mystical materialist. Here the romantic Irishman is much more right than the very rational one; and there is far more truth to life as it is in Lover's couplet—

"*And envied the chicken:* That Peggy was pickin'." than in Eugene's solemn, aesthetic protest against the potato-skins and the lamp-oil. For dramatic purposes, G. B. S., even if he despises romance, ought to comprehend it. But then, if once he comprehended romance, he would not despise it. The series contained, besides its more substantial work, tragic and comic, a comparative frivolity called The Man of Destiny. It is a little comedy about Napoleon, and is chiefly interesting as a foreshadowing of his after sketches of heroes and strong men; it is a kind of parody of Caesar and Cleopatra before it was written. In this connection the mere title of this Napoleonic play is of interest. All Shaw's generation and school of thought remembered Napoleon only by his late and corrupt title of "The Man of Destiny," a title only given to him when he was already fat and tired and destined to exile. They forgot that through all the really thrilling and creative part of his career he was not the man of destiny, but the man who defied destiny. Shaw's sketch is extraordinarily clever; but it is tinged with this unmilitary notion of an inevitable conquest; and this we must remember when we come to those larger canvases on which he painted his more serious heroes. As for the play, it is packed with good things, of which the last is perhaps the best. The long duologue between Bonaparte and the Irish lady ends with the General declaring that he will only be beaten when he meets an English army under an Irish general. It has always been one of Shaw's paradoxes that the English mind has the force to fulfil orders, while the Irish mind has the intelligence to give them, and it is among those of his paradoxes which contain a certain truth. A far more important play is The Philanderer, an ironic comedy which is full of fine strokes and real satire; it is more especially the vehicle of some of Shaw's best satire upon physical science. Nothing could be cleverer than the picture of the young, strenuous doctor, in the utter innocence of his professional ambition, who has discovered a new disease, and is delighted when he finds people suffering from it and cast down to despair when he finds that it does not exist. The point is worth a pause, because it is a good, short way of stating Shaw's attitude, right or wrong, upon the whole of formal morality. What he dislikes in young Doctor Paramore is that he has interposed a secondary and false conscience between himself and the facts. When his disease is disproved, instead of seeing the escape of a human being who thought he was going to die of it, Paramore sees the downfall of a kind of flag or cause. This is the whole contention of The Quintessence of Ibsenism, put better than the book puts it; it is a really sharp exposition of the dangers of "idealism," the sacrifice of people to principles, and Shaw is even wiser in his suggestion that this excessive idealism exists nowhere so strongly as in the world of physical science. He shows that the scientist tends to be more concerned about the sickness than about the sick man; but it was certainly in his mind to suggest here also that the idealist is more concerned about the sin than about the sinner.

This business of Dr. Paramore's disease while it is the most farcical thing in the play is also the most philosophic and important. The rest of the figures, including the Philanderer himself, are in the full sense of those blasting and obliterating words "funny without being vulgar," that is, funny without being of any importance to the masses of men. It is a play about a dashing and advanced "Ibsen Club," and the squabble between the young Ibsenites and the old people who are not yet up to Ibsen. It would be hard to find a stronger example of Shaw's only essential error, modernity—which means the seeking for truth in terms of time. Only a few years have passed and already almost half the wit of that wonderful play is wasted, because it all turns on the newness of a fashion that is no longer new. Doubtless many people still think the Ibsen drama a great thing, like the French classical drama. But going to "The Philanderer" is like going among periwigs and rapiers and hearing that the young men are now all for Racine. What makes such work sound unreal is not the praise of Ibsen, but the praise of the novelty of Ibsen. Any advantage that Bernard Shaw had over Colonel Craven I have over Bernard Shaw; we who happen to be born last have the meaningless and paltry triumph in that meaningless and paltry war. We are the superiors by that silliest and most snobbish of all superiorities, the mere aristocracy of time. All works must become thus old and insipid which have ever tried to be "modern," which have consented to smell of time rather than of eternity. Only those who have stooped to be in advance of their time will ever find themselves behind it. But it is irritating to think what diamonds, what dazzling silver of Shavian wit has been sunk in such an out-of-date warship. In The Philanderer there are five hundred excellent and about five magnificent things. The rattle of repartees between the doctor and the soldier about the humanity of their two trades is admirable. Or again, when the colonel tells Chartaris that "in his young days" he would have no more behaved like Chartaris than he would have cheated at cards. After a pause Chartaris says, "You're getting old, Craven, and you make a virtue of it as usual." And there is an altitude of aerial tragedy in the words of Grace, who has refused the man she loves, to Julia, who is marrying the man she doesn't, "This is what they call a happy ending—these men."

There is an acrid taste in The Philanderer; and certainly he might be considered a super-sensitive person who should find anything acrid in You Never Can Tell. This play is the nearest approach to frank and objectless exuberance in the whole of Shaw's work. Punch, with wisdom as well as wit, said that it might well be called not "You Never Can Tell" but "You Never Can be Shaw." And yet if anyone will read this blazing farce and then after it any of the romantic farces, such as Pickwick or even The Wrong Box, I do not think he will be disposed to erase or even to modify what I said at the beginning about the ingrained grimness and even inhumanity of Shaw's art. To take but one test: love, in an "extravaganza," may be light love or love in idleness, but it should be hearty and happy love if it is to add to the general hilarity. Such are the ludicrous but lucky love affairs of the sportsman Winkle and the Maestro Jimson. In Gloria's collapse before her bullying lover there is something at once cold and unclean; it calls up all the modern supermen with their cruel and fishy eyes. Such farces should begin in a friendly air, in a tavern. There is something very symbolic of Shaw in the fact that his farce begins in a dentist's.

The only one out of this brilliant batch of plays in which I think that the method adopted really fails, is the one called Widower's Houses. The best touch of Shaw is simply in the title. The simple substitution of widowers for widows contains almost the whole bitter and yet boisterous protest of Shaw; all his preference for undignified fact over dignified phrase; all his dislike of those subtle trends of sex or mystery which swing the logician off the straight line. We can imagine him crying, "Why in the name of death and conscience should it be tragic to be a widow but comic to be a widower?" But the rationalistic method is here applied quite wrong as regards the production of a drama. The most dramatic point in the affair is when the open and indecent rack-renter turns on the decent young man of means and proves to him that he is equally guilty, that he also can only grind his corn by grinding the faces of the poor. But even here the point is undramatic because it is indirect; it is indirect because it is merely sociological. It may be the truth that a young man living on an unexamined income which ultimately covers a great deal of house-property is as dangerous as any despot or thief. But it is a truth that you can no more put into a play than into a triolet. You can make a play out of one man robbing another man, but not out of one man robbing a million men; still less out of his robbing them unconsciously.

Of the plays collected in this book I have kept Mrs. Warren's Profession to the last, because, fine as it is, it is even finer and more important because of its fate, which was to rouse a long and serious storm and to be vetoed by the Censor of Plays. I say that this drama is most important because of the quarrel that came out of it. If I were speaking of some mere artist this might be an insult. But there are high and heroic things in Bernard Shaw; and one of the highest and most heroic is this, that he certainly cares much more for a quarrel than for a play. And this quarrel about the censorship is one on which he feels so strongly that in a book embodying any sort of sympathy it would be much better to leave out Mrs. Warren than to leave out Mr. Redford. The veto was the pivot of so very personal a movement by the dramatist, of so very positive an assertion of his own attitude towards things, that it is only just and necessary to state what were the two essential parties to the dispute; the play and the official who prevented the play.

The play of Mrs. Warren's Profession is concerned with a coarse mother and a cold daughter; the mother drives the ordinary and dirty trade of harlotry; the daughter does not know until the end the atrocious origin of all her own comfort and refinement. The daughter, when the discovery is made, freezes up into an iceberg of contempt; which is indeed a very womanly thing to do. The mother explodes into pulverising cynicism and practicality; which is also very womanly. The dialogue is drastic and sweeping; the daughter says the trade is loathsome; the mother answers that she loathes it herself; that every healthy person does loathe the trade by which she lives. And beyond question the general effect of the play is that the trade is loathsome; supposing anyone to be so insensible as to require to be told of the fact. Undoubtedly the upshot is that a brothel is a miserable business, and a brothel-keeper a miserable woman. The whole dramatic art of Shaw is in the literal sense of the word, tragi-comic; I mean that the comic part comes after the tragedy. But just as You Never Can

Tell represents the nearest approach of Shaw to the purely comic, so Mrs. Warren's Profession represents his only complete, or nearly complete, tragedy. There is no twopenny modernism in it, as in The Philanderer. Mrs. Warren is as old as the Old Testament; "for she hath cast down many wounded, yea, many strong men have been slain by her; her house is in the gates of hell, going down into the chamber of death." Here is no subtle ethics, as in Widowers' Houses; for even those moderns who think it noble that a woman should throw away her honour, surely cannot think it especially noble that she should sell it. Here is no lighting up by laughter, astonishment, and happy coincidence, as in You Never Can Tell. The play is a pure tragedy about a permanent and quite plain human problem; the problem is as plain and permanent, the tragedy is as proud and pure, as in OEdipus or Macbeth. This play was presented in the ordinary way for public performance and was suddenly stopped by the Censor of Plays.

The Censor of Plays is a small and accidental eighteenth-century official. Like nearly all the powers which Englishmen now respect as ancient and rooted, he is very recent. Novels and newspapers still talk of the English aristocracy that came over with William the Conqueror. Little of our effective oligarchy is as old as the Reformation; and none of it came over with William the Conqueror. Some of the older English landlords came over with William of Orange; the rest have come by ordinary alien immigration. In the same way we always talk of the Victorian woman (with her smelling salts and sentiment) as the old-fashioned woman. But she really was a quite new-fashioned woman; she considered herself, and was, an advance in delicacy and civilisation upon the coarse and candid Elizabethan woman to whom we are now returning. We are never oppressed by old things; it is recent things that can really oppress. And in accordance with this principle modern England has accepted, as if it were a part of perennial morality, a tenth-rate job of Walpole's worst days called the Censorship of the Drama. Just as they have supposed the eighteenth-century parvenus to date from Hastings, just as they have supposed the eighteenth-century ladies to date from Eve, so they have supposed the eighteenth-century Censorship to date from Sinai. The origin of the thing was in truth purely political. Its first and principal achievement was to prevent Fielding from writing plays; not at all because the plays were coarse, but because they criticised the Government. Fielding was a free writer; but they did not resent his sexual freedom; the Censor would not have objected if he had torn away the most intimate curtains of decency or rent the last rag from private life. What the Censor disliked was his rending the curtain from public life. There is still much of that spirit in our country; there are no affairs which men seek so much to cover up as public affairs. But the thing was done somewhat more boldly and baldly in Walpole's day; and the Censorship of plays has its origin, not merely in tyranny, but in a quite trifling and temporary and partisan piece of tyranny; a thing in its nature far more ephemeral, far less essential, than Ship Money. Perhaps its brightest moment was when the office of censor was held by that filthy writer, Colman the younger; and when he gravely refused to license a work by the author of Our Village. Few funnier notions can ever have actually been facts than this notion that the restraint and chastity of George Colman saved the English public from the eroticism and obscenity of Miss Mitford. Such was the play; and such was the power that stopped the play. A private man wrote it; another private man forbade it; nor was there any difference between Mr. Shaw's authority and Mr. Redford's, except that Mr. Shaw did defend his action on public grounds and Mr. Redford did not. The dramatist had simply been suppressed by a despot; and what was worse (because it was modern) by a silent and evasive despot; a despot in hiding. People talk about the pride of tyrants; but we at the present day suffer from the modesty of tyrants; from the shyness and the shrinking secrecy of the strong. Shaw's preface to Mrs. Warren's Profession was far more fit to be called a public document than the slovenly refusal of the individual official; it had more exactness, more universal application, more authority. Shaw on Redford was far more national and responsible than Redford on Shaw.

The dramatist found in the quarrel one of the important occasions of his life, because the crisis called out something in him which is in many ways his highest quality—righteous indignation. As a mere matter of the art of controversy of course he carried the war into the enemy's camp at once. He did not linger over loose excuses for licence; he declared at once that the Censor was licentious, while he, Bernard Shaw, was clean. He did not discuss whether a Censorship ought to make the drama moral. He declared that it made the drama immoral. With a fine strategic audacity he attacked the Censor quite as much for what he permitted as for what he prevented. He charged him with encouraging all plays that attracted men to vice and only stopping those which discouraged them from it. Nor was this attitude by any means an idle paradox. Many plays appear (as Shaw pointed out) in which the prostitute and the procuress are practically obvious, and in which they are represented as revelling in beautiful surroundings and basking in brilliant popularity. The crime of Shaw was not that he introduced the Gaiety Girl; that had been done, with little enough decorum, in a hundred musical comedies. The crime of Shaw was that he introduced the Gaiety Girl, but did not represent her life as all gaiety. The pleasures of vice were already flaunted before the playgoers. It was the perils of vice that were carefully concealed from them. The gay adventures, the gorgeous dresses, the champagne and oysters, the diamonds and motor-cars, dramatists were allowed to drag all these dazzling temptations before any silly housemaid in the gallery who was grumbling at her wages. But they were not allowed to warn her of the vulgarity and the nausea, the dreary deceptions and the blasting diseases of that life. Mrs. Warren's Profession was not up to a sufficient standard of immorality; it was not spicy enough to pass the Censor. The acceptable and the accepted plays were those which made the fall of a woman fashionable and fascinating; for all the world as if the Censor's profession were the same as Mrs. Warren's profession. Such was the angle of Shaw's energetic attack; and it is not to be denied that there was exaggeration in it, and what is so much worse, omission. The argument might easily be carried too far; it might end with a scene of screaming torture in the Inquisition as a corrective to the too amiable view of a clergyman in The Private Secretary. But the controversy is definitely worth recording, if only as an excellent example of the author's aggressive attitude and his love of turning the tables in debate. Moreover, though this point of view involves a potential overstatement, it also involves an important truth. One of the best points urged in the course of it was this, that though vice is punished in conventional drama, the punishment is not really impressive, because it is not inevitable or even probable. It does not arise out of the evil act. Years afterwards Bernard Shaw urged this argument again in connection with his friend Mr. Granville Barker's play of Waste, in which the woman dies from an illegal operation. Bernard Shaw said, truly enough, that if she had died from poison or a pistol shot it would have left everyone unmoved, for pistols do not in their nature follow female unchastity. Illegal operations very often do. The punishment was one which might follow the crime, not only in that case, but in many cases.

Here, I think, the whole argument might be sufficiently cleared up by saying that the objection to such things on the stage is a purely artistic objection. There is nothing wrong in talking about an illegal operation; there are plenty of occasions when it would be very wrong not to talk about it. But it may easily be just a shade too ugly for the shape of any work of art. There is nothing wrong about being sick; but if Bernard Shaw wrote a play in which all the characters expressed their dislike of animal food by vomiting on the stage, I think we should be justified in saying that the thing was outside, not the laws of morality, but the framework of civilised literature. The instinctive movement of repulsion which everyone has when hearing of the operation in Waste is not an ethical repulsion at all. But it is an aesthetic repulsion, and a right one.

But I have only dwelt on this particular fighting phase because it leaves us facing the ultimate characteristics which I mentioned first. Bernard Shaw cares nothing for art; in comparison with morals, literally nothing. Bernard Shaw is a Puritan and his work is Puritan work. He has all the essentials of the old, virile and extinct Protestant type. In his work he is as ugly as a Puritan. He is as indecent as a Puritan. He is as full of gross words and sensual facts as a sermon of the seventeenth century. Up to this point of his life indeed hardly anyone would have dreamed of calling him a Puritan; he was called sometimes an anarchist, sometimes a buffoon, sometimes (by the more discerning stupid people) a prig. His attitude towards current problems was felt to be arresting and even indecent; I do not think that anyone thought of connecting it with the old Calvinistic morality. But Shaw, who knew better than the Shavians, was at this moment on the very eve of confessing his moral origin. The next book of plays he produced (including The Devil's Disciple, Captain Brassbound's Conversion, and Caesar and Cleopatra), actually bore the title of Plays for Puritans.

The play called The Devil's Disciple has great merits, but the merits are incidental. Some of its jokes are serious and important, but its general plan can only be called a joke. Almost alone among Bernard Shaw's plays (except of course such things as How he Lied to her Husband and The Admirable Bashville) this drama does not turn on any very plain pivot of ethical or philosophical conviction. The artistic idea seems to be the notion of a melodrama in which all the conventional melodramatic situations shall suddenly take unconventional turns. Just where the melodramatic clergyman would show courage he appears to show cowardice; just where the melodramatic sinner would confess his love he confesses his indifference. This is a little too like the Shaw of the newspaper critics rather than the Shaw of reality. There are indeed present in the play two of the writer's principal moral conceptions.

The first is the idea of a great heroic action coming in a sense from nowhere; that is, not coming from any commonplace motive; being born in the soul in naked beauty, coming with its own authority and testifying only to itself. Shaw's agent does not act towards something, but from something. The hero dies, not because he desires heroism, but because he has it. So in this particular play the Devil's Disciple finds that his own nature will not permit him to put the rope around another man's neck; he has no reasons of desire, affection, or even equity; his death is a sort of divine whim. And in connection with this the dramatist introduces another favourite moral; the objection to perpetual playing upon the motive of sex. He deliberately lures the onlooker into the net of Cupid in order to tell him with salutary decision that Cupid is not there at all. Millions of melodramatic dramatists have made a man face death for the woman he loves; Shaw makes him face death for the woman he does not love—merely in order to put woman in her place. He objects to that idolatry of sexualism which makes it the fountain of all forcible enthusiasms; he dislikes the amorous drama which makes the female the only key to the male. He is Feminist in politics, but Anti-feminist in emotion. His key to most problems is, "Ne cherchez pas la femme."

As has been observed, the incidental felicities of the play are frequent and memorable, especially those connected with the character of General Burgoyne, the real full-blooded, free-thinking eighteenth century gentleman, who was much too much of an aristocrat not to be a liberal. One of the best thrusts in all the Shavian fencing matches is that which occurs when Richard Dudgeon, condemned to be hanged, asks rhetorically why he cannot be shot like a soldier. "Now there you speak like a civilian," replies General Burgoyne. "Have you formed any conception of the condition of marksmanship in the British Army?" Excellent, too, is the passage in which his subordinate speaks of crushing the enemy in America, and Burgoyne asks him who will crush their enemies in England, snobbery and jobbery and incurable carelessness and sloth. And in one sentence towards the end, Shaw reaches a wider and more genial comprehension of mankind than he shows anywhere else; "it takes all sorts to make a world, saints as well as soldiers." If Shaw had remembered that sentence on other occasions he would have avoided his mistake about Caesar and Brutus. It is not only true that it takes all sorts to make a world; but the world cannot succeed without its failures.

Perhaps the most doubtful point of all in the play is why it is a play for Puritans; except the hideous picture of a Calvinistic home is meant to destroy Puritanism. And indeed in this connection it is constantly necessary to fall back upon the facts of which I have spoken at the beginning of this brief study; it is necessary especially to remember that Shaw could in all probability speak of Puritanism from the inside. In that domestic circle which took him to hear Moody and Sankey, in that domestic circle which was teetotal even when it was intoxicated, in that atmosphere and society Shaw might even have met the monstrous mother in The Devil's Disciple, the horrible old woman who declares that she has hardened her heart to hate her children, because the heart of man is desperately wicked, the old ghoul who has made one of her children an imbecile and the other an outcast. Such types do occur in small societies drunk with the dismal wine of Puritan determinism. It is possible that there were among Irish Calvinists people who denied that charity was a Christian virtue. It is possible that among Puritans there were people who thought a heart was a kind of heart disease. But it is enough to make one tear one's hair to think that a man of genius received his first impressions in so small a corner of Europe that he could for a long time suppose that this Puritanism was current among Christian men. The question, however, need not detain us, for the batch of plays contained two others about which it is easier to speak.

The third play in order in the series called Plays for Puritans is a very charming one; Captain Brassbound's Conversion. This also turns, as does so much of the Caesar drama, on the idea of vanity of revenge—the idea that it is too slight and silly a thing for a man to allow to occupy and corrupt his consciousness. It is not, of course, the morality that is new here, but the touch of cold laughter in the core of the morality. Many saints and sages have denounced vengeance. But they treated vengeance as something too great for man. "Vengeance is Mine, saith the Lord; I will repay." Shaw treats vengeance as something too small for man—a monkey trick he ought to have outlived, a childish storm of tears which he ought to be able to control. In the story in question Captain Brassbound has nourished through his whole erratic existence, racketting about all the unsavoury parts of Africa—a mission of private punishment which appears to him as a mission of holy justice. His mother has died in consequence of a judge's decision, and Brassbound roams and schemes until the judge falls into his hands. Then a pleasant society lady, Lady Cicely Waynefleet tells him in an easy conversational undertone—a rivulet of speech which ripples while she is mending his coat—that he is making a fool of himself, that his wrong is irrelevant, that his vengeance is objectless, that he would be much better if he flung his morbid fancy away for ever; in short, she tells him he is ruining himself for the sake of ruining a total stranger. Here again we have the note of the economist, the hatred of mere loss. Shaw (one might almost say) dislikes murder, not so much because it wastes the life of the corpse as because it wastes the time of the murderer. If he were endeavouring to persuade one of his moon-lighting fellow-countrymen not to shoot his landlord, I can imagine him explaining with benevolent emphasis that it was not so much a question of losing a life as of throwing away a bullet. But indeed the Irish comparison alone suggests a doubt which wriggles in the recesses of my mind about the complete reliability of the philosophy of Lady Cicely Waynefleet, the complete finality of the moral of Captain Brassbound's Conversion. Of course, it was very natural in an aristocrat like Lady Cicely Waynefleet to wish to let sleeping dogs lie, especially those whom Mr. Blatchford calls under-dogs. Of course it was natural for her to wish everything to be smooth and sweet-tempered. But I have the obstinate question in the corner of my brain, whether if a few Captain Brassbounds did revenge themselves on judges, the quality of our judges might not materially improve.

When this doubt is once off one's conscience one can lose oneself in the bottomless beatitude of Lady Cicely Waynefleet, one of the most living and laughing things that her maker has made. I do not know any stronger way of stating the beauty of the character than by saying that it was written specially for Ellen Terry, and that it is, with Beatrice, one of the very few characters in which the dramatist can claim some part of her triumph.

We may now pass to the more important of the plays. For some time Bernard Shaw would seem to have been brooding upon the soul of Julius Caesar. There must always be a strong human curiosity about the soul of Julius Caesar; and, among other things, about whether he had a soul. The conjunction of Shaw and Caesar has about it something smooth and inevitable; for this decisive reason, that Caesar is really the only great man of history to whom the Shaw theories apply. Caesar was a Shaw hero. Caesar was merciful without being in the least pitiful; his mercy was colder than justice. Caesar was a conqueror without being in any hearty sense a soldier; his courage was lonelier than fear. Caesar was a demagogue without being a democrat. In the same way Bernard Shaw is a demagogue without being a democrat. If he had tried to prove his principle from any of the other heroes or sages of mankind he would have found it much more difficult. Napoleon achieved more miraculous conquest; but during his most conquering epoch he was a burning boy suicidally in love with a woman far beyond his age. Joan of Arc achieved far more instant and incredible worldly success; but Joan of Arc achieved worldly success because she believed in another world. Nelson was a figure fully as fascinating and dramatically decisive; but Nelson was "romantic"; Nelson was a devoted patriot and a devoted lover. Alexander was passionate; Cromwell could shed tears; Bismarck had some suburban religion; Frederick was a poet; Charlemagne was fond of children. But Julius Caesar attracted Shaw not less by his positive than by his negative enormousness. Nobody can say with certainty that Caesar cared for anything. It is unjust to call Caesar an egoist; for there is no proof that he cared even for Caesar. He may not have been either an atheist or a pessimist. But he may have been; that is exactly the rub.

He may have been an ordinary decently good man slightly deficient in spiritual expansiveness. On the other hand, he may have been the incarnation of paganism in the sense that Christ was the incarnation of Christianity. As Christ expressed how great a man can be humble and humane, Caesar may have expressed how great a man can be frigid and flippant. According to most legends Antichrist was to come soon after Christ. One has only to suppose that Antichrist came shortly before Christ; and Antichrist might very well be Caesar.

It is, I think, no injustice to Bernard Shaw to say that he does not attempt to make his Caesar superior except in this naked and negative sense. There is no suggestion, as there is in the Jehovah of the Old Testament, that the very cruelty of the higher being conceals some tremendous and even tortured love. Caesar is superior to other men not because he loves more, but because he hates less. Caesar is magnanimous not because he is warm-hearted enough to pardon, but because he is not warm-hearted enough to avenge. There is no suggestion anywhere in the play that he is hiding any great genial purpose or powerful tenderness towards men. In order to put this point beyond a doubt the dramatist has introduced a soliloquy of Caesar alone with the Sphinx. There if anywhere he would have broken out into ultimate brotherhood or burning pity for the people. But in that scene between the Sphinx and Caesar, Caesar is as cold and as lonely and as dead as the Sphinx.

But whether the Shavian Caesar is a sound ideal or no, there can be little doubt that he is a very fine reality. Shaw has done nothing greater as a piece of artistic creation. If the man is a little like a statue, it is a statue by a great sculptor; a statue of the best period. If his nobility is a little negative in its character, it is the negative darkness of the great dome of night; not as in some "new moralities" the mere mystery of the coal-hole. Indeed, this somewhat austere method of work is very suitable to Shaw when he is serious.

There is nothing Gothic about his real genius; he could not build a mediaeval cathedral in which laughter and terror are twisted together in stone, molten by mystical passion. He can build, by way of amusement, a Chinese pagoda; but when he is in earnest, only a Roman temple. He has a keen eye for truth; but he is one of those people who like, as the saying goes, to put down the truth in black and white. He is always girding and jeering at romantics and idealists because they will not put down the truth in black and white. But black and white are not the only two colours in the world. The modern man of science who writes down a fact in black and white is not more but less accurate than the mediaeval monk who wrote it down in gold and scarlet, sea-green and turquoise. Nevertheless, it is a good thing that the more austere method should exist separately, and that some men should be specially good at it. Bernard Shaw is specially good at it; he is pre-eminently a black and white artist.

And as a study in black and white nothing could be better than this sketch of Julius Caesar. He is not so much represented as "bestriding the earth like a Colossus" (which is indeed a rather comic attitude for a hero to stand in), but rather walking the earth with a sort of stern levity, lightly touching the planet and yet spurning it away like a stone. He walks like a winged man who has chosen to fold his wings. There is something creepy even about his kindness; it makes the men in front of him feel as if they were made of glass. The nature of the Caesarian mercy is massively suggested. Caesar dislikes a massacre, not because it is a great sin, but because it is a small sin. It is felt that he classes it with a flirtation or a fit of the sulks; a senseless temporary subjugation of man's permanent purpose by his passing and trivial feelings. He will plunge into slaughter for a great purpose, just as he plunges into the sea. But to be stung into such action he deems as undignified as to be tipped off the pier. In a singularly fine passage Cleopatra, having hired assassins to stab an enemy, appeals to her wrongs as justifying her revenge, and says, "If you can find one man in all Africa who says that I did wrong, I will be crucified by my own slaves." "If you can find one man in all the world," replies Caesar, "who can see that you did wrong, he will either conquer the world as I have done or be crucified by it." That is the high water mark of this heathen sublimity; and we do not feel it inappropriate, or unlike Shaw, when a few minutes afterwards the hero is saluted with a blaze of swords.

As usually happens in the author's works, there is even more about Julius Caesar in the preface than there is in the play. But in the preface I think the portrait is less imaginative and more fanciful. He attempts to connect his somewhat chilly type of superman with the heroes of the old fairy tales. But Shaw should not talk about the fairy tales; for he does not feel them from the inside. As I have said, on all this side of historic and domestic traditions Bernard Shaw is weak and deficient. He does not approach them as fairy tales, as if he were four, but as "folk-lore" as if he were forty. And he makes a big mistake about them which he would never have made if he had kept his birthday and hung up his stocking, and generally kept alive inside him the firelight of a home. The point is so peculiarly characteristic of Bernard Shaw, and is indeed so much of a summary of his most interesting assertion and his most interesting error, that it deserves a word by itself, though it is a word which must be remembered in connection with nearly all the other plays.

His primary and defiant proposition is the Calvinistic proposition: that the elect do not earn virtue, but possess it. The goodness of a man does not consist in trying to be good, but in being good. Julius Caesar prevails over other people by possessing more virtus than they; not by having striven or suffered or bought his virtue; not because he has struggled heroically, but because he is a hero. So far Bernard Shaw is only what I have called him at the beginning; he is simply a seventeenth-century Calvinist. Caesar is not saved by works, or even by faith; he is saved because he is one of the elect. Unfortunately for himself, however, Bernard Shaw went back further than the seventeenth century; and professing his opinion to be yet more antiquated, invoked the original legends of mankind. He argued that when the fairy tales gave Jack the Giant Killer a coat of darkness or a magic sword it removed all credit from Jack in the "common moral" sense; he won as Caesar won only because he was superior. I will confess, in passing, to the conviction that Bernard Shaw in the course of his whole simple and strenuous life was never quite so near to hell as at the moment when he wrote down those words. But in this question of fairy tales my immediate point is, not how near he was to hell, but how very far off he was from fairyland. That notion about the hero with a magic sword being the superman with a magic superiority is the caprice of a pedant; no child, boy, or man ever felt it in the story of Jack the Giant Killer. Obviously the moral is all the other way. Jack's fairy sword and invisible coat are clumsy expedients for enabling him to fight at all with something which is by nature stronger. They are a rough, savage substitute for psychological descriptions of special valour or unwearied patience. But no one in his five wits can doubt that the idea of "Jack the Giant Killer" is exactly the opposite to Shaw's idea. If it were not a tale of effort and triumph hardly earned it would not be called "Jack the Giant Killer." If it were a tale of the victory of natural advantages it would be called "Giant the Jack Killer." If the teller of fairy tales had merely wanted to urge that some beings are born stronger than others he would not have fallen back on elaborate tricks of weapon and costume for conquering an ogre. He would simply have let the ogre conquer. I will not speak of my own emotions in connection with this incredibly caddish doctrine that the strength of the strong is admirable, but not the valour of the weak. It is enough to say that I have to summon up the physical presence of Shaw, his frank gestures, kind eyes, and exquisite Irish voice, to cure me of a mere sensation of contempt. But I do not dwell upon the point for any such purpose; but merely to show how we must be always casting back to those concrete foundations with which we began. Bernard Shaw, as I have said, was never national enough to be domestic; he was never a part of his past; hence when he tries to interpret tradition he comes a terrible cropper, as in this case. Bernard Shaw (I strongly suspect) began to disbelieve in Santa Claus at a discreditably early age. And by this time Santa Claus has avenged himself by taking away the key of all the prehistoric scriptures; so that a noble and honourable artist flounders about like any German professor. Here is a whole fairy literature which is almost exclusively devoted to the unexpected victory of the weak over the strong; and Bernard Shaw manages to make it mean the inevitable victory of the strong over the weak—which, among other things, would not make a story at all. It all comes of that mistake about not keeping his birthday. A man should be always tied to his mother's apron strings; he should always have a hold on his childhood, and be ready at intervals to start anew from a childish standpoint. Theologically the thing is best expressed by saying, "You must be born again." Secularly it is best expressed by saying, "You must keep your birthday." Even if you will not be born again, at least remind yourself occasionally that you were born once.

Some of the incidental wit in the Caesarian drama is excellent although it is upon the whole less spontaneous and perfect than in the previous plays. One of its jests may be mentioned in passing, not merely to draw attention to its failure (though Shaw is brilliant enough to afford many failures) but because it is the best opportunity for mentioning one of the writer's minor notions to which he obstinately adheres. He describes the Ancient Briton in Caesar's train as being exactly like a modern respectable Englishman. As a joke for a Christmas pantomime this would be all very well; but one expects the jokes of Bernard Shaw to have some intellectual root, however fantastic the flower.

And obviously all historic common sense is against the idea that that dim Druid people, whoever they were, who dwelt in our land before it was lit up by Rome or loaded with varied invasions, were a precise facsimile of the commercial society of Birmingham or Brighton. But it is a part of the Puritan in Bernard Shaw, a part of the taut and high-strung quality of his mind, that he will never admit of any of his jokes that it was only a joke. When he has been most witty he will passionately deny his own wit; he will say something which Voltaire might envy and then declare that he has got it all out of a Blue book. And in connection with this eccentric type of self-denial, we may notice this mere detail about the Ancient Briton. Someone faintly hinted that a blue Briton when first found by Caesar might not be quite like Mr. Broadbent; at the touch Shaw poured forth a torrent of theory, explaining that climate was the only thing that affected nationality; and that whatever races came into the English or Irish climate would become like the English or Irish. Now the modern theory of race is certainly a piece of stupid materialism; it is an attempt to explain the things we are sure of, France, Scotland, Rome, Japan, by means of the things we are not sure of at all, prehistoric conjectures, Celts, Mongols, and Iberians. Of course there is a reality in race; but there is no reality in the theories of race offered by some ethnological professors. Blood, perhaps, is thicker than water; but brains are sometimes thicker than anything. But if there is one thing yet more thick and obscure and senseless than this theory of the omnipotence of race it is, I think, that to which Shaw has fled for refuge from it; this doctrine of the omnipotence of climate. Climate again is something; but if climate were everything, Anglo-Indians would grow more and more to look like Hindoos, which is far from being the case. Something in the evil spirit of our time forces people always to pretend to have found some material and mechanical explanation.

Bernard Shaw has filled all his last days with affirmations about the divinity of the non-mechanical part of man, the sacred quality in creation and choice. Yet it never seems to have occurred to him that the true key to national differentiations is the key of the will and not of the environment. It never crosses the modern mind to fancy that perhaps a people is chiefly influenced by how that people has chosen to behave. If I have to choose between race and weather I prefer race; I would rather be imprisoned and compelled by ancestors who were once alive than by mud and mists which never were. But I do not propose to be controlled by either; to me my national history is a chain of multitudinous choices. It is neither blood nor rain that has made England, but hope, the thing that all those dead men have desired. France was not France because she was made to be by the skulls of the Celts or by the sun of Gaul. France was France because she chose.

I have stepped on one side from the immediate subject because this is as good an instance as any we are likely to come across of a certain almost extraneous fault which does deface the work of Bernard Shaw. It is a fault only to be mentioned when we have made the solidity of the merits quite clear. To say that Shaw is merely making game of people is demonstrably ridiculous; at least a fairly systematic philosophy can be traced through all his jokes, and one would not insist on such a unity in all the songs of Mr. Dan Leno. I have already pointed out that the genius of Shaw is really too harsh and earnest rather than too merry and irresponsible. I shall have occasion to point out later that Shaw is, in one very serious sense, the very opposite of paradoxical. In any case if any real student of Shaw says that Shaw is only making a fool of him, we can only say that of that student it is very superfluous for anyone to make a fool. But though the dramatist's jests are always serious and generally obvious, he is really affected from time to time by a certain spirit of which that climate theory is a case—a spirit that can only be called one of senseless ingenuity. I suppose it is a sort of nemesis of wit; the skidding of a wheel in the height of its speed. Perhaps it is connected with the nomadic nature of his mind.

That lack of roots, this remoteness from ancient instincts and traditions is responsible for a certain bleak and heartless extravagance of statement on certain subjects which makes the author really unconvincing as well as exaggerative; satires that are saugrenu, jokes that are rather silly than wild, statements which even considered as lies have no symbolic relation to truth. They are exaggerations of something that does not exist. For instance, if a man called Christmas Day a mere hypocritical excuse for drunkenness and gluttony that would be false, but it would have a fact hidden in it somewhere. But when Bernard Shaw says that Christmas Day is only a conspiracy kept up by poulterers and wine merchants from strictly business motives, then he says something which is not so much false as startlingly and arrestingly foolish. He might as well say that the two sexes were invented by jewellers who wanted to sell wedding rings. Or again, take the case of nationality and the unit of patriotism. If a man said that all boundaries between clans, kingdoms, or empires were nonsensical or non-existent, that would be a fallacy, but a consistent and philosophical fallacy. But when Mr. Bernard Shaw says that England matters so little that the British Empire might very well give up these islands to Germany, he has not only got hold of the sow by the wrong ear but the wrong sow by the wrong ear; a mythical sow, a sow that is not there at all. If Britain is unreal, the British Empire must be a thousand times more unreal. It is as if one said, "I do not believe that Michael Scott ever had any existence; but I am convinced, in spite of the absurd legend, that he had a shadow." As has been said already, there must be some truth in every popular impression. And the impression that Shaw, the most savagely serious man of his time, is a mere music-hall artist must have reference to such rare outbreaks as these. As a rule his speeches are full, not only of substance, but of substances, materials like pork, mahogany, lead, and leather. There is no man whose arguments cover a more Napoleonic map of detail. It is true that he jokes; but wherever he is he has topical jokes, one might almost say family jokes. If he talks to tailors he can allude to the last absurdity about buttons. If he talks to the soldiers he can see the exquisite and exact humour of the last gun-carriage. But when all his powerful practicality is allowed, there does run through him this erratic levity, an explosion of ineptitude. It is a queer quality in literature. It is a sort of cold extravagance; and it has made him all his enemies.

Chapter 12

Bernard Shaw: The Philosopher

I should suppose that Caesar and Cleopatra marks about the turning tide of Bernard Shaw's fortune and fame. Up to this time he had known glory, but never success. He had been wondered at as something brilliant and barren, like a meteor; but no one would accept him as a sun, for the test of a sun is that it can make something grow. Practically speaking the two qualities of a modern drama are, that it should play and that it should pay. It had been proved over and over again in weighty dramatic criticisms, in careful readers' reports, that the plays of Shaw could never play or pay; that the public did not want wit and the wars of intellect. And just about the time that this had been finally proved, the plays of Bernard Shaw promised to play like Charley's Aunt and to pay like Colman's Mustard. It is a fact in which we can all rejoice, not only because it redeems the reputation of Bernard Shaw, but because it redeems the character of the English people. All that is bravest in human nature, open challenge and unexpected wit and angry conviction, are not so very unpopular as the publishers and managers in their motor-cars have been in the habit of telling us. But exactly because we have come to a turning point in the man's career I propose to interrupt the mere catalogue of his plays and to treat his latest series rather as the proclamations of an acknowledged prophet. For the last plays, especially Man and Superman, are such that his whole position must be re-stated before attacking them seriously.

For two reasons I have called this concluding series of plays not again by the name of "The Dramatist," but by the general name of "The Philosopher." The first reason is that given above, that we have come to the time of his triumph and may therefore treat him as having gained complete possession of a pulpit of his own. But there is a second reason: that it was just about this time that he began to create not only a pulpit of his own, but a church and creed of his own. It is a very vast and universal religion; and it is not his fault that he is the only member of it. The plainer way of putting it is this: that here, in the hour of his earthly victory, there dies in him the old mere denier, the mere dynamiter of criticism. In the warmth of popularity he begins to wish to put his faith positively; to offer some solid key to all creation. Perhaps the irony in the situation is this: that all the crowds are acclaiming him as the blasting and hypercritical buffoon, while he himself is seriously rallying his synthetic power, and with a grave face telling himself that it is time he had a faith to preach. His final success as a sort of charlatan coincides with his first grand failures as a theologian.

For this reason I have deliberately called a halt in his dramatic career, in order to consider these two essential points: What did the mass of Englishmen, who had now learnt to admire him, imagine his point of view to be? and second, What did he imagine it to be? or, if the phrase be premature, What did he imagine it was going to be? In his latest work, especially in Man and Superman, Shaw has become a complete and colossal mystic. That mysticism does grow quite rationally out of his older arguments; but very few people ever troubled to trace the connection. In order to do so it is necessary to say what was, at the time of his first success, the public impression of Shaw's philosophy. Now it is an irritating and pathetic thing that the three most popular phrases about Shaw are false. Modern criticism, like all weak things, is overloaded with words. In a healthy condition of language a man finds it very difficult to say the right thing, but at last says it. In this empire of journalese a man finds it so very easy to say the wrong thing that he never thinks of saying anything else. False or meaningless phrases lie so ready to his hand that it is easier to use them than not to use them. These wrong terms picked up through idleness are retained through habit, and so the man has begun to think wrong almost before he has begun to think at all. Such lumbering logomachy is always injurious and oppressive to men of spirit, imagination or intellectual honour, and it has dealt very recklessly and wrongly with Bernard Shaw. He has contrived to get about three newspaper phrases tied to his tail; and those newspaper phrases are all and separately wrong. The three superstitions about him, it will be conceded, are generally these: first that he desires "problem plays," second that he is "paradoxical," and third that in his dramas as elsewhere he is specially "a Socialist." And the interesting thing is that when we come to his philosophy, all these three phrases are quite peculiarly inapplicable.

To take the plays first, there is a general disposition to describe that type of intimate or defiant drama which he approves as "the problem play." Now the serious modern play is, as a rule, the very reverse of a problem play; for there can be no problem unless both points of view are equally and urgently presented. Hamlet really is a problem play because at the end of it one is really in doubt as to whether upon the author's showing Hamlet is something more than a man or something less. Henry IV and Henry V are really problem plays; in this sense, that the reader or spectator is really doubtful whether the high but harsh efficiency, valour, and ambition of Henry V are an improvement on his old blackguard camaraderie; and whether he was not a better man when he was a thief. This hearty and healthy doubt is very common in Shakespeare; I mean a doubt that exists in the writer as well as in the reader. But Bernard Shaw is far too much of a Puritan to tolerate such doubts about points which he counts essential. There is no sort of doubt that the young lady in Arms and the Man is improved by losing her ideals. There is no sort of doubt that Captain Brassbound is improved by giving up the object of his life. But a better case can be found in something that both dramatists have been concerned with; Shaw wrote Caesar and Cleopatra; Shakespeare wrote Antony and Cleopatra and also Julius Caesar. And exactly what annoys Bernard Shaw about Shakespeare's version is this: that Shakespeare has an open mind or, in other words, that

Shakespeare has really written a problem play. Shakespeare sees quite as clearly as Shaw that Brutus is unpractical and ineffectual; but he also sees, what is quite as plain and practical a fact, that these ineffectual men do capture the hearts and influence the policies of mankind. Shaw would have nothing said in favour of Brutus; because Brutus is on the wrong side in politics. Of the actual problem of public and private morality, as it was presented to Brutus, he takes actually no notice at all. He can write the most energetic and outspoken of propaganda plays; but he cannot rise to a problem play. He cannot really divide his mind and let the two parts speak independently to each other.

He has never, so to speak, actually split his head in two; though I daresay there are many other people who are willing to do it for him. Sometimes, especially in his later plays, he allows his clear conviction to spoil even his admirable dialogue, making one side entirely weak, as in an Evangelical tract. I do not know whether in Major Barbara the young Greek professor was supposed to be a fool. As popular tradition (which I trust more than anything else) declared that he is drawn from a real Professor of my acquaintance, who is anything but a fool, I should imagine not. But in that case I am all the more mystified by the incredibly weak fight which he makes in the play in answer to the elephantine sophistries of Undershaft. It is really a disgraceful case, and almost the only case in Shaw of there being no fair fight between the two sides. For instance, the Professor mentions pity. Mr. Undershaft says with melodramatic scorn, "Pity! the scavenger of the Universe!" Now if any gentleman had said this to me, I should have replied, "If I permit you to escape from the point by means of metaphors, will you tell me whether you disapprove of scavengers?" Instead of this obvious retort, the miserable Greek professor only says, "Well then, love," to which Undershaft replies with unnecessary violence that he won't have the Greek professor's love, to which the obvious answer of course would be, "How the deuce can you prevent my loving you if I choose to do so?" Instead of this, as far as I remember, that abject Hellenist says nothing at all. I only mention this unfair dialogue, because it marks, I think, the recent hardening, for good or evil, of Shaw out of a dramatist into a mere philosopher, and whoever hardens into a philosopher may be hardening into a fanatic.

And just as there is nothing really problematic in Shaw's mind, so there is nothing really paradoxical. The meaning of the word paradoxical may indeed be made the subject of argument. In Greek, of course, it simply means something which is against the received opinion; in that sense a missionary remonstrating with South Sea cannibals is paradoxical. But in the much more important world, where words are used and altered in the using, paradox does not mean merely this: it means at least something of which the antinomy or apparent inconsistency is sufficiently plain in the words used, and most commonly of all it means an idea expressed in a form which is verbally contradictory. Thus, for instance, the great saying, "He that shall lose his life, the same shall save it," is an example of what modern people mean by a paradox. If any learned person should read this book (which seems immeasurably improbable) he can content himself with putting it this way, that the moderns mistakenly say paradox when they should say oxymoron. Ultimately, in any case, it may be agreed that we commonly mean by a paradox some kind of collision between what is seemingly and what is really true. Now if by paradox we mean truth inherent in a contradiction, as in the saying of Christ that I have quoted, it is a very curious fact that Bernard Shaw is almost entirely without paradox. Moreover, he cannot even understand a paradox. And more than this, paradox is about the only thing in the world that he does not understand. All his splendid vistas and startling suggestions arise from carrying some one clear principle further than it has yet been carried. His madness is all consistency, not inconsistency. As the point can hardly be made clear without examples, let us take one example, the subject of education. Shaw has been all his life preaching to grown-up people the profound truth that liberty and responsibility go together; that the reason why freedom is so often easily withheld, is simply that it is a terrible nuisance.

This is true, though not the whole truth, of citizens; and so when Shaw comes to children he can only apply to them the same principle that he has already applied to citizens. He begins to play with the Herbert Spencer idea of teaching children by experience; perhaps the most fatuously silly idea that was ever gravely put down in print. On that there is no need to dwell; one has only to ask how the experimental method is to be applied to a precipice; and the theory no longer exists.

But Shaw effected a further development, if possible more fantastic. He said that one should never tell a child anything without letting him hear the opposite opinion. That is to say, when you tell Tommy not to hit his sick sister on the temple, you must make sure of the presence of some Nietzscheite professor, who will explain to him that such a course might possibly serve to eliminate the unfit. When you are in the act of telling Susan not to drink out of the bottle labelled "poison," you must telegraph for a Christian Scientist, who will be ready to maintain that without her own consent it cannot do her any harm. What would happen to a child brought up on Shaw's principle I cannot conceive; I should think he would commit suicide in his bath. But that is not here the question.

The point is that this proposition seems quite sufficiently wild and startling to ensure that its author, if he escapes Hanwell, would reach the front rank of journalists, demagogues, or public entertainers. It is a perfect paradox, if a paradox only means something that makes one jump. But it is not a paradox at all in the sense of a contradiction. It is not a contradiction, but an enormous and outrageous consistency, the one principle of free thought carried to a point to which no other sane man would consent to carry it. Exactly what Shaw does not understand is the paradox; the unavoidable paradox of childhood. Although this child is much better than I, yet I must teach it. Although this being has much purer passions than I, yet I must control it. Although Tommy is quite right to rush towards a precipice, yet he must be stood in the corner for doing it. This contradiction is the only possible condition of having to do with children at all; anyone who talks about a child without feeling this paradox might just as well be talking about a merman. He has never even seen the animal. But this paradox Shaw in his intellectual simplicity cannot see; he cannot see it because it is a paradox. His only intellectual excitement is to carry one idea further and further across the world. It never occurs to him that it might meet another idea, and like the three winds in Martin Chuzzlewit, they might make a night of it. His only paradox is to pull out one thread or cord of truth longer and longer into waste and fantastic places. He does not allow for that deeper sort of paradox by which two opposite cords of truth become entangled in an inextricable knot. Still less can he be made to realise that it is often this knot which ties safely together the whole bundle of human life.

This blindness to paradox everywhere perplexes his outlook. He cannot understand marriage because he will not understand the paradox of marriage; that the woman is all the more the house for not being the head of it. He cannot understand patriotism, because he will not understand the paradox of patriotism; that one is all the more human for not merely loving humanity. He does not understand Christianity because he will not understand the paradox of Christianity; that we can only really understand all myths when we know that one of them is true. I do not under-rate him for this anti-paradoxical temper; I concede that much of his finest and keenest work in the way of intellectual purification would have been difficult or impossible without it. But I say that here lies the limitation of that lucid and compelling mind; he cannot quite understand life, because he will not accept its contradictions. Nor is it by any means descriptive of Shaw to call him a Socialist; in so far as that word can be extended to cover an ethical attitude. He is the least social of all Socialists; and I pity the Socialist state that tries to manage him. This anarchism of his is not a question of thinking for himself; every decent man thinks for himself; it would be highly immodest to think for anybody else. Nor is it any instinctive licence or egoism; as I have said before, he is a man of peculiarly acute public conscience. The unmanageable part of him, the fact that he cannot be conceived as part of a crowd or as really and invisibly helping a movement, has reference to another thing in him, or rather to another thing not in him.

The great defect of that fine intelligence is a failure to grasp and enjoy the things commonly called convention and tradition; which are foods upon which all human creatures must feed frequently if they are to live. Very few modern people of course have any idea of what they are. "Convention" is very nearly the same word as "democracy." It has again and again in history been used as an alternative word to Parliament. So far from suggesting anything stale or sobre, the word convention rather conveys a hubbub; it is the coming together of men; every mob is a convention. In its secondary sense it means the common soul of such a crowd, its instinctive anger at the traitor or its instinctive salutation of the flag. Conventions may be cruel, they may be unsuitable, they may even be grossly superstitious or obscene; but there is one thing that they never are. Conventions are never dead. They are always full of accumulated emotions, the piled-up and passionate experiences of many generations asserting what they could not explain. To be inside any true convention, as the Chinese respect for parents or the European respect for children, is to be surrounded by something which whatever else it is is not leaden, lifeless or automatic, something which is taut and tingling with vitality at a hundred points, which is sensitive almost to madness and which is so much alive that it can kill. Now Bernard Shaw has always made this one immense mistake (arising out of that bad progressive education of his), the mistake of treating convention as a dead thing; treating it as if it were a mere physical environment like the pavement or the rain. Whereas it is a result of will; a rain of blessings and a pavement of good intentions. Let it be remembered that I am not discussing in what degree one should allow for tradition; I am saying that men like Shaw do not allow for it at all. If Shaw had found in early life that he was contradicted by Bradshaw's Railway Guide or even by the Encyclopaedia Britannica, he would have felt at least that he might be wrong. But if he had found himself contradicted by his father and mother, he would have thought it all the more probable that he was right. If the issue of the last evening paper contradicted him he might be troubled to investigate or explain. That the human tradition of two thousand years contradicted him did not trouble him for an instant. That Marx was not with him was important. That Man was not with him was an irrelevant prehistoric joke. People have talked far too much about the paradoxes of Bernard Shaw.

Perhaps his only pure paradox is this almost unconscious one; that he has tended to think that because something has satisfied generations of men it must be untrue. Shaw is wrong about nearly all the things one learns early in life and while one is still simple. Most human beings start with certain facts of psychology to which the rest of life must be somewhat related. For instance, every man falls in love; and no man falls into free love. When he falls into that he calls it lust, and is always ashamed of it even when he boasts of it. That there is some connection between a love and a vow nearly every human being knows before he is eighteen. That there is a solid and instinctive connection between the idea of sexual ecstasy and the idea of some sort of almost suicidal constancy, this I say is simply the first fact in one's own psychology; boys and girls know it almost before they know their own language. How far it can be trusted, how it can best be dealt with, all that is another matter. But lovers lust after constancy more than after happiness; if you are in any sense prepared to give them what they ask, then what they ask, beyond all question, is an oath of final fidelity. Lovers may be lunatics; lovers may be children; lovers may be unfit for citizenship and outside human argument; you can take up that position if you will. But lovers do not only desire love; they desire marriage. The root of legal monogamy does not lie (as Shaw and his friends are for ever drearily asserting) in the fact that the man is a mere tyrant and the woman a mere slave. It lies in the fact that if their love for each other is the noblest and freest love conceivable, it can only find its heroic expression in both becoming slaves. I only mention this matter here as a matter which most of us do not need to be taught; for it was the first lesson of life. In after years we may make up what code or compromise about sex we like; but we all know that constancy, jealousy, and the personal pledge are natural and inevitable in sex; we do not feel any surprise when we see them either in a murder or in a valentine. We may or may not see wisdom in early marriages; but we know quite well that wherever the thing is genuine at all, early loves will mean early marriages. But Shaw had not learnt about this tragedy of the sexes, what the rustic ballads of any country on earth would have taught him. He had not learnt, what universal common sense has put into all the folk-lore of the earth, that love cannot be thought of clearly for an instant except as monogamous. The old English ballads never sing the praises of "lovers." They always sing the praises of "true lovers," and that is the final philosophy of the question.

The same is true of Mr. Shaw's refusal to understand the love of the land either in the form of patriotism or of private ownership. It is the attitude of an Irishman cut off from the soil of Ireland, retaining the audacity and even cynicism of the national type, but no longer fed from the roots with its pathos or its experience. This broader and more brotherly rendering of convention must be applied particularly to the conventions of the drama; since that is necessarily the most democratic of all the arts. And it will be found generally that most of the theatrical conventions rest on a real artistic basis. The Greek Unities, for instance, were not proper objects of the meticulous and trivial imitation of Seneca or Gabriel Harvey. But still less were they the right objects for the equally trivial and far more vulgar impatience of men like Macaulay. That a tale should, if possible, be told of one place or one day or a manageable number of characters is an ideal plainly rooted in an aesthetic instinct. But if this be so with the classical drama, it is yet more certainly so with romantic drama, against the somewhat decayed dignity of which Bernard Shaw was largely in rebellion. There was one point in particular upon which the Ibsenites claimed to have reformed the romantic convention which is worthy of special allusion.

Shaw and all the other Ibsenites were fond of insisting

that a defect in the romantic drama was its tendency to end with wedding-bells. Against this they set the modern drama of middle-age, the drama which described marriage itself instead of its poetic preliminaries. Now if Bernard Shaw had been more patient with popular tradition, more prone to think that there might be some sense in its survival, he might have seen this particular problem much more clearly. The old playwrights have left us plenty of plays of marriage and middle-age. Othello is as much about what follows the wedding-bells as The Doll's House. Macbeth is about a middle-aged couple as much as Little Eyolf. But if we ask ourselves what is the real difference, we shall, I think, find that it can fairly be stated thus. The old tragedies of marriage, though not love stories, are like love stories in this, that they work up to some act or stroke which is irrevocable as marriage is irrevocable; to the fact of death or of adultery.

Now the reason why our fathers did not make marriage, in the middle-aged and static sense, the subject of their plays was a very simple one; it was that a play is a very bad place for discussing that topic. You cannot easily make a good drama out of the success or failure of a marriage, just as you could not make a good drama out of the growth of an oak tree or the decay of an empire. As Polonius very reasonably observed, it is too long. A happy love-affair will make a drama simply because it is dramatic; it depends on an ultimate yes or no. But a happy marriage is not dramatic; perhaps it would be less happy if it were. The essence of a romantic heroine is that she asks herself an intense question; but the essence of a sensible wife is that she is much too sensible to ask herself any questions at all. All the things that make monogamy a success are in their nature undramatic things, the silent growth of an instinctive confidence, the common wounds and victories, the accumulation of customs, the rich maturing of old jokes. Sane marriage is an untheatrical thing; it is therefore not surprising that most modern dramatists have devoted themselves to insane marriage.

To summarise; before touching the philosophy which Shaw has ultimately adopted, we must quit the notion that we know it already and that it is hit off in such journalistic terms as these three. Shaw does not wish to multiply problem plays or even problems. He has such scepticism as is the misfortune of his age; but he has this dignified and courageous quality, that he does not come to ask questions but to answer them. He is not a paradox-monger; he is a wild logician, far too simple even to be called a sophist. He understands everything in life except its paradoxes, especially that ultimate paradox that the very things that we cannot comprehend are the things that we have to take for granted.

Lastly, he is not especially social or collectivist. On the contrary, he rather dislikes men in the mass, though he can appreciate them individually. He has no respect for collective humanity in its two great forms; either in that momentary form which we call a mob, or in that enduring form which we call a convention.

The general cosmic theory which can so far be traced through the earlier essays and plays of Bernard Shaw may be expressed in the image of Schopenhauer standing on his head. I cheerfully concede that Schopenhauer looks much nicer in that posture than in his original one, but I can hardly suppose that he feels more comfortable. The substance of the change is this. Roughly speaking, Schopenhauer maintained that life is unreasonable. The intellect, if it could be impartial, would tell us to cease; but a blind partiality, an instinct quite distinct from thought, drives us on to take desperate chances in an essentially bankrupt lottery. Shaw seems to accept this dingy estimate of the rational outlook, but adds a somewhat arresting comment. Schopenhauer had said, "Life is unreasonable; so much the worse for all living things." Shaw said, "Life is unreasonable; so much the worse for reason." Life is the higher call, life we must follow. It may be that there is some undetected fallacy in reason itself. Perhaps the whole man cannot get inside his own head any more than he can jump down his own throat. But there is about the need to live, to suffer, and to create that imperative quality which can truly be called supernatural, of whose voice it can indeed be said that it speaks with authority, and not as the scribes.

This is the first and finest item of the original Bernard Shaw creed: that if reason says that life is irrational, life must be content to reply that reason is lifeless; life is the primary thing, and if reason impedes it, then reason must be trodden down into the mire amid the most abject superstitions. In the ordinary sense it would be specially absurd to suggest that Shaw desires man to be a mere animal. For that is always associated with lust or incontinence; and Shaw's ideals are strict, hygienic, and even, one might say, old-maidish. But there is a mystical sense in which one may say literally that Shaw desires man to be an animal. That is, he desires him to cling first and last to life, to the spirit of animation, to the thing which is common to him and the birds and plants. Man should have the blind faith of a beast: he should be as mystically immutable as a cow, and as deaf to sophistries as a fish. Shaw does not wish him to be a philosopher or an artist; he does not even wish him to be a man, so much as he wishes him to be, in this holy sense, an animal. He must follow the flag of life as fiercely from conviction as all other creatures follow it from instinct.

But this Shavian worship of life is by no means lively. It has nothing in common either with the braver or the baser forms of what we commonly call optimism. It has none of the omnivorous exultation of Walt Whitman or the fiery pantheism of Shelley. Bernard Shaw wishes to show himself not so much as an optimist, but rather as a sort of faithful and contented pessimist. This contradiction is the key to nearly all his early and more obvious contradictions and to many which remain to the end. Whitman and many modern idealists have talked of taking even duty as a pleasure; it seems to me that Shaw takes even pleasure as a duty. In a queer way he seems to see existence as an illusion and yet as an obligation. To every man and woman, bird, beast, and flower, life is a love-call to be eagerly followed. To Bernard Shaw it is merely a military bugle to be obeyed. In short, he fails to feel that the command of Nature (if one must use the anthropomorphic fable of Nature instead of the philosophic term God) can be enjoyed as well as obeyed. He paints life at its darkest and then tells the babe unborn to take the leap in the dark. That is heroic; and to my instinct at least Schopenhauer looks like a pigmy beside his pupil. But it is the heroism of a morbid and almost asphyxiated age. It is awful to think that this world which so many poets have praised has even for a time been depicted as a man-trap into which we may just have the manhood to jump. Think of all those ages through which men have talked of having the courage to die. And then remember that we have actually fallen to talking about having the courage to live.

It is exactly this oddity or dilemma which may be said to culminate in the crowning work of his later and more constructive period, the work in which he certainly attempted, whether with success or not, to state his ultimate and cosmic vision; I mean the play called Man and Superman. In approaching this play we must keep well in mind the distinction recently drawn: that Shaw follows the banner of life, but austerely, not joyously. For him nature has authority, but hardly charm. But before we approach it it is necessary to deal with three things that lead up to it. First it is necessary to speak of what remained of his old critical and realistic method; and then it is necessary to speak of the two important influences which led up to his last and most important change of outlook.

First, since all our spiritual epochs overlap, and a man is often doing the old work while he is thinking of the new, we may deal first with what may be fairly called his last two plays of pure worldly criticism. These are Major Barbara and John Bull's Other Island. Major Barbara indeed contains a strong religious element; but, when all is said, the whole point of the play is that the religious element is defeated. Moreover, the actual expressions of religion in the play are somewhat unsatisfactory as expressions of religion—or even of reason. I must frankly say that Bernard Shaw always seems to me to use the word God not only without any idea of what it means, but without one moment's thought about what it could possibly mean. He said to some atheist, "Never believe in a God that you cannot improve on." The atheist (being a sound theologian) naturally replied that one should not believe in a

God whom one could improve on; as that would show that he was not God. In the same style in Major Barbara the heroine ends by suggesting that she will serve God without personal hope, so that she may owe nothing to God and He owe everything to her. It does not seem to strike her that if God owes everything to her He is not God. These things affect me merely as tedious perversions of a phrase. It is as if you said, "I will never have a father unless I have begotten him."

But the real sting and substance of Major Barbara is much more practical and to the point. It expresses not the new spirituality but the old materialism of Bernard Shaw. Almost every one of Shaw's plays is an expanded epigram. But the epigram is not expanded (as with most people) into a hundred commonplaces. Rather the epigram is expanded into a hundred other epigrams; the work is at least as brilliant in detail as it is in design. But it is generally possible to discover the original and pivotal epigram which is the centre and purpose of the play. It is generally possible, even amid that blinding jewellery of a million jokes, to discover the grave, solemn and sacred joke for which the play itself was written.

The ultimate epigram of Major Barbara can be put thus. People say that poverty is no crime; Shaw says that poverty is a crime; that it is a crime to endure it, a crime to be content with it, that it is the mother of all crimes of brutality, corruption, and fear. If a man says to Shaw that he is born of poor but honest parents, Shaw tells him that the very word "but" shows that his parents were probably dishonest. In short, he maintains here what he had maintained elsewhere: that what the people at this moment require is not more patriotism or more art or more religion or more morality or more sociology, but simply more money. The evil is not ignorance or decadence or sin or pessimism; the evil is poverty. The point of this particular drama is that even the noblest enthusiasm of the girl who becomes a Salvation Army officer fails under the brute money power of her father who is a modern capitalist. When I have said this it will be clear why this play, fine and full of bitter sincerity as it is, must in a manner be cleared out of the way before we come to talk of Shaw's final and serious faith. For his serious faith is in the sanctity of human will, in the divine capacity for creation and choice rising higher than environment and doom; and so far as that goes, Major Barbara is not only apart from his faith but against his faith. Major Barbara is an account of environment victorious over heroic will. There are a thousand answers to the ethic in Major Barbara which I should be inclined to offer. I might point out that the rich do not so much buy honesty as curtains to cover dishonesty: that they do not so much buy health as cushions to comfort disease. And I might suggest that the doctrine that poverty degrades the poor is much more likely to be used as an argument for keeping them powerless than as an argument for making them rich. But there is no need to find such answers to the materialistic pessimism of Major Barbara. The best answer to it is in Shaw's own best and crowning philosophy, with which we shall shortly be concerned.

John Bull's Other Island represents a realism somewhat more tinged with the later transcendentalism of its author. In one sense, of course, it is a satire on the conventional Englishman, who is never so silly or sentimental as when he sees silliness and sentiment in the Irishman. Broadbent, whose mind is all fog and his morals all gush, is firmly persuaded that he is bringing reason and order among the Irish, whereas in truth they are all smiling at his illusions with the critical detachment of so many devils. There have been many plays depicting the absurd Paddy in a ring of Anglo-Saxons; the first purpose of this play is to depict the absurd Anglo-Saxon in a ring of ironical Paddies. But it has a second and more subtle purpose, which is very finely contrived.

It is suggested that when all is said and done there is in this preposterous Englishman a certain creative power which comes from his simplicity and optimism, from his profound resolution rather to live life than to criticise it. I know no finer dialogue of philosophical cross-purposes than that in which Broadbent boasts of his commonsense, and his subtler Irish friend mystifies him by telling him that he, Broadbent, has no common-sense, but only inspiration. The Irishman admits in Broadbent a certain unconscious spiritual force even in his very stupidity. Lord Rosebery coined the very clever phrase "a practical mystic." Shaw is here maintaining that all practical men are practical mystics. And he is really maintaining also that the most practical of all the practical mystics is the one who is a fool.

There is something unexpected and fascinating about this reversal of the usual argument touching enterprise and the business man; this theory that success is created not by intelligence, but by a certain half-witted and yet magical instinct. For Bernard Shaw, apparently, the forests of factories and the mountains of money are not the creations of human wisdom or even of human cunning; they are rather manifestations of the sacred maxim which declares that God has chosen the foolish things of the earth to confound the wise. It is simplicity and even innocence that has made Manchester. As a philosophical fancy this is interesting or even suggestive; but it must be confessed that as a criticism of the relations of England to Ireland it is open to a strong historical objection. The one weak point in John Bull's Other Island is that it turns on the fact that Broadbent succeeds in Ireland. But as a matter of fact Broadbent has not succeeded in Ireland. If getting what one wants is the test and fruit of this mysterious strength, then the Irish peasants are certainly much stronger than the English merchants; for in spite of all the efforts of the merchants, the land has remained a land of peasants.

No glorification of the English practicality as if it were a universal thing can ever get over the fact that we have failed in dealing with the one white people in our power who were markedly unlike ourselves. And the kindness of Broadbent has failed just as much as his common-sense; because he was dealing with a people whose desire and ideal were different from his own. He did not share the Irish passion for small possession in land or for the more pathetic virtues of Christianity. In fact the kindness of Broadbent has failed for the same reason that the gigantic kindness of Shaw has failed. The roots are different; it is like tying the tops of two trees together. Briefly, the philosophy of John Bull's Other Island is quite effective and satisfactory except for this incurable fault:

the fact that John Bull's other island is not John Bull's.

This clearing off of his last critical plays we may classify as the first of the three facts which lead up to Man and Superman. The second of the three facts may be found, I think, in Shaw's discovery of Nietzsche.

This eloquent sophist has an influence upon Shaw and his school which it would require a separate book adequately to study. By descent Nietzsche was a Pole, and probably a Polish noble; and to say that he was a Polish noble is to say that he was a frail, fastidious, and entirely useless anarchist. He had a wonderful poetic wit; and is one of the best rhetoricians of the modern world. He had a remarkable power of saying things that master the reason for a moment by their gigantic unreasonableness; as, for instance, "Your life is intolerable without immortality; but why should not your life be intolerable?" His whole work is shot through with the pangs and fevers of his physical life, which was one of extreme bad health; and in early middle age his brilliant brain broke down into impotence and darkness. All that was true in his teaching was this: that if a man looks fine on a horse it is so far irrelevant to tell him that he would be more economical on a donkey or more humane on a tricycle. In other words, the mere achievement of dignity, beauty, or triumph is strictly to be called a good thing. I do not know if Nietzsche ever used the illustration; but it seems to me that all that is creditable or sound in Nietzsche could be stated in the derivation of one word, the word "valour." Valour means valeur; it means a value; courage is itself a solid good; it is an ultimate virtue; valour is in itself valid.

In so far as he maintained this Nietzsche was only taking part in that great Protestant game of see-saw which has been the amusement of northern Europe since the sixteenth century. Nietzsche imagined he was rebelling against ancient morality; as a matter of fact he was only rebelling against recent morality, against the half-baked impudence of the utilitarians and the materialists. He thought he was rebelling against Christianity; curiously enough he was rebelling solely against the special enemies of Christianity, against Herbert Spencer and Mr. Edward Clodd. Historic Christianity has always believed in the valour of St. Michael riding in front of the Church Militant; and in an ultimate and absolute pleasure, not indirect or utilitarian, the intoxication of the spirit, the wine of the blood of God.

There are indeed doctrines of Nietzsche that are not Christian, but then, by an entertaining coincidence, they are also not true. His hatred of pity is not Christian, but that was not his doctrine but his disease. Invalids are often hard on invalids. And there is another doctrine of his that is not Christianity, and also (by the same laughable accident) not common-sense; and it is a most pathetic circumstance that this was the one doctrine which caught the eye of Shaw and captured him. He was not influenced at all by the morbid attack on mercy. It would require more than ten thousand mad Polish professors to make Bernard Shaw anything but a generous and compassionate man. But it is certainly a nuisance that the one Nietzsche doctrine which attracted him was not the one Nietzsche doctrine that is human and rectifying. Nietzsche might really have done some good if he had taught Bernard Shaw to draw the sword, to drink wine, or even to dance. But he only succeeded in putting into his head a new superstition, which bids fair to be the chief superstition of the dark ages which are possibly in front of us—I mean the superstition of what is called the Superman. In one of his least convincing phrases, Nietzsche had said that just as the ape ultimately produced the man, so should we ultimately produce something higher than the man. The immediate answer, of course, is sufficiently obvious: the ape did not worry about the man, so why should we worry about the Superman? If the Superman will come by natural selection, may we leave it to natural selection? If the Superman will come by human selection, what sort of Superman are we to select? If he is simply to be more just, more brave, or more merciful, then Zarathustra sinks into a Sunday-school teacher; the only way we can work for it is to be more just, more brave, and more merciful; sensible advice, but hardly startling. If he is to be anything else than this, why should we desire him, or what else are we to desire? These questions have been many times asked of the Nietzscheites, and none of the Nietzscheites have even attempted to answer them.

The keen intellect of Bernard Shaw would, I think, certainly have seen through this fallacy and verbiage had it not been that another important event about this time came to the help of Nietzsche and established the Superman on his pedestal. It is the third of the things which I have called stepping-stones to Man and Superman, and it is very important. It is nothing less than the breakdown of one of the three intellectual supports upon which Bernard Shaw had reposed through all his confident career. At the beginning of this book I have described the three ultimate supports of Shaw as the Irishman, the Puritan, and the Progressive. They are the three legs of the tripod upon which the prophet sat to give the oracle; and one of them broke. Just about this time suddenly, by a mere shaft of illumination, Bernard Shaw ceased to believe in progress altogether.

It is generally implied that it was reading Plato that did it. That philosopher was very well qualified to convey the first shock of the ancient civilisation to Shaw, who had always thought instinctively of civilisation as modern. This is not due merely to the daring splendour of the speculations and the vivid picture of Athenian life, it is due also to something analogous in the personalities of that particular ancient Greek and this particular modern Irishman. Bernard Shaw has much affinity to Plato—in his instinctive elevation of temper, his courageous pursuit of ideas as far as they will go, his civic idealism; and also, it must be confessed, in his dislike of poets and a touch of delicate inhumanity. But whatever influence produced the change, the change had all the dramatic suddenness and completeness which belongs to the conversions of great men. It had been perpetually implied through all the earlier works not only that mankind is constantly improving, but that almost everything must be considered in the light of this fact.

More than once he seemed to argue, in comparing the dramatists of the sixteenth with those of the nineteenth century, that the latter had a definite advantage merely because they were of the nineteenth century and not of the sixteenth. When accused of impertinence towards the greatest of the Elizabethans, Bernard Shaw had said, "Shakespeare is a much taller man than I, but I stand on his shoulders"—an epigram which sums up this doctrine with characteristic neatness. But Shaw fell off Shakespeare's shoulders with a crash. This chronological theory that Shaw stood on Shakespeare's shoulders logically involved the supposition that Shakespeare stood on Plato's shoulders. And Bernard Shaw found Plato from his point of view so much more advanced than Shakespeare that he decided in desperation that all three were equal.

Such failure as has partially attended the idea of human equality is very largely due to the fact that no party in the modern state has heartily believed in it. Tories and Radicals have both assumed that one set of men were in essentials superior to mankind. The only difference was that the Tory superiority was a superiority of place; while the Radical superiority is a superiority of time. The great objection to Shaw being on Shakespeare's shoulders is a consideration for the sensations and personal dignity of Shakespeare. It is a democratic objection to anyone being on anyone else's shoulders. Eternal human nature refuses to submit to a man who rules merely by right of birth.

To rule by right of century is to rule by right of birth. Shaw found his nearest kinsman in remote Athens, his remotest enemies in the closest historical proximity; and he began to see the enormous average and the vast level of mankind. If progress swung constantly between such extremes it could not be progress at all. The paradox was sharp but undeniable; if life had such continual ups and downs, it was upon the whole flat. With characteristic sincerity and love of sensation he had no sooner seen this than he hastened to declare it. In the teeth of all his previous pronouncements he emphasised and re-emphasised in print that man had not progressed at all; that ninety-nine hundredths of a man in a cave were the same as ninety-nine hundredths of a man in a suburban villa.

It is characteristic of him to say that he rushed into print with a frank confession of the failure of his old theory. But it is also characteristic of him that he rushed into print also with a new alternative theory, quite as definite, quite as confident, and, if one may put it so, quite as infallible as the old one. Progress had never happened hitherto, because it had been sought solely through education. Education was rubbish. "Fancy," said he, "trying to produce a greyhound or a racehorse by education!" The man of the future must not be taught; he must be bred. This notion of producing superior human beings by the methods of the stud-farm had often been urged, though its difficulties had never been cleared up. I mean its practical difficulties; its moral difficulties, or rather impossibilities, for any animal fit to be called a man need scarcely be discussed. But even as a scheme it had never been made clear. The first and most obvious objection to it of course is this: that if you are to breed men as pigs, you require some overseer who is as much more subtle than a man as a man is more subtle than a pig. Such an individual is not easy to find.

It was, however, in the heat of these three things, the decline of his merely destructive realism, the discovery of Nietzsche, and the abandonment of the idea of a progressive education of mankind, that he attempted what is not necessarily his best, but certainly his most important work. The two things are by no means necessarily the same. The most important work of Milton is Paradise Lost; his best work is Lycidas. There are other places in which Shaw's argument is more fascinating or his wit more startling than in Man and Superman; there are other plays that he has made more brilliant. But I am sure that there is no other play that he wished to make more brilliant. I will not say that he is in this case more serious than elsewhere; for the word serious is a double-meaning and double-dealing word, a traitor in the dictionary. It sometimes means solemn, and it sometimes means sincere. A very short experience of private and public life will be enough to prove that the most solemn people are generally the most insincere. A somewhat more delicate and detailed consideration will show also that the most sincere men are generally not solemn; and of these is Bernard Shaw. But if we use the word serious in the old and Latin sense of the word "grave," which means weighty or valid, full of substance, then we may say without any hesitation that this is the most serious play of the most serious man alive.

The outline of the play is, I suppose, by this time sufficiently well known. It has two main philosophic motives. The first is that what he calls the life-force (the old infidels called it Nature, which seems a neater word, and nobody knows the meaning of either of them) desires above all things to make suitable marriages, to produce a purer and prouder race, or eventually to produce a Superman. The second is that in this effecting of racial marriages the woman is a more conscious agent than the man. In short, that woman disposes a long time before man proposes. In this play, therefore, woman is made the pursuer and man the pursued. It cannot be denied, I think, that in this matter Shaw is handicapped by his habitual hardness of touch, by his lack of sympathy with the romance of which he writes, and to a certain extent even by his own integrity and right conscience. Whether the man hunts the woman or the woman the man, at least it should be a splendid pagan hunt; but Shaw is not a sporting man. Nor is he a pagan, but a Puritan. He cannot recover the impartiality of paganism which allowed Diana to propose to Endymion without thinking any the worse of her. The result is that while he makes Anne, the woman who marries his hero, a really powerful and convincing woman, he can only do it by making her a highly objectionable woman. She is a liar and a bully, not from sudden fear or excruciating dilemma; she is a liar and a bully in grain; she has no truth or magnanimity in her. The more we know that she is real, the more we know that she is vile. In short, Bernard Shaw is still haunted with his old impotence of the unromantic writer; he cannot imagine the main motives of human life from the inside. We are convinced successfully that Anne wishes to marry Tanner, but in the very process we lose all power of conceiving why Tanner should ever consent to marry Anne. A writer with a more romantic strain in him might have imagined a woman choosing her lover without shamelessness and magnetising him without fraud. Even if the first movement were feminine, it need hardly be a movement like this. In truth, of course, the two sexes have their two methods of attraction, and in some of the happiest cases they are almost simultaneous. But even on the most cynical showing they need not be mixed up. It is one thing to say that the mousetrap is not there by accident. It is another to say (in the face of ocular experience) that the mousetrap runs after the mouse.

But whenever Shaw shows the Puritan hardness or even the Puritan cheapness, he shows something also of the Puritan nobility, of the idea that sacrifice is really a frivolity in the face of a great purpose. The reasonableness of Calvin and his followers will by the mercy of heaven be at last washed away; but their unreasonableness will remain an eternal splendour. Long after we have let drop the fancy that Protestantism was rational it will be its glory that it was fanatical. So it is with Shaw. To make Anne a real woman, even a dangerous woman, he would need to be something stranger and softer than Bernard Shaw. But though I always argue with him whenever he argues, I confess that he always conquers me in the one or two moments when he is emotional.

There is one really noble moment when Anne offers for all her cynical husband-hunting the only defence that is really great enough to cover it. "It will not be all happiness for me. Perhaps death." And the man rises also at that real crisis, saying, "Oh, that clutch holds and hurts. What have you grasped in me? Is there a father's heart as well as a mother's?" That seems to me actually great; I do not like either of the characters an atom more than formerly; but I can see shining and shaking through them at that instant the splendour of the God that made them and of the image of God who wrote their story.

A logician is like a liar in many respects, but chiefly in the fact that he should have a good memory. That cutting and inquisitive style which Bernard Shaw has always adopted carries with it an inevitable criticism. And it cannot be denied that this new theory of the supreme importance of sound sexual union, wrought by any means, is hard logically to reconcile with Shaw's old diatribes against sentimentalism and operatic romance. If Nature wishes primarily to entrap us into sexual union, then all the means of sexual attraction, even the most maudlin or theatrical, are justified at one stroke. The guitar of the troubadour is as practical as the ploughshare of the husbandman. The waltz in the ballroom is as serious as the debate in the parish council. The justification of Anne, as the potential mother of Superman, is really the justification of all the humbugs and sentimentalists whom Shaw had been denouncing as a dramatic critic and as a dramatist since the beginning of his career.

It was to no purpose that the earlier Bernard Shaw said that romance was all moonshine. The moonshine that ripens love is now as practical as the sunshine that ripens corn. It was vain to say that sexual chivalry was all rot; it might be as rotten as manure—and also as fertile. It is vain to call first love a fiction; it may be as fictitious as the ink of the cuttle or the doubling of the hare; as fictitious, as efficient, and as indispensable. It is vain to call it a self-deception; Schopenhauer said that all existence was a self-deception; and Shaw's only further comment seems to be that it is right to be deceived.

To Man and Superman, as to all his plays, the author attaches a most fascinating preface at the beginning. But I really think that he ought also to attach a hearty apology at the end; an apology to all the minor dramatists or preposterous actors whom he had cursed for romanticism in his youth. Whenever he objected to an actress for ogling she might reasonably reply, "But this is how I support my friend Anne in her sublime evolutionary effort." Whenever he laughed at an old-fashioned actor for ranting, the actor might answer, "My exaggeration is not more absurd than the tail of a peacock or the swagger of a cock; it is the way I preach the great fruitful lie of the life-force that I am a very fine fellow." We have remarked the end of Shaw's campaign in favour of progress. This ought really to have been the end of his campaign against romance. All the tricks of love that he called artificial become natural;

because they become Nature. All the lies of love become truths; indeed they become the Truth.

The minor things of the play contain some thunderbolts of good thinking. Throughout this brief study I have deliberately not dwelt upon mere wit, because in anything of Shaw's that may be taken for granted. It is enough to say that this play which is full of his most serious quality is as full as any of his minor sort of success. In a more solid sense two important facts stand out: the first is the character of the young American; the other is the character of Straker, the chauffeur. In these Shaw has realised and made vivid two most important facts. First, that America is not intellectually a go-ahead country, but both for good and evil an old-fashioned one. It is full of stale culture and ancestral simplicity, just as Shaw's young millionaire quotes Macaulay and piously worships his wife. Second, he has pointed out in the character of Straker that there has arisen in our midst a new class that has education without breeding. Straker is the man who has ousted the hansom-cabman, having neither his coarseness nor his kindliness. Great sociological credit is due to the man who has first clearly observed that Straker has appeared. How anybody can profess for a moment to be glad that he has appeared, I do not attempt to conjecture.

Appended to the play is an entertaining though somewhat mysterious document called "The Revolutionist's Handbook." It contains many very sound remarks; this, for example, which I cannot too much applaud: "If you hit your child, be sure that you hit him in anger." If that principle had been properly understood, we should have had less of Shaw's sociological friends and their meddling with the habits and instincts of the poor. But among the fragments of advice also occurs the following suggestive and even alluring remark: "Every man over forty is a scoundrel." On the first personal opportunity I asked the author of this remarkable axiom what it meant. I gathered that what it really meant was something like this: that every man over forty had been all the essential use that he was likely to be, and was therefore in a manner a parasite. It is gratifying to reflect that Bernard Shaw has sufficiently answered his own epigram by continuing to pour out treasures both of truth and folly long after this allotted time. But if the epigram might be interpreted in a rather looser style as meaning that past a certain point a man's work takes on its final character and does not greatly change the nature of its merits, it may certainly be said that with Man and Superman, Shaw reaches that stage. The two plays that have followed it, though of very great interest in themselves, do not require any revaluation of, or indeed any addition to, our summary of his genius and success. They are both in a sense casts back to his primary energies; the first in a controversial and the second in a technical sense. Neither need prevent our saying that the moment when John Tanner and Anne agree that it is doom for him and death for her and life only for the thing unborn, is the peak of his utterance as a prophet.

The two important plays that he has since given us are The Doctor's Dilemma and Getting Married. The first is as regards its most amusing and effective elements a throw-back to his old game of guying the men of science. It was a very good game, and he was an admirable player. The actual story of the Doctor's Dilemma itself seems to me less poignant and important than the things with which Shaw had lately been dealing. First of all, as has been said, Shaw has neither the kind of justice nor the kind of weakness that goes to make a true problem. We cannot feel the Doctor's Dilemma, because we cannot really fancy Bernard Shaw being in a dilemma. His mind is both fond of abruptness and fond of finality; he always makes up his mind when he knows the facts and sometimes before. Moreover, this particular problem (though Shaw is certainly, as we shall see, nearer to pure doubt about it than about anything else) does not strike the critic as being such an exasperating problem after all. An artist of vast power and promise, who is also a scamp of vast profligacy and treachery, has a chance of life if specially treated for a special disease. The modern doctors (and even the modern dramatist) are in doubt whether he should be specially favoured because he is aesthetically important or specially disregarded because he is ethically anti-social. They see-saw between the two despicable modern doctrines, one that geniuses should be worshipped like idols and the other that criminals should be merely wiped out like germs. That both clever men and bad men ought to be treated like men does not seem to occur to them. As a matter of fact, in these affairs of life and death one never does think of such distinctions. Nobody does shout out at sea, "Bad citizen overboard!" I should recommend the doctor in his dilemma to do exactly what I am sure any decent doctor would do without any dilemma at all: to treat the man simply as a man, and give him no more and no less favour than he would to anybody else. In short, I am sure a practical physician would drop all these visionary, unworkable modern dreams about type and criminology and go back to the plain business-like facts of the French Revolution and the Rights of Man.

The other play, Getting Married, is a point in Shaw's career, but only as a play, not, as usual, as a heresy. It is nothing but a conversation about marriage; and one cannot agree or disagree with the view of marriage, because all views are given which are held by anybody, and some (I should think) which are held by nobody. But its technical quality is of some importance in the life of its author. It is worth consideration as a play, because it is not a play at all. It marks the culmination and completeness of that victory of Bernard Shaw over the British public, or rather over their official representatives, of which I have spoken. Shaw had fought a long fight with business men, those incredible people, who assured him that it was useless to have wit without murders, and that a good joke, which is the most popular thing everywhere else, was quite unsalable in the theatrical world. In spite of this he had conquered by his wit and his good dialogue; and by the time of which we now speak he was victorious and secure. All his plays were being produced as a matter of course in England and as a matter of the fiercest fashion and enthusiasm in America and Germany. No one who knows the nature of the man will doubt that under such circumstances his first act would be to produce his wit naked and unashamed. He had been told that he could not support a slight play by mere dialogue. He therefore promptly produced mere dialogue without the slightest play for it to support. Getting Married is no more a play than Cicero's dialogue De Amicitia, and not half so much a play as Wilson's Noctes Ambrosianae. But though it is not a play, it was played, and played successfully. Everyone who went into the theatre felt that he was only eavesdropping at an accidental conversation. But the conversation was so sparkling and sensible that he went on eavesdropping. This, I think, as it is the final play of Shaw, is also, and fitly, his final triumph. He is a good dramatist and sometimes even a great dramatist. But the occasions when we get glimpses of him as really a great man are on these occasions when he is utterly undramatic. From first to last Bernard Shaw has been nothing but a conversationalist. It is not a slur to say so; Socrates was one, and even Christ Himself. He differs from that divine and that human prototype in the fact that, like most modern people, he does to some extent talk in order to find out what he thinks; whereas they knew it beforehand. But he has the virtues that go with the talkative man; one of which is humility. You will hardly ever find a really proud man talkative; he is afraid of talking too much. Bernard Shaw offered himself to the world with only one great qualification, that he could talk honestly and well. He did not speak; he talked to a crowd. He did not write; he talked to a typewriter. He did not really construct a play; he talked through ten mouths or masks instead of through one. His literary power and progress began in casual conversations—and it seems to me supremely right that it should end in one great and casual conversation. His last play is nothing but garrulous talking, that great thing called gossip. And I am happy to say that the play has been as efficient and successful as talk and gossip have always been among the children of men.

Of his life in these later years I have made no pretence of telling even the little that there is to tell. Those who regard him as a mere self-advertising egotist may be surprised to hear that there is perhaps no man of whose private life less could be positively said by an outsider. Even those who know him can make little but a conjecture of what has lain behind this splendid stretch of intellectual self-expression; I only make my conjecture like the rest. I think that the first great turning-point in Shaw's life (after the early things of which I have spoken, the taint of drink in the teetotal home, or the first fight with poverty) was the deadly illness which fell upon him, at the end of his first flashing career as a Saturday Reviewer. I know it would goad Shaw to madness to suggest that sickness could have softened him. That is why I suggest it. But I say for his comfort that I think it hardened him also; if that can be called hardening which is only the strengthening of our souls to meet some dreadful reality. At least it is certain that the larger spiritual ambitions, the desire to find a faith and found a church, come after that time. I also mention it because there is hardly anything else to mention; his life is singularly free from landmarks, while his literature is so oddly full of surprises. His marriage to Miss Payne-Townsend, which occurred not long after his illness, was one of those quite successful things which are utterly silent. The placidity of his married life may be sufficiently indicated by saying that (as far as I can make out) the most important events in it were rows about the Executive of the Fabian Society. If such ripples do not express a still and lake-like life, I do not know what would. Honestly, the only thing in his later career that can be called an event is the stand made by Shaw at the Fabians against the sudden assault of Mr. H. G. Wells, which, after scenes of splendid exasperations, ended in Wells' resignation. There was another slight ruffling of the calm when Bernard Shaw said some quite sensible things about Sir Henry Irving. But on the whole we confront the composure of one who has come into his own.

The method of his life has remained mostly unchanged. And there is a great deal of method in his life; I can hear some people murmuring something about method in his madness. He is not only neat and business-like; but, unlike some literary men I know, does not conceal the fact. Having all the talents proper to an author, he delights to prove that he has also all the talents proper to a publisher; or even to a publisher's clerk. Though many looking at his light brown clothes would call him a Bohemian, he really hates and despises Bohemianism; in the sense that he hates and despises disorder and uncleanness and irresponsibility. All that part of him is peculiarly normal and efficient. He gives good advice; he always answers letters, and answers them in a decisive and very legible hand. He has said himself that the only educational art that he thinks important is that of being able to jump off tram-cars at the proper moment. Though a rigid vegetarian, he is quite regular and rational in his meals; and though he detests sport, he takes quite sufficient exercise. While he has always made a mock of science in theory, he is by nature prone to meddle with it in practice. He is fond of photographing, and even more fond of being photographed. He maintained (in one of his moments of mad modernity) that photography was a finer thing than portrait-painting, more exquisite and more imaginative; he urged the characteristic argument that none of his own photographs were like each other or like him. But he would certainly wash the chemicals off his hands the instant after an experiment; just as he would wash the blood off his hands the instant after a Socialist massacre. He cannot endure stains or accretions; he is of that temperament which feels tradition itself to be a coat of dust; whose temptation it is to feel nothing but a sort of foul accumulation or living disease even in the creeper upon the cottage or the moss upon the grave. So thoroughly are his tastes those of the civilised modern man that if it had not been for the fire in him of justice and anger he might have been the most trim and modern among the millions whom he shocks: and his bicycle and brown hat have been no menace in Brixton.

But God sent among those suburbans one who was a prophet as well as a sanitary inspector. He had every qualification for living in a villa—except the necessary indifference to his brethren living in pigstyes. But for the small fact that he hates with a sickening hatred the hypocrisy and class cruelty, he would really accept and admire the bathroom and the bicycle and asbestos-stove, having no memory of rivers or of roaring fires. In these things, like Mr. Straker, he is the New Man. But for his great soul he might have accepted modern civilisation; it was a wonderful escape. This man whom men so foolishly call crazy and anarchic has really a dangerous affinity to the fourth-rate perfections of our provincial and Protestant civilisation. He might even have been respectable if he had had less self-respect.

His fulfilled fame and this tone of repose and reason in his life, together with the large circle of his private kindness and the regard of his fellow-artists, should permit us to end the record in a tone of almost patriarchal quiet. If I wished to complete such a picture I could add many touches: that he has consented to wear evening dress; that he has supported the Times Book Club; and that his beard has turned grey; the last to his regret, as he wanted it to remain red till they had completed colour-photography. He can mix with the most conservative statesmen; his tone grows continuously more gentle in the matter of religion. It would be easy to end with the lion lying down with the lamb, the wild Irishman tamed or taming everybody, Shaw reconciled to the British public as the British public is certainly largely reconciled to Shaw.

But as I put these last papers together, having finished this rude study, I hear a piece of news. His latest play, The Showing Up of Blanco Posnet, has been forbidden by the Censor. As far as I can discover, it has been forbidden because one of the characters professes a belief in God and states his conviction that God has got him. This is wholesome; this is like one crack of thunder in a clear sky. Not so easily does the prince of this world forgive. Shaw's religious training and instinct is not mine, but in all honest religion there is something that is hateful to the prosperous compromise of our time. You are free in our time to say that God does not exist; you are free to say that He exists and is evil; you are free to say (like poor old Renan) that He would like to exist if He could. You may talk of God as a metaphor or a mystification; you may water Him down with gallons of long words, or boil Him to the rags of metaphysics; and it is not merely that nobody punishes, but nobody protests. But if you speak of God as a fact, as a thing like a tiger, as a reason for changing one's conduct, then the modern world will stop you somehow if it can. We are long past talking about whether an unbeliever should be punished for being irreverent. It is now thought irreverent to be a believer. I end where I began: it is the old Puritan in Shaw that jars the modern world like an electric shock. That vision with which I meant to end, that vision of culture and common-sense, of red brick and brown flannel, of the modern clerk broadened enough to embrace Shaw and Shaw softened enough to embrace the clerk, all that vision of a new London begins to fade and alter. The red brick begins to burn red-hot; and the smoke from all the chimneys has a strange smell. I find myself back in the fumes in which I started.... Perhaps I have been misled by small modernities. Perhaps what I have called fastidiousness is a divine fear. Perhaps what I have called coldness is a predestinate and ancient endurance. The vision of the Fabian villas grows fainter and fainter, until I see only a void place across which runs Bunyan's Pilgrim with his fingers in his ears. Bernard Shaw has occupied much of his life in trying to elude his followers. The fox has enthusiastic followers, and Shaw seems to regard his in much the same way.

This man whom men accuse of bidding for applause seems to me to shrink even from assent. If you agree with Shaw he is very likely to contradict you; I have contradicted Shaw throughout, that is why I come at last almost to agree with him. His critics have accused him of vulgar self-advertisement; in his relation to his followers he seems to me rather marked with a sort of mad modesty. He seems to wish to fly from agreement, to have as few followers as possible. All this reaches back, I think, to the three roots from which this meditation grew. It is partly the mere impatience and irony of the Irishman. It is partly the thought of the Calvinist that the host of God should be thinned rather than thronged; that Gideon must reject soldiers rather than recruit them. And it is partly, alas, the unhappy Progressive trying to be in front of his own religion, trying to destroy his own idol and even to desecrate his own tomb. But from whatever causes, this furious escape from popularity has involved Shaw in some perversities and refinements which are almost mere insincerities, and which make it necessary to disentangle the good he has done from the evil in this dazzling course. I will attempt some summary by stating the three things in which his influence seems to me thoroughly good and the three in which it seems bad. But for the pleasure of ending on the finer note I will speak first of those that seem bad.

The primary respect in which Shaw has been a bad influence is that he has encouraged fastidiousness. He has made men dainty about their moral meals. This is indeed the root of his whole objection to romance. Many people have objected to romance for being too airy and exquisite. Shaw objects to romance for being too rank and coarse. Many have despised romance because it is unreal; Shaw really hates it because it is a great deal too real. Shaw dislikes romance as he dislikes beef and beer, raw brandy or raw beefsteaks. Romance is too masculine for his taste. You will find throughout his criticisms, amid all their truth, their wild justice or pungent impartiality, a curious undercurrent of prejudice upon one point: the preference for the refined rather than the rude or ugly. Thus he will dislike a joke because it is coarse without asking if it is really immoral. He objects to a man sitting down on his hat, whereas the austere moralist should only object to his sitting down on someone else's hat. This sensibility is barren because it is universal. It is useless to object to man being made ridiculous. Man is born ridiculous, as can easily be seen if you look at him soon after he is born. It is grotesque to drink beer, but it is equally grotesque to drink soda-water; the grotesqueness lies in the act of filling yourself like a bottle through a hole. It is undignified to walk with a drunken stagger; but it is fairly undignified to walk at all, for all walking is a sort of balancing, and there is always in the human being something of a quadruped on its hind legs. I do not say he would be more dignified if he went on all fours; I do not know that he ever is dignified except when he is dead. We shall not be refined till we are refined into dust. Of course it is only because he is not wholly an animal that man sees he is a rum animal; and if man on his hind legs is in an artificial attitude, it is only because, like a dog, he is begging or saying thank you. Everything important is in that sense absurd from the grave baby to the grinning skull; everything practical is a practical joke. But throughout Shaw's comedies, curiously enough, there is a certain kicking against this great doom of laughter. For instance, it is the first duty of a man who is in love to make a fool of himself; but Shaw's heroes always seem to flinch from this, and attempt, in airy, philosophic revenge, to make a fool of the woman first. The attempts of Valentine and Charteris to divide their perceptions from their desires, and tell the woman she is worthless even while trying to win her, are sometimes almost torturing to watch; it is like seeing a man trying to play a different tune with each hand. I fancy this agony is not only in the spectator, but in the dramatist as well. It is Bernard Shaw struggling with his reluctance to do anything so ridiculous as make a proposal. For there are two types of great humorist: those who love to see a man absurd and those who hate to see him absurd. Of the first kind are Rabelais and Dickens; of the second kind are Swift and Bernard Shaw. So far as Shaw has spread or helped a certain modern reluctance or mauvaise honte in these grand and grotesque functions of man I think he has definitely done harm. He has much influence among the young men; but it is not an influence in the direction of keeping them young. One cannot imagine him inspiring any of his followers to write a war-song or a drinking-song or a love-song, the three forms of human utterance which come next in nobility to a prayer.

It may seem odd to say that the net effect of a man so apparently impudent will be to make men shy. But it is certainly the truth. Shyness is always the sign of a divided soul; a man is shy because he somehow thinks his position at once despicable and important. If he were without humility he would not care; and if he were without pride he would not care. Now the main purpose of Shaw's theoretic teaching is to declare that we ought to fulfil these great functions of life, that we ought to eat and drink and love. But the main tendency of his habitual criticism is to suggest that all the sentiments, professions, and postures of these things are not only comic but even contemptibly comic, follies and almost frauds. The result would seem to be that a race of young men may arise who do all these things, but do them awkwardly. That which was of old a free and hilarious function becomes an important and embarrassing necessity. Let us endure all the pagan pleasures with a Christian patience. Let us eat, drink, and be serious.

The second of the two points on which I think Shaw has done definite harm is this: that he has (not always or even as a rule intentionally) increased that anarchy of thought which is always the destruction of thought. Much of his early writing has encouraged among the modern youth that most pestilent of all popular tricks and fallacies; what is called the argument of progress. I mean this kind of thing. Previous ages were often, alas, aristocratic in politics or clericalist in religion; but they were always democratic in philosophy; they appealed to man, not to particular men. And if most men were against an idea, that was so far against it. But nowadays that most men are against a thing is thought to be in its favour; it is vaguely supposed to show that some day most men will be for it. If a man says that cows are reptiles, or that Bacon wrote Shakespeare, he can always quote the contempt of his contemporaries as in some mysterious way proving the complete conversion of posterity.

The objections to this theory scarcely need any elaborate indication. The final objection to it is that it amounts to this: say anything, however idiotic, and you are in advance of your age. This kind of stuff must be stopped. The sort of democrat who appeals to the babe unborn must be classed with the sort of aristocrat who appeals to his deceased great-grandfather. Both should be sharply reminded that they are appealing to individuals whom they well know to be at a disadvantage in the matter of prompt and witty reply. Now although Bernard Shaw has survived this simple confusion, he has in his time greatly contributed to it. If there is, for instance, one thing that is really rare in Shaw it is hesitation. He makes up his mind quicker than a calculating boy or a county magistrate. Yet on this subject of the next change in ethics he has felt hesitation, and being a strictly honest man has expressed it. "I know no harder practical question than how much selfishness one ought to stand from a gifted person for the sake of his gifts or on the chance of his being right in the long run. The Superman will certainly come like a thief in the night, and be shot at accordingly; but we cannot leave our property wholly undefended on that account. On the other hand, we cannot ask the Superman simply to add a higher set of virtues to current respectable morals; for he is undoubtedly going to empty a good deal of respectable morality out like so much dirty water, and replace it by new and strange customs, shedding old obligations and accepting new and heavier ones. Every step of his progress must horrify conventional people; and if it were possible for even the most superior man to march ahead all the time, every pioneer of the march towards the Superman would be crucified."

When the most emphatic man alive, a man unmatched in violent precision of statement, speaks with such avowed vagueness and doubt as this, it is no wonder if all his more weak-minded followers are in a mere whirlpool of uncritical and unmeaning innovation. If the superior person will be apparently criminal, the most probable result is simply that the criminal person will think himself superior. A very slight knowledge of human nature is required in the matter. If the Superman may possibly be a thief, you may bet your boots that the next thief will be a Superman. But indeed the Supermen (of whom I have met many) have generally been more weak in the head than in the moral conduct; they have simply offered the first fancy which occupied their minds as the new morality. I fear that Shaw had a way of encouraging these follies. It is obvious from the passage I have quoted that he has no way of restraining them.

The truth is that all feeble spirits naturally live in the future, because it is featureless; it is a soft job; you can make it what you like. The next age is blank, and I can paint it freely with my favourite colour. It requires real courage to face the past, because the past is full of facts which cannot be got over; of men certainly wiser than we and of things done which we could not do. I know I cannot write a poem as good as Lycidas. But it is always easy to say that the particular sort of poetry I can write will be the poetry of the future. This I call the second evil influence of Shaw: that he has encouraged many to throw themselves for justification upon the shapeless and the unknown. In this, though courageous himself, he has encouraged cowards, and though sincere himself, has helped a mean escape. The third evil in his influence can, I think, be much more shortly dealt with. He has to a very slight extent, but still perceptibly, encouraged a kind of charlatanism of utterance among those who possess his Irish impudence without his Irish virtue. For instance, his amusing trick of self-praise is perfectly hearty and humorous in him; nay, it is even humble; for to confess vanity is itself humble. All that is the matter with the proud is that they will not admit that they are vain. Therefore when Shaw says that he alone is able to write such and such admirable work, or that he has just utterly wiped out some celebrated opponent, I for one never feel anything offensive in the tone, but, indeed, only the unmistakable intonation of a friend's voice. But I have noticed among younger, harder, and much shallower men a certain disposition to ape this insolent ease and certitude, and that without any fundamental frankness or mirth. So far the influence is bad. Egoism can be learnt as a lesson like any other "ism." It is not so easy to learn an Irish accent or a good temper. In its lower forms the thing becomes a most unmilitary trick of announcing the victory before one has gained it.

When one has said those three things, one has said, I think, all that can be said by way of blaming Bernard Shaw. It is significant that he was never blamed for any of these things by the Censor. Such censures as the attitude of that official involves may be dismissed with a very light sort of disdain. To represent Shaw as profane or provocatively indecent is not a matter for discussion at all; it is a disgusting criminal libel upon a particularly respectable gentleman of the middle classes, of refined tastes and somewhat Puritanical views. But while the negative defence of Shaw is easy, the just praise of him is almost as complex as it is necessary; and I shall devote the last few pages of this book to a triad corresponding to the last one—to the three important elements in which the work of Shaw has been good as well as great.

In the first place, and quite apart from all particular theories, the world owes thanks to Bernard Shaw for having combined being intelligent with being intelligible. He has popularised philosophy, or rather he has repopularised it, for philosophy is always popular, except in peculiarly corrupt and oligarchic ages like our own. We have passed the age of the demagogue, the man who has little to say and says it loud. We have come to the age of the mystagogue or don, the man who has nothing to say, but says it softly and impressively in an indistinct whisper. After all, short words must mean something, even if they mean filth or lies; but long words may sometimes mean literally nothing, especially if they are used (as they mostly are in modern books and magazine articles) to balance and modify each other. A plain figure 4, scrawled in chalk anywhere, must always mean something; it must always mean 2 + 2. But the most enormous and mysterious algebraic equation, full of letters, brackets, and fractions, may all cancel out at last and be equal to nothing. When a demagogue says to a mob, "There is the Bank of England, why shouldn't you have some of that money?" he says something which is at least as honest and intelligible as the figure 4. When a writer in the Times remarks, "We must raise the economic efficiency of the masses without diverting anything from those classes which represent the national prosperity and refinement," then his equation cancels out; in a literal and logical sense his remark amounts to nothing.

There are two kinds of charlatans or people called quacks to-day. The power of the first is that he advertises—and cures. The power of the second is that though he is not learned enough to cure he is much too learned to advertise. The former give away their dignity with a pound of tea; the latter are paid a pound of tea merely for being dignified. I think them the worse quacks of the two. Shaw is certainly of the other sort. Dickens, another man who was great enough to be a demagogue (and greater than Shaw because more heartily a demagogue), puts for ever the true difference between the demagogue and the mystagogue in Dr. Marigold: "Except that we're cheap-jacks and they're dear-jacks, I don't see any difference between us." Bernard Shaw is a great cheap-jack, with plenty of patter and I dare say plenty of nonsense, but with this also (which is not wholly unimportant), with goods to sell. People accuse such a man of self-advertisement. But at least the cheap-jack does advertise his wares, whereas the don or dear-jack advertises nothing except himself. His very silence, nay his very sterility, are supposed to be marks of the richness of his erudition. He is too learned to teach, and sometimes too wise even to talk. St. Thomas Aquinas said: "In auctore auctoritas." But there is more than one man at Oxford or Cambridge who is considered an authority because he has never been an author.

Against all this mystification both of silence and verbosity Shaw has been a splendid and smashing protest. He has stood up for the fact that philosophy is not the concern of those who pass through Divinity and Greats, but of those who pass through birth and death. Nearly all the most awful and abstruse statements can be put in words of one syllable, from "A child is born" to "A soul is damned." If the ordinary man may not discuss existence, why should he be asked to conduct it? About concrete matters indeed one naturally appeals to an oligarchy or select class. For information about Lapland I go to an aristocracy of Laplanders; for the ways of rabbits to an aristocracy of naturalists or, preferably, an aristocracy of poachers. But only mankind itself can bear witness to the abstract first principles of mankind, and in matters of theory I would always consult the mob. Only the mass of men, for instance, have authority to say whether life is good. Whether life is good is an especially mystical and delicate question, and, like all such questions, is asked in words of one syllable. It is also answered in words of one syllable, and Bernard Shaw (as also mankind) answers "yes."

This plain, pugnacious style of Shaw has greatly clarified all controversies. He has slain the polysyllable, that huge and slimy centipede which has sprawled over all the valleys of England like the "loathly worm" who was slain by the ancient knight. He does not think that difficult questions will be made simpler by using difficult words about them. He has achieved the admirable work, never to be mentioned without gratitude, of discussing Evolution without mentioning it. The good work is of course more evident in the case of philosophy than any other region; because the case of philosophy was a crying one. It was really preposterous that the things most carefully reserved for the study of two or three men should actually be the things common to all men. It was absurd that certain men should be experts on the special subject of everything. But he stood for much the same spirit and style in other matters; in economics, for example. There never has been a better popular economist; one more lucid, entertaining, consistent, and essentially exact. The very comicality of his examples makes them and their argument stick in the mind; as in the case I remember in which he said that the big shops had now to please everybody, and were not entirely dependent on the lady who sails in "to order four governesses and five grand pianos." He is always preaching collectivism; yet he does not very often name it. He does not talk about collectivism, but about cash; of which the populace feel a much more definite need. He talks about cheese, boots, perambulators, and how people are really to live.

For him economics really means housekeeping, as it does in Greek. His difference from the orthodox economists, like most of his differences, is very different from the attacks made by the main body of Socialists. The old Manchester economists are generally attacked for being too gross and material. Shaw really attacks them for not being gross or material enough. He thinks that they hide themselves behind long words, remote hypotheses or unreal generalisations. When the orthodox economist begins with his correct and primary formula, "Suppose there is a Man on an Island——" Shaw is apt to interrupt him sharply, saying, "There is a Man in the Street."

The second phase of the man's really fruitful efficacy is in a sense the converse of this. He has improved philosophic discussions by making them more popular. But he has also improved popular amusements by making them more philosophic. And by more philosophic I do not mean duller, but funnier; that is more varied. All real fun is in cosmic contrasts, which involve a view of the cosmos. But I know that this second strength in Shaw is really difficult to state and must be approached by explanations and even by eliminations. Let me say at once that I think nothing of Shaw or anybody else merely for playing the daring sceptic. I do not think he has done any good or even achieved any effect simply by asking startling questions. It is possible that there have been ages so sluggish or automatic that anything that woke them up at all was a good thing. It is sufficient to be certain that ours is not such an age. We do not need waking up; rather we suffer from insomnia, with all its results of fear and exaggeration and frightful waking dreams. The modern mind is not a donkey which wants kicking to make it go on. The modern mind is more like a motor-car on a lonely road which two amateur motorists have been just clever enough to take to pieces, but are not quite clever enough to put together again. Under these circumstances kicking the car has never been found by the best experts to be effective. No one, therefore, does any good to our age merely by asking questions—unless he can answer the questions. Asking questions is already the fashionable and aristocratic sport which has brought most of us into the bankruptcy court. The note of our age is a note of interrogation. And the final point is so plain; no sceptical philosopher can ask any questions that may not equally be asked by a tired child on a hot afternoon. "Am I a boy?—Why am I a boy?—Why aren't I a chair?—What is a chair?" A child will sometimes ask questions of this sort for two hours. And the philosophers of Protestant Europe have asked them for two hundred years.

If that were all that I meant by Shaw making men more philosophic, I should put it not among his good influences but his bad. He did do that to some extent; and so far he is bad. But there is a much bigger and better sense in which he has been a philosopher. He has brought back into English drama all the streams of fact or tendency which are commonly called undramatic. They were there in Shakespeare's time; but they have scarcely been there since until Shaw. I mean that Shakespeare, being interested in everything, put everything into a play. If he had lately been thinking about the irony and even contradiction confronting us in self-preservation and suicide, he put it all into Hamlet. If he was annoyed by some passing boom in theatrical babies he put that into Hamlet too. He would put anything into Hamlet which he really thought was true, from his favourite nursery ballads to his personal (and perhaps unfashionable) conviction of the Catholic purgatory. There is no fact that strikes one, I think, about Shakespeare, except the fact of how dramatic he could be, so much as the fact of how undramatic he could be.

In this great sense Shaw has brought philosophy back into drama—philosophy in the sense of a certain freedom of the mind. This is not a freedom to think what one likes (which is absurd, for one can only think what one thinks); it is a freedom to think about what one likes, which is quite a different thing and the spring of all thought. Shakespeare (in a weak moment, I think) said that all the world is a stage. But Shakespeare acted on the much finer principle that a stage is all the world. So there are in all Bernard Shaw's plays patches of what people would call essentially undramatic stuff, which the dramatist puts in because he is honest and would rather prove his case than succeed with his play. Shaw has brought back into English drama that Shakespearian universality which, if you like, you can call Shakespearian irrelevance. Perhaps a better definition than either is a habit of thinking the truth worth telling even when you meet it by accident. In Shaw's plays one meets an incredible number of truths by accident.

To be up to date is a paltry ambition except in an almanac, and Shaw has sometimes talked this almanac philosophy. Nevertheless there is a real sense in which the phrase may be wisely used, and that is in cases where some stereotyped version of what is happening hides what is really happening from our eyes. Thus, for instance, newspapers are never up to date. The men who write leading articles are always behind the times, because they are in a hurry. They are forced to fall back on their old-fashioned view of things; they have no time to fashion a new one. Everything that is done in a hurry is certain to be antiquated; that is why modern industrial civilisation bears so curious a resemblance to barbarism. Thus when newspapers say that the Times is a solemn old Tory paper, they are out of date; their talk is behind the talk in Fleet Street. Thus when newspapers say that Christian dogmas are crumbling, they are out of date; their talk is behind the talk in public-houses. Now in this sense Shaw has kept in a really stirring sense up to date.

He has introduced into the theatre the things that no one else had introduced into a theatre—the things in the street outside. The theatre is a sort of thing which proudly sends a hansom-cab across the stage as Realism, while everybody outside is whistling for motor-cabs. Consider in this respect how many and fine have been Shaw's intrusions into the theatre with the things that were really going on. Daily papers and daily matinees were still gravely explaining how much modern war depended on gunpowder. Arms and the Man explained how much modern war depends on chocolate. Every play and paper described the Vicar who was a mild Conservative. Candida caught hold of the modern Vicar who is an advanced Socialist. Numberless magazine articles and society comedies describe the emancipated woman as new and wild. Only You Never Can Tell was young enough to see that the emancipated woman is already old and respectable. Every comic paper has caricatured the uneducated upstart. Only the author of Man and Superman knew enough about the modern world to caricature the educated upstart—the man Straker who can quote Beaumarchais, though he cannot pronounce him. This is the second real and great work of Shaw—the letting in of the world on to the stage, as the rivers were let in upon the Augean Stable. He has let a little of the Haymarket into the Haymarket Theatre. He has permitted some whispers of the Strand to enter the Strand Theatre. A variety of solutions in philosophy is as silly as it is in arithmetic, but one may be justly proud of a variety of materials for a solution. After Shaw, one may say, there is nothing that cannot be introduced into a play if one can make it decent, amusing, and relevant. The state of a man's health, the religion of his childhood, his ear for music, or his ignorance of cookery can all be made vivid if they have anything to do with the subject. A soldier may mention the commissariat as well as the cavalry; and, better still, a priest may mention theology as well as religion. That is being a philosopher; that is bringing the universe on the stage.

Lastly, he has obliterated the mere cynic. He has been so much more cynical than anyone else for the public good that no one has dared since to be really cynical for anything smaller. The Chinese crackers of the frivolous cynics fail to excite us after the dynamite of the serious and aspiring cynic. Bernard Shaw and I (who are growing grey together) can remember an epoch which many of his followers do not know: an epoch of real pessimism. The years from 1885 to 1898 were like the hours of afternoon in a rich house with large rooms; the hours before tea-time. They believed in nothing except good manners; and the essence of good manners is to conceal a yawn. A yawn may be defined as a silent yell.

The power which the young pessimist of that time showed in this direction would have astonished anyone but him. He yawned so wide as to swallow the world. He swallowed the world like an unpleasant pill before retiring to an eternal rest. Now the last and best glory of Shaw is that in the circles where this creature was found, he is not. He has not been killed (I don't know exactly why), but he has actually turned into a Shaw idealist. This is no exaggeration. I meet men who, when I knew them in 1898, were just a little too lazy to destroy the universe. They are now conscious of not being quite worthy to abolish some prison regulations. This destruction and conversion seem to me the mark of something actually great. It is always great to destroy a type without destroying a man. The followers of Shaw are optimists; some of them are so simple as even to use the word. They are sometimes rather pallid optimists, frequently very worried optimists, occasionally, to tell the truth, rather cross optimists: but they not pessimists; they can exult though they cannot laugh. He has at least withered up among them the mere pose of impossibility. Like every great teacher, he has cursed the barren fig-tree. For nothing except that impossibility is really impossible.

I know it is all very strange. From the height of eight

hundred years ago, or of eight hundred years hence, our age must look incredibly odd. We call the twelfth century ascetic. We call our own time hedonist and full of praise and pleasure. But in the ascetic age the love of life was evident and enormous, so that it had to be restrained. In an hedonist age pleasure has always sunk low, so that it has to be encouraged. How high the sea of human happiness rose in the Middle Ages, we now only know by the colossal walls that they built to keep it in bounds. How low human happiness sank in the twentieth century our children will only know by these extraordinary modern books, which tell people that it is a duty to be cheerful and that life is not so bad after all. Humanity never produces optimists till it has ceased to produce happy men. It is strange to be obliged to impose a holiday like a fast, and to drive men to a banquet with spears. But this shall be written of our time: that when the spirit who denies besieged the last citadel, blaspheming life itself, there were some, there was one especially, whose voice was heard and whose spear was never broken.

Chapter 13

Criticism

Puncturing puffery with Hilberry's Spear

Never content with a single target of opportunity, George Bernard Shaw takes on foolish chauvinism of every stripe in *Arms and the Man*. It's an exercise in with that can still be enjoyed as well as appreciated, as the Hilberry's merry new production demonstrates.

We look to Shaw for verbal virtuosity, but we don't really expect to have a belly-laughing good time. And we are surprised when a director like Margaret Spear and a cast like this smart Hilberry ensemble show us one.

The war that rages in the play is a laughably useless one between Bulgaria and Serbia. It ends with a solemn cessation of fighting but not, perish the thought, an end to the warlike posturing that was deemed politically correct a the time.

Shaw's hero is a Swiss mercenary fighting for the Serbs, Captain Bluntschli, who matter-of-factly compares to the reality of war to the drumbeatings of the warlike. His view of all this - as well as Shaw's - is wryly bemused. Honor and idealism are mere poses. Real warriors, he says, carry chocolate instead of bullets.

Indeed, *Arms and the Man* is about poses of all kinds - romantic, social, patriotic - and Shaw delights in lampooning them. But his characters aren't cartoons (as always with Shaw there's too much reality behind the wit for that), and Spear's cast finds the right tone of deadpan pomposity and human foolishness.

To the role of Bluntschli, Peter Toran brings the chiseled

good looks of a film actor and a sense of authority that makes him, as Shaw intended, the only truly capable man in uniform on stage, the instrument Shaw uses to deflate the others.

His exact opposite is the mustached twit Major Sergius (Thorsten Kaye), who strikes languid poses upon each entrance and revels in his idiotic notions about chivalry and flashing cavalry charges.

In the course of things, his fiancee Raina a quintessentially robust Shavian heroine, as played by Roxanne Wellington - falls for Bluntschli and learns a thing or two about how it really is between men and women.

Her parents, who still measure their worth by the number of horses they own, are hilariously puffed-up small-time aristocrats, as played impeccably by Michael S. Ouimet and Nancy Lipschultz. And Henry Lide and Janet Clarkson are very good, too, as the entrepreneurial servant Nicola and the lusty maid Louka.

The Hilberry has had more downs than ups lately. This *Arms and the Man* is a joyous up.

Chattering Classes: George Bernard Shaw Receives a Witty, Pretty Make-Over.

You need a bit of gusto and confidence to "do" a George Bernard Shaw play, I've always thought. It could so easily go horribly wrong. "I suppose we won't be home in time for Crimewatch?" I said to my companion, wearily. Long and wordy, cerebral and self-satisfied were my general anticipations. But I was wrong. I was gripped by Peter Hall's new production of You Never Can Tell from the start. I settled back, as if in front of a roaring fire, and didn't want it to end. The hours flew by.

A cunning device is used whereby, the moment the lights come up, we hear a woman scream before we even register that she is in a dentist's chair having a tooth extracted by a handsome dentist. We, the audience, are jolted to attention, like it or not. After that it's a kind of Upstairs, Downstairs affair, complete with a charismatic "lady", sexually repressed daughter and a sage, all-seeing butler.

But You Never Can Tell offers much more than that: fantastic spats of withering dialogue and intellectual swordplay that would have had me on the edge of my seat if I hadn't had a lap full of plain Belgian at the time.

Diana Quick, as the principled Mrs Clandon (or, as she calls herself, "an advanced woman"), is wonderfully concise and natural in her delivery. If there were an Olivier Award for Acting by a Body Part, her chest should surely be nominated: resolute and unmoved in the first act, by the third it heaves about like a badger under a bedspread, dramatising her anguish in the most innovative fashion.

Mrs Clandon arrives in an English seaside town in the 1890s with her three children. It is 18 years since she separated from their father, about whom she has divulged nothing, not even his name. Wouldn't you know it, but her ex is there too, and the lot of them are thrown together along with a handsome, if financially challenged, chap called Valentine.

Ryan Kiggell relishes this role, acting with such a lightness of touch that we believe him when he says: "The whole world is like a feather dancing in the light." As you can imagine, much hilarity ensues.

Valentine is soon embroiled with the eldest daughter, Gloria, haughtily played as a young Sue Lawley by Nancy Carroll, who maintains a heady mix of aloofness and barely concealed desire right up until the final triumph of lust over Victorian propriety, feelings over conscience and, ultimately, common humanity (or sex) over science and (if we're looking at the bigger picture) freedom over slavery.

These were the concerns of the thinking classes at the time. By sheer artistry—both Shaw's and the combined talents of Peter Hall and this wonderful cast—we are drawn into the debate.

The servile waiter (a perfectly measured and droll performance by Edward Fox) is a kind of geriatric Ariel/ Volpone arrangement (with just a touch of Churchill), who deflates his superiors' attempts to control the future with their ideological beliefs by repeating the handy perennial: "You never can tell."

It is grown-up comedy with intelligent and pithy lines. The pompous, eminent QC Mr Bohun (Michael Mears) informs the family: "My speciality is being right when other people are wrong."

The dialogue is witty and frequently poetic, but engages us emotionally in a way Oscar Wilde, for instance, could never have contemplated. A product of its time maybe, but these are the Little Britain characters of their day, and they are just as recognisable and relevant.

You Never Can Tell makes a satisfying evening's entertainment. It is a beautifully crafted play, funny and moving, performed with effortless skill by an accomplished set of actors. Sinead Matthews is a joy as the disarmingly bold minx Dolly, and the rather wonderfully named Ken Bones brings great humanity to the part of her brutal, estranged father, Mr Crampton. When the time inevitably comes and a reckless producer stages a play (or musical) about Harold Shipman, he's my top tip for the title role. (While we're on the subject, I also nominate Dame Judi for the part of Primrose. Or, if she's not available, try Vanessa Feltz.) Even the usherettes at the elegant Garrick Theatre were charming, a credit to their drama schools.

I couldn't have had a better night out if I'd then dined at J Sheekey's and sat next to Jude and Sienna. Which, in fact, I did. My earlier predictions for a dreary evening were laughably off the mark. As Edward Fox's wise waiter tells us: "It's the unexpected that always happens, isn't it? You never can tell." Which made me think... Sienna couldn't keep her eyes off me tonight. I wonder...?

Prostitution and Social Purity in the 1880s and 1890s.

The social purity 'crusade' that gathered force after 1885 initiated a change both in ways of representing prostitution and in public opinion about ways of dealing with the sexually deviant woman. Since the 1860s the police had been granted the power under the Contagious Diseases Acts to apprehend women of doubtful virtue in the streets and insist that they be medically examined; if found to be diseased, they could then be detained in lock hospitals. Once these acts were repealed in 1885, prostitutes had greater freedom but were also kept under surveillance by philanthropists and the medical profession. A variety of discourses constructed the prostitute either as an innocent victim of male lust or as a 'demon' and 'contagion of evil'. Judith Walkowitz has argued that such an ideological framework excluded the experience of women who drifted into this lifestyle temporarily, and provided 'a restrictive and moralistic image' of the fallen woman. Arguably, literary representations of prostitutes tended to flesh out the potentially restrictive images used in feminist, medical and periodical writing on the subject, though no form of discourse was immune to the strong influence of the language of purity used by the members of the National Vigilance Association and its advocates.

In this article I will consider representations of the prostitute and her relationship with the philanthropist or New Woman in fiction and drama of the late-Victorian period. Novels that flirted with the concept of a prostitute heroine, such as George Gissing's The Unclassed and Annie Holdsworth's New Woman novel, Joanna Traill, Spinster, were perceived to be rather scandalous, particularly if they bordered on the sexually explicit. George Bernard Shaw's attempts to dramatize a discussion about prostitution and the existence of brothels had to be banned from the late-Victorian stage. According to Frank Mort, 'positive representations of active female sexuality' were extremely rare in debates on prostitution, an additional constraint on writers in an age of censorship. Borrowing from feminist accounts which often revealed an uneasiness about working-class female sexuality and lack of faith in the reclamation of fallen women, literary texts exposed the fears and fantasies surrounding the sexually experienced woman, particularly in the New Woman's reaction to her 'fallen sister'. The sympathy that is elicited on behalf of the prostitute is then often achieved at the cost of an acceptance of stereotypical ways of thinking about working-class women and female sexuality.

Images of the Prostitute in Non-literary Discourses

It has been argued that after 1886 debate on prostitution steadily faded as it became tacitly accepted as an inevitable evil. The repressive actions of the NVA, which sought to regulate street prostitution and music halls, to ban obscene books and close brothels, did not prevent feminists and members of the medical profession from speaking out about fallen women but sometimes even helped them to frame their arguments about sexual vice. Feminist accounts of prostitution tended to promote the importance of philanthropy and to stress woman's vital role in 'leading [the prostitute] back to a better life'. Josephine Butler, whose prominent campaigning for repeal from the 1870s onwards included nursing dying prostitutes in her own home, spoke of 'this wonderful and beautiful solidarity of the women of the world before God' and challenged entrenched views of the fallen by highlighting 'the sacredness of every woman even at her lowest, most degraded, and most despised estate'. Her belief in the reclamation of prostitutes enabled by sisterhood between middle and working-class women was not shared by other philanthropists of the time, nor were such positive images of 'degraded' women always endorsed. Mary Jeune, who published a series of articles in The Fortnightly Review of 1885 about her experience of helping the fallen, distinguished between 'the woman who has just fallen' and can be 'easily reached by sympathy and kindness', most probably a victim of seduction and what she referred to as 'the lowest class of fallen women' who are 'too degraded to accept or wish for any help'. In speaking of the problems of finding work for reclaimed prostitutes, she went on to claim that some would be 'too degraded for an ordinary home and domestic service'. Resistance to the project of reclamation, including a refusal to accept that prostitution was morally wrong, was then explained in terms of working-class women being 'too degraded' to accept the terms of their middle-class sisters, rather than as a potential failure of philanthropy. As Walkowitz has argued, women seen as innocent victims of male lust and medical and police tyranny were felt to be 'appropriate objects of solicitude', whereas those women who fell outside this classification were branded as shameless, degraded and evil, not deserving of a feminist's sympathy and care. Elizabeth Blackwell, the first woman doctor and a prominent member of the NVA, referred to this group as a 'growing army of shameless women'. Those women who refused to be reclaimed spoilt the feminists' 'protective surveillance' of their sisters and their anger at such refusals was 'easily coopted and rechannelled into repressive anti-vice campaigns'.

This tendency betrayed a wider desire in society to police the dangerous classes, and a fear of uncontrolled working-class sexuality. Frank Mort has highlighted the 'renewed official panic over the urban poor in the 1880s', which clearly informed feminist attitudes to poor women. Middle-class distaste, or even disgust, is signalled in Blackwell's comments on those engaging in 'free lust and indulging the impulses of a sexual caprice', which blurs the distinctions between commercial sex and extra-marital sexuality; free lust was not a specifically working-class phenomenon. She also railed against those women who were 'desecrating the sanctity of sexual relations, proving the ease with which the rewards of vice are gained', seeking to impose her own standards of sexual morality on working-class women but also criticising women who had sex before marriage. Feminist definitions of what constituted sexual vice were slippery; in the crusade for purity Butler's condemnation of the 'still greater evil—official and tolerated vice' J4 could also have extended beyond the practice of prostitution, as vice was applied to other forms of sexual activity at the time. Working-class women could always be attacked on the grounds of their sexual knowledge and consequent impurity, as this passage from Mary Jeune indicates:

> The poorer girl is not necessarily impure... perhaps in some ways her completer knowledge acts as a shield. When she is obliged to leave home for service we have no fight to blame her, if chaste personally, because she is not pure-minded; pure-minded in the sense in which the term is ordinarily used she cannot be... While she may be deprived

of the freshness and delicacy of an ignorant woman, she does not run the same danger of falling.

By arguing that working-class girls are always already fallen, given that they have a 'familiarity' with and 'completer knowledge' of sexual matters than middle-class girls, Jeune accuses them of being very close to the shameless prostitute, even if they do not sell their bodies on the street. This reflects the wider 'anxiety over the sexual precocity of working-class girls' which feminists sought to control; the suggestion that working-class women can never be 'pure-minded' because of the sexual characteristics of their class seems to render the feminist project of reclamation inoperable and to reinforce images of working-class women as sexually deviant. Medical accounts were even more heavily influenced by the language of purity. Although this linguistic register was used by women 'to develop a trenchant critique of male sexuality' in feminist writing such as the New Woman novel which targeted male vice, in the medical press prostitutes were still being singled out for blame for spreading syphilis. The Repeal of the Contagious Diseases Acts was viewed as 'disastrous' in the light of the greater freedom that streetwalkers now appeared to enjoy. The Lancet ridiculed any attempts to instigate compulsory examination of male clients, as it was assumed that women were the main carriers of the disease, and announced that 'the [CD] Acts were their best friends—much better, indeed, than the neglect and filth to which the repealers of these Acts have abandoned them'. If prostitution were not regulated, this argument implied that the freedom of such women might increase 'filth', or the active sexuality which made social purists uneasy. The Lancet claimed that women were the 'aggressive parties' in initiating encounters with potential clients and that 'men should be able to walk to and from their business without having the social evil thrust upon them night after night and year after year'. This clearly attributed women's aggression to their over-active sexualities and ignored the economic factors which forced women to 'thrust' themselves on 'innocent' men who frequented districts known as the haunts of prostitutes. Such images of sexually active working-class women were used by feminists and social purists to enlist women's help in what Butler called 'the purification of society'; by advocating alternative standards of sexual morality, middle-class women would be able to 'strengthen and guide the sexual virtue of a people' according to Blackwell. The social purity campaigners, ostensibly working in women's interests, were by now creating the same climate of surveillance and repression which the repealers had protested against, seeking to keep working-class women and their sexualities under control. Stereotypical views of the diseased streetwalker proved difficult to edit out of official discourses on prostitution, reinforcing the view of the sexually active women as dangerous. Although feminists such as Butler might proclaim the sacredness of her fallen sisters, images of prostitutes as degraded and shameless, corrupted by their sexual knowledge, persisted, particularly under the influence of purity crusaders intent on outlawing vice in all its forms.

Prostitutes in the Novel: degraded or pure?

The question of whether degraded prostitutes could ever be purified and reclaimed into a better life underpinned fictional treatment of fallen women at this time, which attempted to provide authentic accounts of the lives and behaviour of working-class women. In George Gissing's The Unclassed and Annie Holdsworth's New Woman novel Joanna Traill, Spinster, fallen women are allowed to tell their stories in a way that solicits the sympathies of the reader and attacks preconceptions about working-class sexual deviance; a contemporary review of Gissing's text promised that, 'it will give to many readers a very different notion of the "unfortunate" class'.23 Whereas images of suffering and degraded women had been used as propaganda in the repeal cause, as it was 'politically expedient' to aim for this kind of representation, novels allowed writers to explore the prostitute's experience in greater detail, though this did not of course guarantee an unbiased opinion. Gissing's depiction of Osmond Waymark, who toys with marrying a fallen woman, was clearly influenced by his own unhappy marriage to Neil Harrison, whom he had rescued from the streets, whereas Holdsworth's position as a feminist and co-editor of The Woman's Signal obviously informed her views on philanthropy and female sexuality. Whilst the novels followed the agenda of the purists in 'speaking out about sex' and taking immorality seriously, their work was potentially more radical in abandoning pruriency and questioning the sexual double standard. Interestingly, whilst Holdsworth's novel did not offend the Athenaeum reviewer and even inspired praise for its portrayal of the prostitute, a 'delightful personage', Gissing came up against more adverse criticism in the 1880s when his text was perceived to be more scandalous, one of the reasons why he published a revised version in 1895 after editing out supposedly inappropriate scenes. In this section I will consider the differences between the two texts and the attitudes to prostitution they explore in the light of the growth of the social purity movement and changing images of the prostitute in the 1880s and 1890s.

Different reasons for entering prostitution are given in the texts, highlighting both economic factors and the sexual behaviour of working-class women. Gissing focuses on fallen women as victims of economic circumstances, who walk the streets either to supplement meagre wages from working in match factories, workrooms or in domestic service, or as a 'rest' from the hard labour such employment involved. One of the minor characters, Sally Fisher, proclaims, 'All us girls are the same; we have to keep on two jobs at the same time'. The narrator's comment on Lotty Starr, 'by no means a vicious girl', reinforces the idea of sexual deviance as a necessary characteristic of poor young women: 'A girl who says that she is occupied in a workroom is never presumed to be able to afford the luxury of strict virtue'. In contrast Holdsworth's heroine Christine Dow, despite her attempts to convince the philanthropists that 'I had never a chance... I didn't know', seems to have chosen her lifestyle to suit her needs, a type of prostitute recognised by the Lancet who condemned those who chose the profession as 'an easy and luxurious [life], much preferable to the life of drudgery they had hitherto led' She refuses to go to a penitentiary, claiming, 'I don't want to be a good woman—not that sort, leastways' and does not suffer from shame about her profession. Here economic factors are combined with the working woman's enjoyment of her sexual activity or the prostitute's lifestyle. However, this text also contains a more conventionalised vision of prostitutes en masse, when the philanthropists search Piccadilly Circus at night for Christine and look into 'evil faces... eyes bold, defiant and wretched... those sad ghosts of womanhood'. This reflects the way in which philanthropists sought to stereotype prostitutes as a homogenous group, though the novel is to demonstrate that individual women have different stories to tell and different attitudes to reclamation.

The possible defiance of the prostitute was linked to her evil nature in contemporary accounts, which distinguished between the bold, degraded women and the younger, more innocent victims of male lust. The stories of the bolder women were felt to be much more dangerous as they associated sexual activity with freedom and fun, rather than unnatural vice. Mary Jeune describes the situation in which:

> In recounting the downward history of her career, the more abandoned and hardened woman would dwell on the fun, the excitement, the gaiety of its different phases, always keeping silent... about the squalor, misery, and degradation of the other side of it. Foul, coarse language, oaths, and jests, were used, and the darkest page of the woman's life discussed with such freedom and absence of shame that the least corrupted of women would become habituated to thoughts and aspects of vice from which they would have shrunk in horror a few weeks before.

Philanthropists were unhappy about prostitutes' stories, which were silent about degradation because they presented a more subversive image of the prostitute and gestured towards the 'emergence of a much clearer subculture of prostitution' in the wake of social-purity legislation. The 'absence of shame' identified in fallen women was probably evident in the speech and behaviour of many working women who enjoyed their sexualities. Christine has many of the characteristics of a degraded woman, despite her youth, though she is presented in contradictory terms as 'a luxurious, ambitious, little creature, with nothing but an instinct female purity and a strong love of cleanliness to save her from the uttermost degradation'. Although both Ida and Christine are presented as independent, unconventional women, who gain their 'spirit' and 'passion' from their streetwalking, Ida is eager to escape from her 'vile trade' whereas Christine resists reclamation and longs for the pleasures of her old life. Gissing seems to lean towards a purified version of the prostitute in Ida, allowing her to explicitly refuse the tag of 'degraded' and to criticise Waymark for 'speak[ing] contemptuously, like that'. Christine's case is more contradictory in that her 'instinct female purity' atones for her behaviour even as Holdsworth refuses to apologise for her depiction of a shameless woman who never entirely rejects her sexual forwardness. The reclamation of prostitutes is given a specific gendered resonance in the novels, as both examine the nature of the relationship between philanthropist and fallen woman, classified by Walkowitz as 'hierarchical, controlling, and punitive'. Holdsworth satirises the 'fashion' for philanthropy, described by the contemporary feminist writer Mrs Roy Devereux as 'a morbid appetite for coquetting with sin', and explicitly uses terms and images familiar from feminist accounts. We are told that Joanna Traill 'claimed sisterhood with the fallen, and yearned to reach hands of help to them'. Her male associate, Boas, also stresses the need for sisterhood and has no qualms about commenting on Christine's 'wild', 'undisciplined' nature and the difficulties of taming her. Joanna is initially frightened by 'the girl's stormy passions', but proves herself adept at moulding her into a quiet and passive Victorian woman and reprimanding her for her 'easy familiarity' with men. In Gissing's novel Waymark's repressed erotic interest in Ida and his belief that she is no 'common' prostitute prevent him from seeking to control her through reclamation. After giving money to a suffering prostitute outside a theatre, he is unable to repeat his philanthropic action with Ida because he recognises that she is of a 'different kind':

In the case of an ordinary pretty and good-natured girl

falling in his way as Ida Starr had done, he would have exerted whatever influence he might acquire over her to persuade her into better paths. Any such direct guidance was, he felt, out of the question here. The girl had independence of judgement, she would resent anything said by him on the assumption of her moral inferiority, and, for aught he knew, with justice.

The admission that working-class women may resent guidance and judgement of their sexual behaviour suggests a criticism of philanthropy and the hierarchies it creates, though Waymark's later attempts to educate Ida, whilst lending her money and introducing her to his friends, seem to negate his good intentions. Jenne's belief that philanthropy was 'essentially a woman's work;... too fraught with risk for any man to attempt', is demonstrated in the increasingly risky nature of Waymark's encounters with Ida as his sexual desires compete with his feelings of sympathy. Despite his reservations, however, both Ida and her friend Sally appear happy to accept both financial and emotional support, without feeling that they are sacrificing their independence and identity in the way that Christine does. The prostitute's inferiority cannot be so easily glossed over when it comes to questions of marriage. Patricia Ingham has argued that Ida 'resists classification as a degenerate fallen woman by force of character', refusing to 'accept and internalise society's image of her. Yet, the prostitute's force of character offers no protection from the entrenched views of patriarchal society figured through Waymark and Christine's admirer, Bevan. Despite his enlightened attitude towards fallen women, Waymark still has stereotypical views about working-class sexual deviance, finding the prostitute's social inferiority and sexual morality both repulsive and desirable. He questions her about her clients and has to deny himself the pleasure of passionate imaginings' about her sexual experiences. Whilst recognising that his passions are aroused by her rather than the 'timid conventionality' of the middleclass heroine Maud, his knowledge of the characteristics of girls of this class' assures him that she does not have 'the capacity for love', nor the ability to tell the truth, making her unsuitable as a potential wife. Typically, Gissing is interested in the difficulties of reconciling sexual desire with the need to marry, dwelling on Waymark's fears that 'the alliance between them could only be a mere caprice on her part, such as girls of her kind are very subject to'. Branding Ida as a girl of a particular kind and class, who exhibits specific 'characteristics', betrays his belief in 'society's image' of the sexual deviance of the working classes. For the 1895 edition, Gissing toned down the sexual content of the novel, including editing out a scene in which Waymark kisses Ida; for the later edition his repression of his desires until he is convinced of Ida's purity is more important. Contemporary reviewers failed to believe in his honourable intentions, the Academy offering the view that 'a long-continued platonic attachment between a normal young man—even of aesthetic tastes—and a London prostitute is an incident hardly within the range of probability'. The prostitute's sexual deviance makes her an object of desire but she cannot suddenly adopt the sexual characteristics of another class in order to satisfy requirements for an ideal wife; Ida's pleas that Waymark treat her as if she were 'a modest girl' are denied by the inferiority she cannot escape.

In Joanna Traill, Spinster the prostitute can only be figured as an object of desire when her sexual knowledge remains hidden. Attracted to Christine's independence as well as her capacity to fill the role of domestic angel after her reclamation, Bevan is horrified by the revelation that his intended wife has inhabited the dens and streets of London. In a conversation about reclaiming the fallen with Boas early in the novel, he voices his lack of confidence in the project of introducing reformed prostitutes into middle-class homes: 'She'd demoralise the butler, and run away with the spoons... I don't think a woman once polluted would ever be clean, no matter where you put her'. Holdsworth uses the New Woman plot to critique male sexuality in the style of Sarah Grand, overtly condemning Bevan for his conventional views about female sexuality. His 'loathing' of his potential wife, whose sexual deviance suddenly becomes apparent in her 'bare throat' and 'flesh', is denounced by Boas, who accuses him of 'judg[ing] her like a common prostitute' and 'send[ing] her to the devil'. Again, it is behaviour learned on the streets which has enabled Christine to attract Bevan in the first place; like Waymark, he is attracted to the prostitute's sexual agency and control as both women are confident about initiating encounters with men, whether money is involved or not. Male attitudes to working-class women are then shaped by their repressed desires; Waymark's need for a 'pliant and docile' wife cannot be squared with his attraction to the passionate, sexually experienced woman.

Significantly, the discussion of sexuality is diverted away from Christine onto the spinster heroine as the novel develops, as Joanna is alerted not only to her possible degradation of streetwalking but to the dangers of repression. Her new-found interest in helping the fallen is interpreted by her sisters as an attempt to attract Boas: 'Did you hear that she goes twice a week to the slums and meets Mr Boas there?—philanthropy, they call it'. Such work gives her a knowledge of sexuality which sets her apart from other women as in the streets she witnesses 'scenes that, imagined only... would have made her die of shame'. Rather than the philanthropist controlling the prostitute, the novel seems to suggest an alternative relationship where the 'feminist identification with outcast women' is taken to the extreme of the feminist wanting to emulate the behaviour of her fallen sister. Mrs Devereux commented derisively on the feminist's 'fascination' with 'the kind of sin which she has neither the opportunity nor the desire to commit', yet the text suggests that feminists did desire to engage in the 'sin' of sexuality. By the end of the novel Joanna admits to herself 'the depth of her passion' now she has moved on from her 'empty and valueless' life as a celibate spinster. She represses her desire for Boas, even to the extent of encouraging him to marry Christine, until it is too late and she dies with her purity intact. The text implies that policing sexuality ultimately leads to repression and that it is men's attitudes towards sexually active women which need to change, rather than women's sexual behaviour and desires.

Both texts reflect the influence of the social purity movement in their final statements about prostitution, but challenge the more conservative views of philanthropists in indicating that working-class girls can retain their purity even after life on the streets. Gissing ultimately allows Ida to become Waymark's 'ideal woman', though this is achieved by first rescuing her into the middle class after a reconciliation with her rich grandfather. In a speech she imagines delivering to Waymark, she proclaims, 'it is no arrogance to say that I have become a pure woman'. Ingham sees this as one of the strengths of Gissing's novel, as the heroine 'confounds the usual oppositional signs of respectable and fallen woman'. Contemporary reviewers were not so positive, perceiving the purification of a prostitute as problematic and unrealistic. One remarked, 'the notion that the mind of a prostitute can remain pure and unsullied in the midst of her profession is simply contrary to fact, however well it may fit in with this or that theory. On the other hand, we fail to see how any objection can be taken to the theory that love can save the streetwalker from her life of degradation, and even purify her heart from the pollution of the past'. The purification of degraded women is given more credence in Holdsworth's novel, which exhibits Christine as a 'good pure woman', endorsing the value of philanthropy and criticising men for their preconceptions about female sexuality, though the Bookman reviewer still voiced his disbelief in Christine's reclamation. Bonds between women are cemented by the purity of the female philanthropist, who, it is implied, can only extend the hand of friendship because she is pure: 'her purity made her face and forgive the sin less spotless women would have shunned and condemned'. More influenced by the language of purity feminism, the text is also at times more radical in its emphasis on the need to alter public opinion about fallen women and its blaming of men for women's ruin. Boas proclaims in one of his speeches, 'the man plunges the woman into a sink of iniquity, and holds her there while he screams for purity. The women are as bad... it's this attitude of men and women towards the fallen that prevents their redemption'. Similarly,

Joanna calls for women to be braver, 'to recognise the trade and fight it' rather than remaining ignorant of the experiences of working-class women. Perhaps one of the reasons for the greater popularity of this novel was its avoidance of the issue of men's desire for sexually experienced working-class women; Gissing's explicit references to Waymark's desire for sexually deviant women revealed the more risky subtext of men's dissatisfaction with the conventionally pure heroine. Male screams for purity could not be silenced but the degraded nature of the prostitute could be called into question and alternative images of the sexually active woman made available.

White Slavery and the Prostitute as Victim: Encouraged by the popularity of the daring drama of Heurik Ibsen in the late 1880s and early 1890s, Victorian dramatists became increasingly interested in debates around female sexuality. As a Fabian socialist, George Bernard Shaw saw prostitution as a primarily economic social problem, to be discussed in relation to wider issues such as women's work and earnings. Rather than focussing on the difficulties of reclaiming prostitutes or women's experiences of the streets, he chose to reconsider the question of white slavery, the abduction or deception of women forced to work in brothels on the Continent. This had previously been addressed in W.T. Stead's famous expose of child prostitution, The Maiden Tribute of Modern Babylon, which employed the language and conventions of melodrama and pornography both to titillate readers of the sensationalist Pall Mall Gazette in which it was first published and to push through reforms in social policy. As Judith Walkowitz has argued, in Stead's narrative 'class criticism was immediately undercut by sentimental moralism and a focus on passive, innocent female victims and individual evil men that diverted attention away from the economic and social issues relating to prostitution'. As Lesley Hall has shown, 'the image of "white slavery" in the media and popular perception was of the helpless innocent victim decoyed by procurers'. However, Shaw refused to reproduce the image of the prostitute as helpless victim in his play Mrs Warren's Profession, preferring to emphasise the economic issues which prompted women's choice of this trade. The mass closing of brothels in England and Wales between 1885 and 1914 resulted in an increased policing and sentencing of women, rather than alleviating the problem which, as Shaw suggested, was more to do with the alternatives available for working women. He asserted in his 1902 Preface to his play, 'No normal woman would be a professional prostitute if she could better herself by being respectable', the Fabian argument developed in Mrs Warren's key speeches. Although his play was much less scandalous than The Maiden Tribute, it was still refused a licence by the Lord Chamberlain, with only 2 private performances by the Stage Society in 1902 and 2 public performances in America in 1905, before censorship was eventually relaxed in 1925.

Like Holdsworth's novel, written in the same year, Mrs Warren "s Profession focuses on the relationship between the New Woman and the prostitute, though the situation is reversed so that here the prostitute is the mature woman and also a biological rather than a surrogate mother. Rather than conforming to restrictive images of the prostitute, Shaw represented Kitty Warren as a vulgar flirt who cannot be accepted into polite society, referring to her in his letters as 'a most deplorable old rip'. Due to her promotion from prostitute to brothel-manager, Mrs Warren is as much of a business-woman as her daughter Vivie, who earns her New Woman credentials as a legal actuary in Chancery Lane. Her narrative of her fall into prostitution at the end of Act II presents her neither as an abducted innocent nor a degraded woman but as a self-respecting, working girl trying to escape economic exploitation, who refuses to feel the shame 'expected from a woman' in her position. Prostitution is seen as 'far better than any other employment open to her', including working as a bar-maid, waitress, scullery-maid or in the white-lead factory where her half-sister died. Drawing on feminist and philanthropic rhetoric, one of her most forceful lines is 'it can't be right... that there shouldn't be better opportunities for women'. Shaw also borrows from contemporary Fabian research into women's work and earnings, specifying women's 'starvation wages' such as the barmaid's 4 shillings a week plus bed and board, which makes saving almost impossible. However, his representations of the European brothel seem much less well-informed:

> The house in Brussels was real high class: a much better place for a woman to be in than the factory where Anne Jane got poisoned. None of our girls were ever treated as I was treated in the scullery of that temperance place, or at the Waterloo bar, or at home.

Although historians have commented on the disconcertingly vague' stories about the White Slave Traffic, this disclaimer seems to be twisting historical evidence about the conditions endured by white slaves. By valorising the existence of brothels, Shaw is attacking the repressive measures taken in England, which effectively forced women back onto the streets. A continental system of tolerated areas might protect women from police harassment, but it seems unlikely that all prostitutes in European brothels were well-treated and watched over by maternal figures, as this suggests. In a postscript to his Preface written in 1930, Shaw remarked on the agents of the trade who set 'traps' for women 'lured to London by offers of situations', a more familiar scenario. In the play 'slavery' is associated with badly paid work in general, though Kitty is quick to point out that prostitution 'is not work that any woman would do for pleasure... though to hear the pious people talk you would suppose it was a bed of roses'. Shaw then seeks to correct the misconceptions of the 'pious people' with his socialist account, characterising his prostitute as a struggling working woman who has no need of philanthropic intervention. Despite his attempts to detach himself from the language and attitudes of social purity groups, however, Shaw also uses his New Woman as a mouthpiece for repression. She articulates the more stereotypical view of white slavery in which prostitutes are the helpless victims of male 'capitalist bullies' like George Crofts, Kitty's business partner. The revelation in Act III that Mrs Warren is still reaping the financial benefits of her houses prompts a shift in Vivie's way of thinking: she revises her opinion of her mother, now an 'unmentionable woman' and confronts Crofts with the accusation: 'When I think of the society that tolerates you, and the laws that protect you! When I think of how helpless 9 out of 10 girls would be in the hands of you and my mother!'. As Mrs Warren has no desire to be reclaimed and Vivie no philanthropic intentions, the New Woman expresses disgust rather than sympathy for the immorality of her fallen sister. This represents a development in ways of representing the relationship between the fallen woman and the New Woman; although Vivie shares her fellow spinster Joanna Traill's repressive tendencies, she is not made to question them as Joanna does after her philanthropic work, nor is she prompted into new ways of thinking about female sexuality. Her horror at her mother's lifestyle, intensified by Kitty's attempts to advertise the profession in the style of a procuress, effectively translates into a horror of sexuality in general. Whereas in an earlier scene Kitty yields to temptation and kisses Frank, Vivie shies away from sexual contact. There are however possibilities for a lesbian reading, suggested by Vivie's long nights in with her boss, Honoria Fraser; it may be male sexuality which Vivie fears. She cannot bring herself to say her mother's profession out loud and like Frank, who is quick to label Kitty 'thoroughly immoral' and 'a very bad lot' despite kissing her, is too proud to accept financial help from such a source. By reproducing male attitudes to the prostitute and refusing philanthropic identification, Vivie distances herself from a modern audience; her final speeches have been interpreted in terms of 'coldness and calculation', so that her mother's charge that she is a 'stuck-up prude' seems all too true. Vivie's attitudes towards prostitution, representative of the harsher, repressive views of purity feminism, are ultimately seen as more dangerous than the flourishing of European brothels, again reiterating the point that the repression of the New Woman may be just as problematic as the active sexuality of the prostitute.

All three texts then sought to educate the public about fallen women by exploding myths of prostitutes as either innocent victims or degraded demons. Reworking images from feminist and medical discourses, they also provided greater insight into the experiences of working-class women and mobilised debates on female sexuality and the consequences of repression. The economic causes of prostitution, often ignored in contemporary vilifications of 'vicious' women, were also reinforced. However, in promoting 'the feeling of sympathy and fellowship with even the most degraded' that philanthropists advocated, this new generation of writers had to tread carefully in their battle against censorship; Shaw's demythologisation of the White Slave Trade was still seen as too scandalous for Victorian audiences.

In the climate of the 1880s and 1890s such texts were perceived as scandalous, as they refused to endorse accepted views of female sexuality, instead contributing to new images of female sexual identity through representations of the prostitute. Despite their radical intentions, however, the texts also reproduced some of the more conventional attitudes of philanthropists and purity feminists. The Unclassed tackled the thorny question of male desire for sexually active women, though this was harnessed to a quite conventional vision of the philanthropist controlling his social inferior. Holdsworth endorsed the prostitute's sexual agency but also celebrated the project of reclamation which reinstalled female purity. Shaw attacked repression and valorised the existence of brothels, but used his New Woman as a mouthpiece for purity feminism. Ultimately, all three texts were scandalous in validating active female sexuality, suggesting that women's repression of their sexuality was just as much a social problem as Mrs Warren's profession

G.B. SHAW: Creative Evolutionist.

Michael Timko is professor emeritus of the City University of New York. His article "Florence Nightingale: Fantasy and Fact" appeared in the July 2003 issue of The World & I.

The death of paleontologist Stephen Jay Gould caused many to think once again about evolution, specifically about Gould's hero, Charles Darwin. Few would connect Gould and Darwin to George Bernard Shaw. When we think of Shaw, we think of My Fair Lady, the musical based on his drama Pygmalion. While many remember him chiefly as a dramatist, others might think of him in one of his many other roles: vegetarian, nonsmoker, total abstainer (not even tea; he drank carrot juice and water only), and antivivisectionist. He also was a staunch advocate for language reform, socialism, and Wagner. One commentator on Shaw points out that he brought a new adjective into English: Shavian, a term that sums up his brilliance. Another wrote: "His plays were superb exercises in high- level argument on every issue under the sun, from feminism and God, to war and eternity, but they were also hits—and still are."

What we tend to forget is that he was also seriously interested in the question of evolution and that he was a bitter opponent of Darwin. Shaw, who thought Darwin's theory emphasized the element of chance far too much, put forward his own hypothesis based on the ideas of Lamarck and Samuel Butler. Unhappy with the Darwinian emphasis on circumstance and environment, Shaw insisted that human beings, as "spiritual" creatures, had much to say about their own development and future progress; he expounded these ideas in two plays in particular: Man and Superman and Back to Methuselah. In one sense, of course, he was simply dramatizing his own life, which had evolved by means of his particular brand of creative wit and thought.

Early Life and Ibsen; His life before he became a prominent figure can be briefly summarized, but even that brief summary demonstrates his creativity. He was born in 1856 in Dublin, the only son and third child of an unsuccessful grain merchant. Shaw's mother, disgusted with her husband's drinking, lost herself in music and left the bringing up of her child to the servants. According to some, she found solace with her singing teacher, George John Vandeleur Lee, who lived with the family in Dublin for a time and whom she followed when he moved to London. Shaw, who joined his mother in London in 1876, after she had left Lee, learned to love music, art, and the theater; he served as music and drama critic for various magazines and papers. An autodidact, he overcame his shyness, became a skilled debater, and joined the recently founded Fabian Society, a socialist group. Always fascinated by the theater, inspired by Ibsen, the founder of modern drama, Shaw became one of the foremost playwrights of his time.

Shaw's interest in Ibsen is linked to his passionate hatred of Darwin and his defence of creative evolution, or the life force. Like Ibsen, Shaw championed the drama of ideas rather than of action, which usually, in his day, was more melodramatic than dramatic. He was not only an active socialist but an author who tackled "unpleasant" subjects; in fact his early plays were called "Plays Unpleasant." One of them, Mrs. Warren's Profession, deals with prostitution. Mrs. Warren's daughter finds out that her mother has financed her university education with money earned as a madam; she is so incensed that she berates her mother and wants to return all the money given her. In his preface to the play, Shaw points out that in most instances the cause of prostitution is not depravity but poverty. Prostitution, he insists, is not limited to women selling their bodies. Real prostitution is that of intelligent men and women debasing their intellect. People tend to romanticize it instead of seriously discussing the problem and its causes. There is no doubt in the minds of many that Shaw, in writing of Mrs. Warren, was embodying Fabian socialistic ideas. He was also thinking of Ibsen's dramas Hedda Gabler and A Doll's House, especially the latter, in which the heroine leaves her husband for refusing to treat her as an equal.

Shaw himself provides clues to his views on both socialism and evolution in a passage in The Quintessence of Ibsenism. His remarks on the king, women, and the church are revealing:

The point to seize is that social progress takes effect through the replacement of old institutions by new ones; and since every institution involves the recognition of the duty of conforming to it, progress must involve the repudiation of an established duty at every step. If the Englishman had not repudiated the duty of absolute obedience to his king, his political progress would have been impossible. If women had not repudiated the duty of absolute submission to their husbands, and defied public opinion as to the limits set by modesty to their education, they would never have gained the protection of the Married Women's Act, the municipal vote, or the power to qualify themselves as medical practitioners.

Darwin, we know, was not the first to bring up the question of evolution, progress, and the interdependence of all things. Jacques Barzun, the famous critic, cites four sources of evolutionary thought: German philosophy, geological and astronomic history, biological evolutionary thought, and history in general. Darwin's immediate predecessors in evolutionary thought were Buffon; Erasmus Darwin (1731–1802), Charles' grandfather; and Lamarck (1744–1829). According to Samuel Butler, whose novel The Way of All Flesh emphasized the Lamarckian belief in man's ability to will change: "Buffon planted, Erasmus Darwin and Lamarck watered, but it was Mr. Darwin who said 'That fruit is ripe,' and shook it into his lap." Lamarck is largely discredited today, and the reasons for that illustrate why Darwin's ideas were accepted and became famous. Both Darwin and Lamarck were arguing in favour of organic evolution and against the immutability of species and plants. They both held that living things were not (in spite of what the Bible said) independently created but are mutable or transmutable and evolve from one form to another by a process of what came to be called "descent by modification." Lamarck's views, however, contained two principles that Darwin rejected (and most biologists today reject). Lamarck maintained, first, that acquired characteristics could be transmitted from parent to offspring; and, second, that changes in physical form could occur as the result of conscious willing on the part of the living beings experiencing these changes. (He used the famous example of the giraffe stretching its neck.) Darwin on the other hand, while an evolutionist like Lamarck, provided the answers that many accept today, although, it must be said, even followers of his insist on pointing out variations of Darwinism. After gathering facts for many years, Darwin with great reluctance presented his findings, the main points being the struggle for existence and the survival of the fittest through natural selection.

Shaw the Lamarckian: Shaw, who admired Lamarck, vehemently disagreed with Darwin. This disagreement was based largely on the notion that Darwin had deprived man of any kind of free choice. If man is not free to choose, and everything he does is already determined by circumstance and environment, what is the purpose of life itself? In both Man and Superman and Back to Methuselah, Shaw argues that the Darwinian concept of evolution is simply wrong, and that most people accept it because, as he states in the preface to Back to Methuselah, "there is nothing to puzzle you in Darwinism. That was the secret of Darwin's popularity. He never puzzled anybody." More to the point, Darwinism, for Shaw, deprived man of free will or any sort of will. "Whenever the Neo-Darwinian doctrine was preached," Shaw writes, "I made no attempt to conceal my intellectual contempt for its blind coarseness and shallow logic, or my natural abhorrence of its sickening inhumanity."

Shaw's own belief, based on Lamarckian thought, was in what he called creative evolution, which did allow for free will. Instead of being mere machines, Darwinian creatures of circumstance and adaptation, human beings have a sense of purpose and achieve what they aspire to in this life by means of this will to live and succeed. Shaw quotes Schopenhauer: "The driving force behind evolution is a will to live, and to live, as Christ said long before, more abundantly."

The mention of Christ is no accident. In his preface to Back to Methuselah, Shaw seems anxious to avoid being branded antireligious. Indeed, in proclaiming his gospel of creative evolution, Shaw endeavors to provide it with a historical and religious basis. In 1562, he writes, the Church of England, meeting in convocation in London, "proclaimed that God is without body, parts, or passions, or, as we say, an Elan Vital or Life Force. Unfortunately neither parents, parsons, nor pedagogues could be induced to adopt that article." It is this concept of the life force that Shaw adopts as gospel, one that he preaches in both Man and Superman and Back to Methuselah. It is what he calls "the metaphysical side of Evolution," as opposed to the "scientific" Darwinian gospel.

In Shaw's opinion, Darwin and the scientific evolutionists are responsible for keeping millions of people from believing that "we are continually urged upwards by a force called the Will of God."

In Man and Superman, written during the years 1901 and 1903, Shaw presents his radical "evolutionary" ideas: his view of the real relationship between man and woman; and his anti-Darwinian concept of nature, one in direct contrast to Darwin's notion of the survival of the fittest, or, as Tennyson wrote, "Nature red in tooth and claw." In his drama Shaw contends that Darwin ignored the first idea completely and was utterly mistaken about the second. While the plot of the play can be simply summarized, Shaw's witty and satiric treatment of it is anything but simple. "I took the legend of Don Juan in its Mozartian form and made it a dramatic parable," Shaw wrote. He also, as commentators have pointed out, made his Don Juan a Byronic character. Byron, in his treatment of that rake, becomes the pursued instead of the pursuer. In Shaw's play, Jack Tanner, a wealthy socialist, is appointed guardian of Ann Whitfield and her sister. Jack thinks that Ann wants to marry Octavius, an artist, but soon realizes that Ann has her sights on him instead. His attempt to run away to Spain is foiled by Ann, and in the end he accepts his "capture."

In Shaw's view, Mozart portrays Ann as a "womanly woman"; in his play, he portrays her as a woman in the grip of the life force or creative evolution. "Man," he writes in the epistle dedicatory to Man and Superman, "is no longer like Don Juan, victor in the duel of sex." Woman, on the other hand, is no longer the pursued but the pursuer. "My Don Juan," he writes, "is the quarry instead of the huntsman. The woman's need of him to enable her to carry on Nature's most urgent work does not prevail against him until his resistance gathers her energy to a climax at which she dares to throw away her customary exploitations of the conventional affectionate and dutiful poses, and claim him by natural right for a purpose that far transcends their mortal personal purposes."

The Shavian purpose that far transcends mortal personal purposes is, of course, creative evolution. In one passage in the epistle, Shaw writes: "It is assumed that the woman must wait, motionless, before she is wooed. Nay, she often does wait motionless. That is how the spider waits for the fly. But the spider spins her web. And, if the fly, like my hero, shows a strength that promises to extricate him, how swiftly does he abandon her pretense of passiveness, and openly fling coil after coil about him until he is secured forever!"

The scene that best illustrates the new woman and the new Don Juan occur in act 4 of the play. Ann, the pursuer, has made it clear to Jack that he is her choice. He replies, "But why me?" As Ann continues her pursuit, Jack finally caves in. The following dialogue takes place:

Ann: Flatterer. Why are you trying to fascinate me, Jack, if you don't want to marry me?

Tanner: The Life Force. I am in the grip of the Life Force.

Ann: [Rising quietly and shaking her finger at him] Now, Jack, behave yourself.

Tanner: Infamous, abandoned woman! Devil!

Ann: Boa-constrictor! Elephant!

Tanner: Hypocrite!

Ann: [Softly] I must be, for my future husband's sake.

Tanner: Oh, you are witty: at the supreme moment the Life Force endows you with every quality. The trap was laid from the beginning.

Ann: [Concentrating all her magic] From the beginning—from our childhood—for both of us—by the Life Force.

Tanner: [Seizing her in his arms] I love you. The Life Force enchants me. I have the whole world in my arms when I clasp you.

The Life Force

The second point that Shaw emphasizes in the play, the specifically anti-Darwinian one, concerns the role of Nature. Act 3, the famous "Don Juan in Hell," is seldom performed because of its length and sheer verbal effusion. An evocation of Mozart's opera, it is Jack Tanner's dream as he is fleeing from Ann through the mountains. The four characters in this "philosophical interlude" are similar to those in the other three acts (Jack being a distant relation to the legendary Don Juan

Tenerio), and one of the chief lessons they learn, besides finding out that heaven is boring and hell is really a more exciting place, is the Shavian notion of the life force.

There are far too many attempts to explain this notion in act 3, which is one of the reasons it is seldom done, but two are explicit and reveal the Shavian wit. In one of the exchanges between Don Juan and Do-a Ana, she asks him, "Is there nothing in heaven but contemplation, Juan?" and he replies: "In the heaven I seek, no other joy. But there is the work of helping Life in its struggle upward. Think of how it wastes and scatters itself, how it raises up obstacles to itself and destroys itself in its ignorance and blindness. It needs a brain, this irresistible force, lest in its ignorance it should resist itself."

In what is perhaps the most explicit Shavian explanation of the life force, the Devil tells Don Juan that as heaven is boring, he should come to live in Hell. Don Juan, in what is perhaps the most famous speech in all of Shaw's plays, explains: "I, my friend, am as much a part of Nature as my own finger is a part of me. If my finger is the organ by which I grasp the sword or the mandoline [sic], my brain is the organ by which Nature strives to understand itself. My dog's brain serves my dog's purposes; but my own brain labors at a knowledge which does nothing for me personally but make my body bitter to me and decay and death a calamity. Were I not possessed with a purpose beyond my own I had better be a ploughman than a philosopher."

Don Juan then drives home Shaw's basic anti-Darwinian view of life and man:

This is because the philosopher is in the grip of the Life Force. This Life Force says to him, "I have done a thousand wonderful things unconsciously by merely willing to live and following the line of least resistance: now I want to know myself and my destination, and choose my path... And this," says the Life Force to the philosopher, "must thou strive to do for me until thou diest, when I will make another brain and another philosopher to carry on the work."

When the Devil objects, Don Juan replies in the best-known lines from the play, "The philosopher is Nature's pilot.

And there you have our difference: to be in hell is to drift; to be in heaven is to steer."

Back To Methuselah: Even though Man and Superman was a success, Shaw himself evidently felt that he had not succeeded in making creative evolution a popular religion, and in 1918 he began writing Back to Methuselah. It took him two years. "I now find myself inspired to make a second legend of Creative Evolution," he wrote in the preface to the play. " I abandon the legend of Don Juan with its erotic associations, and go back to the legend of the Garden of Eden. I am not, I hope, under more illusion than is humanly inevitable as to the crudity of this my beginning of a Bible for Creative Evolution." While the play, which has five parts, is not as long as the Bible, it does, in fact, begin with the Garden of Eden and end far in the future, part 5 taking place on a summer afternoon in the year a.d. 31,920.

Eric Bentley, the best contemporary critic on Shaw, has given an excellent summary of the play: While Man and Superman presented Shaw's idea that man's brain enables him to understand life and thus control it, Back to Methuselah, Bently writes, uses "slightly different categories and emphases" to make the same point. "Life and Matter are the two basic realities. At first Life is enslaved by Matter. But the higher man fights against his enslavement, and when his existence is released from Matter at the time called Death, he reverts to the pure stream of Life. Thus Life spirals upwards. Eventually Matter will be enslaved by Life, and Death thereby will be abolished. Immortality will have been achieved, and Life will be pure idea."

While all this may sound abstract, and, as one might expect, there have not been many successful productions of the play, Shaw did succeed in presenting to his audiences and readers by means of various scenes his "Bible for Creative Evolution." Several clearly illustrate both the Shavian message and wit. In part 1, "In the Beginning," the Serpent delivers the first of many anti-Darwinian utterances, as it tells Eve: "When Lilith [the heroine of this Shavian drama] told me what she had imagined in our silent language I bade her desire it and will it; and then, to our great wonder, the thing she had desired and willed created itself in her under the urging of her will. Then I too willed to renew myself as two instead of one; and after many days the miracle happened, and I burst from my skin another snake interlaced with me; and now there are two imaginations, two desires, two wills to create with." Eve replies, "To desire, to imagine, to will, to create. Find me one word for it all: you, who are so clever at words." In typical Shavian fashion, the Serpent replies: "In one word, to conceive."

In part 2, "The Gospel of the Brothers Barnabas," Shaw drives home his message of creative evolution. Conrad, one of the leaders of the Longevity Party, assures his followers that the men of science support his position. "Ever since the reaction against Darwin set in at the beginning of the present century," he tells them, "all scientific opinion worth counting has been converging rapidly upon Creative Evolution."

Franklyn, another supporter, chimes in: "Poetry has been converging on it: religion has been converging on it. It is going to be the religion of the twentieth century: a religion that has its intellectual roots in philosophy and science, just as medieval Christianity had its intellectual roots in Aristotle." Just to be sure that his followers (and the audience) understand, Franklyn spells out the Shavian concept. "The force behind evolution, call it what you will, is determined to solve the problem of civilization; and if it cannot do it through us, it will produce some more capable agents. Man is not God's last word: God can still create. If you cannot do His work, He will produce some being who can."

In part 5, "As Far as Thought Can Reach," Shaw presents the ultimate existence, "life as pure thought." One of the ancients, Martellus, a Shavian voice, tells the others: "The body always ends by being a bore. Nothing remains beautiful and interesting except thought, because the thought is the life." One of the sceptics asks: "But if life is thought, can you live without a head?" One of the He-Ancients, who seems to be mostly a head, replies: "Not now perhaps. But prehistoric men thought they could not live without tails. I can live without a tail. Why should I not live without a head?" A She-Ancient supports him: "None of us now believe that all this machinery of flesh and blood is necessary. It does [believe it]."

The "death of the flesh" is the ultimate answer for Shaw, for it will be the death of death. Humans will have achieved immortality through creative evolution. In typical fashion, Shaw gives the final words of the drama to Lilith, "in whom the father and mother were one." Adam complains to Lilith of the changes brought about by creative evolution: "What is it all for? We were well enough in the garden. And now the fools have killed all the animals; and they are dissatisfied because they cannot be bothered with their bodies! Foolishness, I call it." Lilith responds: "They have accepted the burden of eternal life. Best of all, they are still not satisfied: the impulse I gave them in that day when I sundered myself in twain and launched Man and Woman on the earth still urges them: after passing a million goals they press on to the goal of redemption from the flesh, to the vortex freed from matter, to the whirlpool in pure intelligence that, when the world began, was a whirlpool in pure force. I will not supersede them until they have forded this last stream that lies between flesh and spirit, and disentangled their life from the matter that has always mocked it."

This goal may seem much too unattractive to most of us, but it is one that seems inevitable in the light of Shaw's anti-Darwinian view of man's evolutionary development. Shaw and Darwin never doubted that human beings were evolving; their basic disagreement was not on the question of evolution itself but on one's approach toward evolution. Darwin, scientist that he was, insisted always on circumstance and environment, what came to be seen as the "survival of the fittest"; while Shaw, with his concern with man's free will, focused on what he preferred to call "vitalism." This conviction was the key to his creative evolution, or elan vital.

Darwin, although he struggled with moral and religious questions for years, could never bring himself to such a view. Shaw, on the other hand, was convinced that the vital human spirit could transcend any self-imposed standards or conventions, natural or otherwise. The great difference between these two can be seen in Shaw's assertion of his position in one of his many letters: "I am a moral revolutionary," he wrote, "interested, not in class war, but in the struggle between human vitality and the artificial systems of morality." In the light of this Shavian approach to evolution, it seems ironic that Darwin, not Shaw, has become the target of so much controversy and opprobrium in our own time.

Bibliography

Bernard Shaw by G.K. Chesterton (1909);

Bernard Shaw by H.Pearson (1942);

Bernard Shaw by E. Bentley (1957);

Bernard Shaw: Man and Writer by A. Williamson (1963);

A Guide to the Plays of Bernard Shaw by C.B. Purdom (1963);

Bermard Shaw by E.R. Bentley (1967);

Concordance to the Plays and Prefaces of Bernard Shaw by E.D. Bevan (1971, 10 vols.);

Bernard Shaw: Art and Socialism by E. Strauss (1978);

The Genius of Shaw, ed. M. Holroyd (1979);

Bernard Shaw: The Darker Side by A. Silver (1982);

Bernard Shaw: A Guide to Research by S. Weintraub (1992);

Bernard Shaw: The Ascent of the Superman by Sally Peters (1996);

Shaw by M. Holroyd (1988-93, 4 vols., authorized biography) Suom.: Suomeksi julkaistu myös Järjen sanoja sodasta.